To Joy and John

Affectionately —

Piet

20 June 1977

F. O. Matthiessen: The Critical Achievement

F. O. MATTHIESSEN:
THE CRITICAL ACHIEVEMENT

By Giles B. Gunn

UNIVERSITY OF WASHINGTON PRESS

SEATTLE AND LONDON

Library of Congress Cataloging in Publication Data

Gunn, Giles B
   F. O. Matthiessen : the critical achievement.

   "Bibliography of the works of F. O. Matthiessen": p.
   Includes bibliographical references and index.
   1. Matthiessen, Francis Otto, 1902–1950.
PS29.M35G8   810'.9'0052   75-20363
ISBN 0-295-95430-2

This book was published with the assistance of a grant from the Andrew W. Mellon
Foundation.

For Janet

To lend himself, to project himself and steep himself, to feel and feel till he understands and to understand so well that he can say, to have perception at the pitch of passion and expression as embracing as the air, to be infinitely curious and incorrigibly patient, and yet plastic and inflammable and determinable, stooping to conquer and serving to direct—these are fine chances for an active mind, chances to add the idea of independent beauty to the conception of success. Just in proportion as he is sentient and restless, just in proportion as he reacts and reciprocates and penetrates, is the critic a valuable instrument; for in literature assuredly criticism is the critic, just as art is the artist; it being assuredly the artist who invented art and the critic who invented criticism, and not the other way around.

And it is with the kinds of criticism exactly as it is with the kinds of art—the best kind, the only kind worth speaking of, is the kind that springs from the liveliest experience.

HENRY JAMES
"Criticism"

Acknowledgments

IN THE course of a project of this kind, one inevitably becomes indebted to others in ways too numerous to mention and too personal to acknowledge in any but the most superficial manner. Nonetheless, I here wish to express my thanks to several individuals who, though lacking any responsibility for the final outcome, still played an important part in the completion of this book: to Preston T. Roberts, Jr., who first introduced me to the literary and cultural criticism of F. O. Matthiessen; to Nathan A. Scott, Jr., who put at my disposal his broad knowledge of the modern tradition and, in addition to lending support and encouragement, provided me with the stimulus of astute and challenging criticism; to James E. Miller, Jr., who read the entire manuscript, some of it in several versions, and helped me recast and strengthen various parts of it; to Leo Marx, who also read the manuscript in its entirety, listened to me talk about it, and never failed to respond to appeals for assistance by giving me the benefit of his intimate familiarity with Matthiessen's work and his humane and balanced view of the American tradition as a whole; to Henry Nash Smith and C. L. Barber, who on separate and very memorable occasions gave me added insight into the rich complexity of Matthiessen's personal life and helped to clarify my own sense of the nature of his critical achievement; to various of my former students in Religion and Literature 403, who have shared with me their own interest in the problems of modern American literary and cultural historiography; and, finally, to my wife, Janet, who in ways that go beyond telling has remained, as Matthiessen might have said, "an indispensable resource."

I should add that I have been most fortunate over the past several years to be able to draw upon the wise counsel and sympathetic understanding of two of my former colleagues at the University of Chicago, Anthony C. Yu and Joseph Sittler; to have been able to rely upon the generosity of the University of Chicago, and particularly the Divinity School and its dean, Joseph M. Kitagawa, when I needed time for research and writing; and to have been blessed with the services of Mrs. Rehova Arthur and her staff, who typed and retyped successive drafts. For preparing the final draft with care and dispatch, I wish to thank Mrs. Minerva Bell. And for her valiant labor in bringing both consistency and clarity to these pages, special thanks are due Mrs. Grace H. Stimson.

Parts of chapters 1 and 5 are drawn from my essay "Criticism as Repossession and Responsibility: F. O. Matthiessen and the Ideal Critic," *American Quarterly* 22, no. 5 (Fall, 1970): 629–48, Copyright 1970, Trustees of the University of Pennsylvania, and are here reprinted by permission. For permission to quote from copyrighted material by F. O. Matthiessen, I am grateful to the following publishers: to Houghton Mifflin Company for quotations from *Sarah Orne Jewett,* Copyright 1929, by Francis Otto Matthiessen; to Harvard University Press for quotations from *Translation: An Elizabethan Art,* Copyright 1931 by the President and Fellows of Harvard College; to Oxford University Press for quotations from *The Achievement of T. S. Eliot,* Copyright 1935, 1958 by Oxford University Press, from *American Renaissance,* Copyright 1941 by Oxford University Press, from *Henry James: The Major Phase,* Copyright 1944 by Oxford University Press, from *From the Heart of Europe,* Copyright 1948 by Oxford University Press, from *The Responsibilities of the Critic,* selected by John Rackliffe, Copyright 1952 by Oxford University Press; to William Morrow & Co. for quotations from *Theodore Dreiser,* Copyright 1951 by William Sloane Associates, Inc. I am also grateful to the editors of the *Monthly Review* for permission to quote from material published in the special issue devoted to F. O. Matthiessen, *Monthly Review* 2, no. 6 (Oct., 1950), Copyright 1950 by *Monthly Review*.

January 1, 1975

Contents

ABBREVIATIONS

AR   *American Renaissance* (New York: Oxford University Press, 1941)

ATSE   *The Achievement of T. S. Eliot: An Essay on the Nature of Poetry* (3rd ed., with additional chapter by C. L. Barber, Galaxy Books; New York: Oxford University Press, 1959)

FHE   *From the Heart of Europe* (New York: Oxford University Press, 1948)

HJ   *Henry James: The Major Phase* (New York: Oxford University Press, 1944)

JF   *The James Family: Including Selections from the Writings of Henry James, Senior, William, Henry, and Alice James* (New York: Knopf, 1947)

SOJ   *Sarah Orne Jewett* (Boston: Houghton Mifflin, 1929)

T   *Translation: An Elizabethan Art* (Cambridge: Harvard University Press, 1931)

TD   *Theodore Dreiser* (New York: William Sloane Associates, 1951)

Introduction

IN 1963, more than twenty years after the publication of *American Renaissance*, Roy Harvey Pearce acknowledged in the essay, "Literature, History and Humanism," what he described in his subtitle as "an Americanist's dilemma." Noting that much of the criticism of American letters which had been written after the appearance of *American Renaissance* deserved to be called "post-Matthiessenian," Professor Pearce nonetheless argued that we have yet to comprehend or fully absorb Matthiessen's achievement. Taking as his example Matthiessen's twofold assumption that "an artist's use of language is the most sensitive index to cultural history, since a man can articulate only who he is, and what he has been made by the society of which he is a willing or an unwilling part," and that to read cultural history in this fashion is to "feel the challenge of our still undiminished resources," Professor Pearce pointedly asked:

Do we yet know how to define the terms: "artist," "use of language," "sensitive index," "articulation," "being a willing or an unwilling part"? Do we yet understand what it is to be "challenged" thus? Have we understood what it means to have "undiminished resources"?[1]

I have written this book on the assumption that the best way to come to terms with these questions, and others like them, is to start with Matthiessen's own work. I have been motivated

[1] Roy Harvey Pearce, "Literature, History and Humanism: An Americanist's Dilemma," *College English* 34 (Feb., 1963): 372.

throughout by my conviction that Matthiessen's collected criticism—a corpus comprising nine books, five anthologies, and approximately 150 essays, articles, and reviews—presents precisely the same kind of "challenge" Matthiessen himself found in the literature of our past. Not simply because it has for so long been neglected, but also because it is so rich in substance and mode of approach, I have become convinced that Matthiessen's achievement constitutes one of "our still undiminished resources."

In seeking evidence to support my claim, I have tried to confine myself to the testimony presented by Matthiessen's own criticism. It is not that I lack interest in the flesh-and-blood man who did the writing, but that I think Matthiessen deserves to be viewed as he endeavored to view others, by seeking the man within the work rather than the man behind it. To whatever degree this study is concerned with the story of a life, it should be regarded less as the biography of a person than of a mind. My focus is largely restricted to the development of Matthiessen's ideas about literature, criticism, and life generally as they emerge in and shape the course of his published writing. Whenever I have departed from this procedure, I have still tried to select only such details as would further illumine this approach.[2]

Yet because Matthiessen regarded his ideas—to employ one of his own figures—not as mere counters in a stale game but rather as modes of action and forms of belief, there is an unusually intimate relation between what Matthiessen thought and wrote and who he was. It is no accident, I think, that one of his favorite words was *integrity*. Requiring that "uncompromising honesty," as he once termed it, which characterizes those who strive to give expression only to what they know to be true to their own experience, integrity was the quality he most prized in others and sought most vigorously to embody in himself. His

[2] For explicitly biographical information I have relied heavily on the remarkable series of impressions left by Matthiessen's associates, colleagues, and friends in the commemorative issue of the *Monthly Review*, published soon after his death. With an extraordinary combination of devotion and candor, the contributors created as faithful and coherent a portrait of the man as we are ever likley to have. This special issue, edited by Paul Sweezy and Leo Huberman, came out in October 1950; later that same year it was published as a book by Henry Schuman of New York. May Sarton, in *Faithful Are the Wounds* (1955), presents a fictionalized portrait of Matthiessen in the character of Edward Cavan.

life and his achievement exhibit what a fellow critic and close friend once described as a heroic struggle for "unity of being,"[3] and that struggle is nowhere more evident than in the way Matthiessen fought, if not always successfully, to relate the inner to the outer, the private to the public, the mental and the emotional to the civic and the professional.

As with many of the best critical minds in America, however, Matthiessen presents something of a paradox. The author of the first book in America on the poetry and criticism of T. S. Eliot, and hence instrumental in introducing critical formalism to the United States, Matthiessen was nonetheless inveterately opposed to formalism's politically conservative implications and strongly resisted its habitual tendency to divorce works of literature from their cultural matrix. In spite of devoting a large part of his critical energies to the work of Hawthorne, Melville, James, and Eliot, and thus of helping to confirm the philosophy of tragic skepticism during the 1940s and early 1950s, Matthiessen himself was deeply religious rather than agnostic and remained highly critical of the modishness of the existential pessimism that swept across the country after World War II. Further, though Matthiessen belonged to the progressive social tradition in American intellectual history, he repudiated its naïve theory of progress and criticized its image of man as simpleminded and doctrinaire. While his deepest political affinities lay in the earlier Populist and agrarian frontier tradition, with its strong belief in the fundamental goodness of the common man, Matthiessen nonetheless became a distinguished professor of English at Harvard, lived on Beacon Hill, and directed his published research almost exclusively to the New England literary tradition. Again, though he did more writing in twenty years than most men could complete in sixty, he was firmly convinced that action is the proper extension of thought and continually deplored the assumptions behind the notion of "publish or perish." The greatest paradox, however, was the most tragic: in spite of his conviction that love is the highest value in human life and, moreover, that love has been incarnate in diverse ways throughout human history, he nevertheless ultimately found it

[3] C. L. Barber, "Preface to the Third Edition (1958)," *ATSE,* p. xii.

impossible to reconcile himself to life and committed suicide in the predawn hours of April 1, 1950.

It is tempting to make light of these paradoxes by noting that Matthiessen put little faith in perfect intellectual consistency. One of his former students has observed that "perhaps the most profound and elusive lesson he taught was that a smooth and absolutely logical structure of ideas is not necessarily a sign of the greatest intellectual maturity."[4] But if Matthiessen presumed that experience always outruns our conceptions of it and that theory inevitably trails behind practice, there is all the more reason for taking the paradoxical nature of his own commitments seriously. Whatever they may disclose of Matthiessen's internal divisions, they were still a part of the very fabric of his being. The loyal Yale alumnus who was as proud of his membership in Skull and Bones as of his Phi Beta Kappa key was the same man who fought economic exploitation in the famous case of the New Mexican coal miners in 1934, who twice served as president of the Harvard Teachers' Union, who was a trustee of the Sam Adams Labor School, and who campaigned for Henry Wallace in 1948; the man who entered politics to satisfy his desperate need for fellowship found solace in a writer like Henry James because of James's cultivation of the dimension of personal inwardness; the man who criticized the official morality of downtown America at virtually every opportunity was able to make generous contributions to worthy causes and impecunious friends largely because of a modest inheritance from his grandfather's stock in a watch company; the man who vigorously criticized the competitive spirit was himself driven by an almost compulsive desire to measure himself against his peers; the man who wrote so often and so well about the necessity of valuing things for their own sake could not give himself seriously to anything if it did not lead somewhere or count for something; the man who was sometimes aggressive to the point of belligerence was also passionately opposed to violence except as a last resort and considered himself a lifelong pacifist.

In lesser men such paradoxes might have suggested weakness or confusion, but in Matthiessen they were for the most part

---

[4] Leo Marx, "The Teacher," *Monthly Review* 2 (1950): 211.

evidence of strength and diversity, constituting the boundaries in terms of which he fought to sustain his wholeness. Though that wholeness was perhaps less a matter of completely realized fact than of aspiration and will, Matthiessen's view of the person clearly reserved a large place for the element of conflict. Without conflict, he believed, life lost much of its interest and the person gave up all opportunity for significant choice and development. The integrity of the self, Matthiessen seemed to assume, had to be maintained under the pressure of conflicting loyalties and allegiances; otherwise the self would lose its requisite margin of tension, alertness, and, above all, complexity.

If Matthiessen's approach sounds somewhat unconventional as a theory of personality, it was by no means uncharacteristically American. Matthiessen was far too close a student of the classic writers of the nineteenth century not to have learned, as they so vividly exemplified, that the "very essence" of persons, as well as of culture, often resides in their central conflicts, "their meaning and power lying in their contradictions."[5] To try to minimize or explain away Matthiessen's own contradictions, therefore, would be to strip him of those very qualities that in no small measure determined his unique strength both as a critic and as a man. Matthiessen was, or at least tried to be, the master of his own disorder, and in learning some of its constructive uses he made his most vital contribution to American life and letters.

To accept Matthiessen's incongruities, however, is not to assert that his life and work lacked a coherent center. In spite of obvious conflicts, such as the contradiction between his commitment to democracy and his criticism of the American way of life, or between his faith as a Christian and his tragic view of existence, Matthiessen's thought, like Matthew Arnold's before him, exhibits "a logic and architecture which is none the less strict for being organic and not mechanical."[6] The key to that logic is best expressed, I believe, in a remark C. L. Barber once made about T. S. Eliot. After observing that most of Eliot's literary criticism has little to do with religion per se, Barber was yet

[5] Lionel Trilling, *The Liberal Imagination* (Garden City, N.Y.: Doubleday Anchor Books, 1957), p. 7.
[6] Lionel Trilling, *Matthew Arnold* (New York: Norton, 1939), p. x.

obliged to point out that very nearly all "his comments on literature and culture . . . still prove to be adjusted to religious actuality as he conceives it."[7] I do not say that Matthiessen, any more than Eliot, always derived his critical norms from Christian theology or that he ever regarded the spiritual factor in literature as paramount. I merely suggest that virtually everything Matthiessen ever thought or wrote acquired its sanctions from concerns that to him were essentially religious and, further, that those concerns defined the range of experience in terms of which he considered any question.

Matthiessen himself acknowledged his religious orientation, if somewhat obliquely, at a dinner given in honor of the publication of *American Renaissance* by the Student and Faculty unions at Harvard in the spring of 1941. The event was significant for Matthiessen because it seemed to mark a definite moment in his career when his personal and public selves had almost perfectly coalesced. The book in which he had invested so much of his own interior life as scholar and critic was being honored, not least because it provided a usable past for all those who believed, as he did, in the necessity of radically reconstituting the social order. Nor was the symbolism of the occasion lost on Matthiessen himself. Realizing that many in his audience, because of his own demonstrated interest in economic and political reform, might regard the book only as the interpretation and expression of an adversary tradition within American writing which might itself be categorized as a radical critique of American society, Matthiessen was anxious not to be misunderstood. When he rose to acknowledge the tribute paid him, he was at pains to clarify the nature of his intentions:

I feel that I am among friends, and I do not want there to be any misunderstanding. Some of you are Marxists. I am not a Marxist. I have been influenced by Marx as anyone has who has seriously thought about political matters in the last fifty years. But Marx was often more successful in coining effective slogans for immediate political action than in arriving at statements of philosophical truth. If any of you really believe that religion is only "the opiate of the people," you cannot hope to understand the five figures I have tried to write about in *American Renaissance.*[8]

[7] C. L. Barber, "The Power of Development . . . in a Different World" (*ATSE*, 202).
[8] Joseph H. Summers, in *Monthly Review* 2 (1950): 310.

Matthiessen makes it difficult to follow the thread of unity which winds its way throughout his criticism, because, in spite of his absorption with religious concerns, he assiduously avoided extensive systematic treatments of most of the issues that mattered to him. One looks in vain for a clear statement not only of his religious position but also of his theory of literature or his view of criticism.[9] It is not that he was averse to systematic thought as such, but only that his mind was too heavily concrete and empirical, too preoccupied with the variety and the complexity of the particular, either to enjoy or to trust sustained flights of theoretical inquiry. When he reflected on theoretical matters, as he frequently did, he felt more comfortable in using the thought of someone else, by way of comparison or contrast, to suggest his own position.

This tendency gives to many of Matthiessen's firmest theoretical convictions a strongly derivative flavor. But we should not be misled into thinking that his own commitments were less important to him because they had first been articulated by someone else. If he frequently employed the ideas of others to suggest his own positions, he also utilized such occasions to address what he regarded as vital issues. Virtually all his books and articles—from *Sarah Orne Jewett* (1929) to *Theodore Dreiser* (1951)—were designed both to deal with the subject at hand and to display its special bearing on a particular problem. What kept all his writing from becoming merely topical was his unfailing ability to meet the demands of the subject itself before attempting to assess what he once referred to as its "unspent potential."

In writing about Matthiessen I have tried—with two exceptions—to follow his own development, which falls roughly into three overlapping phases. The earliest phase, constituting the substance of my second chapter, includes his first three book-length studies: *Sarah Orne Jewett* (1929), *Translation: An Elizabethan Art* (1931), and *The Achievement of T. S. Eliot: An Essay on the Nature of Poetry* (1935). The second or middle phase, to which chapters iii and iv are largely devoted, is best represented by

---

[9] The exception is the Hopwood lecture entitled "The Responsibilities of the Critic," which Matthiessen delivered at the University of Michigan in the spring of 1948, but in no sense does it articulate all Matthiessen's ideas about the nature and the function of criticism.

Matthiessen's major and defining work, *American Renaissance: Art and Expression in the Age of Emerson and Whitman* (1941). The final phase, dealt with in chapter v, includes *Henry James: The Major Phase* (1944), *From the Heart of Europe* (1948), and *Theodore Dreiser* (1951). Two additional chapters, preceding and following these central ones, explore other aspects of Matthiessen's achievement. To place Matthiessen's work in the context of the influences he felt and responded to, I have written an initial chapter, "The Shaping Environment." To assess the critical legacy Matthiessen left behind, I have written a final chapter, "The Nature and Quality of Matthiessen's Achievement."

In order to articulate without falsifying the complex unity of Matthiessen's thought, I have let him speak for himself, insofar as possible, by quoting generously from his own writing. When this procedure seemed inadvisable, I attempted to follow as closely as possible the shifting, often devious, course of Matthiessen's own arguments, thus taking the risks of paraphrase. I defend my procedure on the grounds that no other approach seems quite so satisfactory in light of the peculiar nature of Matthiessen's criticism. Matthiessen designed his writing, as Raymond Williams once said of Edmund Burke, less as a series of formulations to be accepted as true or false than as a kind of "articulated experience, and as such . . . [it] has a validity which can survive even the demolition of its general conclusions." The remainder of Williams's comment is also germane: "It is not that the eloquence survives where the cause has failed; the eloquence, if it were merely the veneer of a cause, would now be worthless. What survives is an experience, a particular kind of learning; the writing is important only to the extent that it communicates this. It is, finally, a personal experience become a landmark."[10]

It is no coincidence that the same words might be applied to the essays of Ralph Waldo Emerson, who, like Matthiessen, endeavored to make his writing an articulation of experience. If Burke, Emerson, and Matthiessen were united in nothing else, they were at one in the assumption that a man writes not merely to express but also to enable. Each strove to make his work an

---

[10] Raymond Williams, *Culture and Society, 1780–1950* (New York: Columbia University Press, 1958), p. 5.

expression of mind in the act of finding and realizing itself, and all left a literary corpus that will survive as a mode of learning or a form of experience long after it has been forgotten as a body of knowledge.

Characteristics such as these, which Matthiessen shared with Emerson, have finally led me to think of him as a signal instance of Emerson's "American Scholar." Nor, but for reasons of modesty, would Matthiessen have objected to this designation. The standards he set for himself in writing *American Renaissance,* and indeed for all his books, were, as he admitted, "the inevitable and right extension of Emerson's demands in The American Scholar" (*AR,* xvi). Like his Emersonian prototype, Matthiessen was committed to extending the perimeters of conscious experience by bringing as much life as possible to the level of moral and intellectual awareness. There were enormous hazards in this undertaking but enormous rewards as well. What was at stake was a repossession of the very nature of experience itself; and in this, I believe, Matthiessen displayed no less a "genius for the essential"[11] than Emerson had before him.

[11] This phrase is used in the introduction to *Emerson: A Modern Anthology,* ed. Alfred Kazin and Daniel Aaron (Boston: Houghton Mifflin, 1958), p. 13.

F. O. Matthiessen: The Critical Achievement

CHAPTER ONE

The Shaping Environment

The key word in our time is not rebellion but knowledge. Man's very nature is a predicament to him; and society is not a collection of philistines who have rigid values which he opposes but a collection of people whose own traditions are dead, and who are looking for convictions. This is why the critical imagination plays so large a role in modern-day culture, for ideas bring life; and why the best writers of our time—whether it be Malraux in *The Voices of Silence,* or Edmund Wilson searching into the deep, deep well of the past—have the effect not of opposing a status quo but of creating the new reality of mind where, in all our unexpectedness, we can live.

ALFRED KAZIN
On Native Grounds

MATTHIESSEN'S interest in critical theory sprang largely from his strong reaction to the kind of narrowly historical and biographical scholarship which had, since well before the turn of the century, characterized so much American literary study. Matthiessen revealed that reaction as early as 1929 when, just two years out of graduate school, he stated flatly in a review of two books on the achievements and prospects of American criticism that "it is time for the history of American literature to be rewritten" (*RC,* 181).[1] Significantly, Matthiessen not only predicted the kind of fresh historical scholarship a new generation of American critics would subsequently undertake, but he also defined the kind of literary and cultural historian he himself would eventually become.

Matthiessen's bold assertion was elicited by his already firm belief that American literature had been studied for too long in "a vacuum without relation to anything but itself, a genealogy of printed works, one book begetting another" (*RC,* 181). Fur-

[1] The two books reviewed were Norman Foerster, *American Criticism* (1928), and *The Reinterpretation of American Literature* (1928), ed. Norman Foerster.

thermore, previous efforts to study the development of American literature in its wider historical and cultural implications had been dominated by political and geographical concerns, thus obscuring the two factors Matthiessen considered most important: the intimate relationship between American and European culture, and the crucial implications of native American conditions. Matthiessen was convinced that no adequate history of American literature could be written until literary and cultural historians were willing to consider all aspects of American culture, from education to politics and from religion to economics, without forgetting that their primary responsibility was literary and not historical. Such historians would be every bit as interested in the effect of the Puritan heritage upon the development of American culture as in the influence of the frontier on the development of the American character. And when these new historians turned their attention to more conventional subjects, such as the nature of American romanticism or the tradition of American realism, they would treat these movements more as complex reactions to the spirit of the times than merely as ways of writing and feeling.

Though one can easily discern in this tentative portrait of the literary historian of the future the shadow of such men as Frederick Jackson Turner, Henry Adams, Charles A. Beard, and Vernon Louis Parrington, Matthiessen was careful to qualify the extent of their influence. These figures, Matthiessen suggested, might serve as partial models for his ideal literary historian only because he should strive, as they did, to give us "a new vision of the forces dominant in our political and social past" (*RC*, 182). But the historian's material, Matthiessen insisted, would be primarily aesthetic and literary, whereas theirs was political, social, or economic; he would remember, as sometimes they did not, that "one does not have to master the importance of Jacksonian democracy to read intelligently 'Rappaccini's Daughter' " (*RC*, 182).

At a time when the American academic community, or at least that part of it concerned with the life of letters, was bitterly divided over the obligations of scholarship versus the imperatives of criticism, these were strong words indeed. Nearly half a century later, we can see that the great gulf which then separated scholars from critics and critics from scholars was largely an artificial one, but in the heated intellectual atmosphere of the 1920s it was regarded as almost unbridgeable. To those who gave their allegiance to scholarship, with its insistence upon the academic virtues of accuracy, breadth, and disinterestedness, criticism often seemed like so much "belletristic trifling" (the phrase is Parrington's) or, worse, impressionistic special pleading. To those who identified themselves with the urgencies and engagements of criticism, scholarship, by contrast, frequently seemed encrusted with outworn conventions and irrelevant to the common welfare. It was difficult to remain impartial, but it was even more difficult to honor the claims of both.

Yet concordance between the two is precisely what Matthiessen hoped to accomplish by his call for new standards in American criticism. He wanted a criticism that could illumine the meaning of the present without distorting the materials of the past, an objective that called for the creation of standards at once wise, tough, and yet flexible. He did not believe that such standards could be found simply by turning to the past on the assumption that they already existed fully formed in the work of a Plato, an Aristotle, or a Sidney. Adequate standards, Matthiessen believed, would have to be created, not only by studying the works of the past but also by meeting the demands of the present, particularly as those demands were influenced by the American environment.

Matthiessen's conclusion reveals that almost at the outset of his career he was in firm possession of the two basic components of his own theory of criticism. His insistence on adequate critical standards emphasized his belief that criticism must be evaluative as well as explicative in order to fulfill its unique function in society, that the critic's real business is the discrimination of qualities, not the description of quantities. In maintaining further that those standards should be recreated from an assessment of America's relation to the past and of her circumstances in the present, he was stipulating that criticism must have an organic basis—springing as literature itself should from an awareness of the needs of the community—in order to have integrity and relevance, that the critic must write for all the people instead of for a special coterie.

1

Since Matthiessen arrived at these convictions early in his career, it is somewhat astonishing to realize how thoroughly conventional and undistinguished his intellectual life was at the beginning. By his own admission, his first moment of intellectual awakening did not occur until 1918, when in his freshman year at Yale he began to read Shakespeare and other major writers under the direction of a young English instructor named Bob French. It was the first time in Matthiessen's educational experience that ideas had been treated as anything more than a kind of furniture of the mind, albeit a graceful and serviceable kind of furniture, and he responded with all the enthusiasm, absorption, and newly awakened sense of dedication of a religious neophyte. In four short years Matthiessen was transformed from an undeveloped college freshman, whose outside reading in preparatory school had been concerned chiefly with the fortunes of Baseball Joe of the Silver Stars, to a Rhodes scholar eager to pursue a teaching career. Yet it was not until he returned to Harvard after his two years in England that he finally settled on American literature (his B.Litt. thesis at Oxford was on Oliver Goldsmith). Looking back on his early life in his disarmingly personal book, *From the Heart of Europe* (1948), he expressed regret that his middle-class upbringing and schooling had kept him from realizing personal and intellectual opportunities.

One such disappointment concerned the importance of the region associated with many of his happiest boyhood memories, the town of La Salle, Illinois, on the banks of the Illinois River, where his grandparents lived. The youngest of four children in a family that suffered disruption and painful marital conflict— his mother was a gentle New Englander and a distant relation of Sarah Orne Jewett's, his father a rancher and engineer from California with a penchant for irresponsibility and untrustworthiness—Matthiessen was raised partly in Pasadena, where his parents had originally settled, and partly in Illinois and the East, where his mother withdrew to escape an increasingly uncomfortable domestic situation. It was particularly in La Salle that

Matthiessen found that sense of inner peace and harmony with his surroundings and his family for which every child longs. And yet it would subsequently strike him as appallingly ironic that it was not until many years later, when he had become an English instructor at Harvard and was reading Francis Parkman's *La Salle and the Great West*, that he was finally able to connect Starved Rock and the Illinois River, where he and his grandfather had frequently gone canoeing, with some of the great episodes in the opening of the American West. "La Salle had simply been the name of my grandfather's town," he recalled. "That it was the name also of a French explorer was lodged somewhere abstractly in my memory, but I had not had the irreplaceable experience of sharing, as a boy, in a rich consciousness of history" (*FHE*, 74).

The same experience of missed education was repeated when Matthiessen went to preparatory school. After attending the Polytechnic School in Pasadena, he was sent to the Hackley School in Tarrytown, New York, to prepare for meeting college entrance requirements. Though Hackley did give the boy the needed education, it apparently did little more. According to Matthiessen's own report, Hackley in no way helped him to develop his own tastes—since his best subject there was mathematics, he entered Yale thinking that subject would probably be his major—and, whether through carelessness, ignorance, or indifference, the school also effectively prevented him and the other boys from having the one significant intellectual encounter it might have provided. Hackley's music teacher and choir director was the able American composer Charles Griffes; yet Matthiessen was compelled to observe that "in the barren atmosphere of a conventional boys' school, that was apparently not assumed to be a matter of interest" (*FHE*, 74). When Matthiessen finally got around to reading a biography of Griffes (who died in the flu epidemic of 1919), he was further shocked to learn that during his senior year at Hackley "this shy bird-like little man" was sitting in isolation and loneliness at the end of another corridor in his own dormitory reading such writers as Flaubert and Dostoevsky. "Even if I was not ready for them at sixteen," Matthiessen remarked bitterly, "there is an unforgivable wastage in any institution where the important things are never mentioned, and where communication withers through disuse" (*FHE,* 74).

The fact that Matthiessen's family ties were stretched so thin by lengthy absences from home and that his early educational experiences did little to help form him as a person may in part explain why he could eventually write with such intense feeling about the American sense of rootlessness, and why, further, he would stress that every generation must repossess the past for itself. The early experiences also help to explain why Matthiessen's introduction to Yale had so strong an impact upon him. The transition from Tarrytown to New Haven must have been rather like the arrival of one of Henry James's young heroines in Europe. Thirty years later Matthiessen still vividly remembered those first few months at Yale, which produced "the giddy sensation of a limitless domain opening out before you" (*FHE,* 71). In addition to the university's own colorful past—various aspects of which were always to hold a fascination for Matthiessen out of all proportion to his strong antipathy to anything that smacked of special privilege—there was the opportunity to study with outstanding teachers and scholars like Lorande Woodruff in biology and Chauncey Tinker in English, men who were able to communicate a living and intimate knowledge of their subjects even to beginning students. The very accessibility of such people meant that Yale was still small enough in those days to enjoy a genuine sense of intellectual community. However scholarly their learning, many of Matthiessen's teachers at Yale regarded knowledge as something to be shared as well as preserved; they made their students feel that the educational process was a collaborative endeavor to which the young could make a vital contribution.

Nevertheless, Matthiessen's interest in the academic profession developed slowly, and mainly by accident. The discovery that literature was extremely important to him was owing largely to the influence of acquaintances he made while contributing to the *Yale Literary Magazine* as an undergraduate. Having arrived at Yale just after the departure of Archibald MacLeish, Phelps Putnam, and Stephen Vincent Benét, Matthiessen and his friends were encouraged to think that they, too, might be participating in a Yale renaissance. Although more than half his classmates had served in World War I—Matthiessen himself had enlisted and served for a few months in the Royal Canadian Air Force—they shared in the general sense of release and of renewed hope after the war; they were touched hardly at all by the mood of depression afflicting members of the Lost Generation who stayed on in Paris. Talk at the Elizabethan Club, of which Matthiessen was an active member, was often heady and exciting, and this stimulation, plus his own increasing interest in writing—he was eventually to become managing editor of the *Yale Daily News*—finally confirmed his commitment to literature. Yet it was not until his senior year at Yale that Matthiessen decided to become a teacher and not until he had gone to England as a Rhodes scholar in 1923 that he started to read major American writers. English literature at Yale had been restricted to British writers (*Moby-Dick* was still catalogued in the Yale Library under cetology), and Matthiessen had supplemented this program with work in Greek and the classics. Whitman's *Children of Adam* and *Calamus* poems, which Matthiessen started to read in a dingy little tearoom near the British Museum, were his first native discoveries, and he later took *Walden* with him, very self-consciously, he later admitted, on a trip up the Rhine to Freiburg and the Schwarzwald. He did not get around to *Moby-Dick* until after he had finished his work at Oxford and returned to America to resume graduate study at Harvard.

Matthiessen was originally drawn to Harvard because of the possibility of working with George Lyman Kittredge on the Elizabethans; indeed, his doctoral dissertation was to be a study of six Elizabethan translations of Greek, Roman, and French classics. Yet in another of the accidents that often shaped his career, the appearance of Lewis Mumford's *The Golden Day* in 1927 awakened him to the earlier work of Van Wyck Brooks, which in turn stimulated him to direct his attention to American literature. Oddly enough, much of the impetus for this decision came from Matthiessen's exposure to the ideas of Irving Babbitt, who was then preparing for the last major battle of his life, this time with Brooks, Mumford, Mencken, Sherman, and other critics who hoped to encourage a rediscovery of native American authors. In that contest Matthiessen found himself at odds with most of Babbitt's reactions to modern and American literature, but he later praised Babbitt's lectures as "by far the most living experience in my graduate study at Harvard. . . . The vigor with which he objected to almost every author since the eighteenth century forced me to fight for my tastes, which grew stronger by the exercise" (*FHE*, 74).

When Matthiessen first became a teacher, on a two-year instructorship at Yale (the rest of his academic career was spent at Harvard), it was Babbitt's integrity of purpose and commitment, together with Bob French's devotion, honesty, and sensitivity, which served as his chief models. In the credo Matthiessen contributed to the *Harvard Progressive* in 1940, he referred to his acceptance of the job at Harvard as "accepting a call"; Leo Marx has surmised that a century earlier Matthiessen might well have become a minister.[2] Teaching was for Matthiessen a vocation in the most old-fashioned sense of the word, something one does with every fiber of his being. There was no real separation between his work in the classroom and his work in the study; it was all part of a single-minded attempt to share with others the fruits (as well as the frustrations) of his own agonized effort to bring as much experience as possible under the scrutiny of the moral and critical imagination. This endeavor was enormously taxing, simply because Matthiessen gave himself to it so completely. As John Rackliffe has suggested, he could do nothing by halves:

He threw himself wholly into anything he even touched. The result was a life certainly of great variety and richness, a life at the same time intensely taut and strained. His standards, for himself even more than for others, were high, exacting, and necessarily exhausting. He himself wanted to be alert and "aware" (one of his favorite words), missing nothing, evading nothing, permitting himself no retreats and no ambiguous compromises, allowing no blurred edges. He seemed compelled to follow—no doubt long before he knew the phrase itself—the advice of Henry James, to be "one of the people on whom nothing is lost."[3]

---

[2] Leo Marx, "The Teacher," *Monthly Review* 2 (1950): 211. For much of the following discussion of Matthiessen's teaching career, I am indebted to Marx's superb essay.

[3] John Rackliffe, "Notes for a Character Study," *Monthly Review* 2 (1950): 244–45. This extraordinarily probing article, written by one of Matthiessen's former students, is still the finest portrait of Matthiessen the man.

In later life his high standards no doubt often made Matthiessen seem formidable and unyielding as a teacher. He could be ruthless with students who took things for granted or supposed that Harvard owed them an education merely for having admitted them, but he was warmly encouraging to those who consciously tried to surpass themselves. As demanding as he was, Matthiessen was always ready to acknowledge achievement, even in a form that held no particular interest for him; he frequently let his best students know that they were teaching him as much as he was teaching them. That kind of relationship was in fact what he desired and expected. Sharing Lincoln Steffens's frustration with professors who ask questions to which they already know the answers, Matthiessen believed that no real learning could occur unless students were free to ask questions themselves. If occasionally the professor was forced beyond the range of his competence, so much the better, for the only hope of initiating fresh thought was the discovery of heretofore unexplored areas.

This approach to education was much better suited to the small seminar or discussion section than to the lecture hall, and it was in the former that Matthiessen felt most comfortable. Though in time he was to become famous for certain of his heavily attended lecture courses, his heart was never fully in them. Lacking interest in the dramatics of the podium, frequently used as an attention-gathering device, Matthiessen was at his best in a more informal setting where student and teacher could think together, inching their way through a complicated issue until the particular details under examination suddenly fused into a rounded picture. For this reason Matthiessen was an avid supporter of Harvard's tutorial system almost from its inception; from 1931 to 1948 he served as chairman of the Board of Tutors in history and literature, under the program he helped found with Perry Miller and one or two others. Here is where he felt he could be most effective in assisting students, while at the same time pursuing those relations between art and culture which were closest to his own interests. Further, the tutorial system gave him and his students the opportunity to combine the close inspection of particulars with a search for the large overview. Matthiessen needed to see things both ways, both in detail and against a broad background.

Matthiessen also valued the tutorial system because, more than most professors, he not only enjoyed working with students but also needed them. Because of the lack of close family relationships and because of his own temperament, Matthiessen dreaded the thought of loneliness. Instinctively he realized that young people understand the importance of close human contacts more readily than their elders. His relationships with students enabled him to strike a balance between society and solitude, to borrow one of his favorite formulations from Emerson. Moreover, these relationships satisfied his deep personal need to give of himself, to spend himself in behalf of others. His willingness to give can be seen not merely in his affection for close friends or his generous donation of time, money, and talents to causes he believed in, but also in his availability to students, his consenting to read and evaluate manuscripts submitted to him even by strangers, his desire to promote the careers of younger scholars who struck him as promising, his constant efforts, sometimes painful as well as awkward, to understand and associate with those whose social and cultural backgrounds differed markedly from his own, and finally his unfailing readiness to sympathize with the underdog and the outcast.

Matthiessen's personal associations with others, however, were not without stress or even pain. To him, friendship was a distinct privilege, even a gift, which carried with it certain responsibilities. Friends were cherished not only for their devotion and loving-kindness but also for their forebearance and constancy; if Matthiessen detected the slightest lapse in a friend's loyalty, he could react with bitterness and hostility. The relation with a friend was too costly for him and entailed too heavy an emotional expense to permit him to suffer disruptions of it lightly. One side of him was tempted to interpret basic disagreements over important issues as outright betrayals, but there was another side that was more than willing to go the extra mile.

Extremely vulnerable as he was to the experience of loneliness, Matthiessen needed support from those whose affection he most deeply valued. When that support was forthcoming, he was not above expressing his gratitude, even in public. One particularly moving example of this is found in the dedication of his book on the later novels of Henry James. Though conscious at the time he wrote *Henry James: The Major Phase* of the debts he owed other scholars and interested colleagues, he was even more conscious of his debt to a small group of Harvard undergraduates who had insisted upon staying in college until they were needed by the armed services. Refusing "to be distracted from primary values," his three "instigators," as he referred to them in the dedication, had been a constant source of strength and inspiration by helping him to believe that even during wartime the preservation of the humanities "should be a leading aim" (*HJ,* xvi).

2

The belief that one cannot afford to neglect art and culture in time of war was but the corollary to Matthiessen's conviction that art and culture are indisputably related to social well-being, and that an individual work of literature achieves a life of its own because it has at once a social as well as an aesthetic purpose.[4] The rigor with which he held to this perception is perhaps unique in modern American criticism, and he is consequently somewhat difficult to place on any conventional map of the critical landscape. Instead of associating himself with one critical group rather than another, he made it his business to become familiar with them all and then sought to define what he might have described as the "usable truth" of each. To place him accurately in any other terms but the ones he chose for himself would require a rehearsal of nearly the entire history of modern criticism, or at least of that part of it which made its influence felt in America after 1900. Among moderns alone from whom Matthiessen seems to have learned are such diverse figures as I. A. Richards, T. E. Hulme, T. S. Eliot, Kenneth Burke, John Crowe Ransom, Allen Tate, Van Wyck Brooks, Stuart P. Sherman, Irving Babbitt, Paul Elmer More, Edmund Wilson, T. K. Whipple, Christopher Caudwell, Yvor Winters, Granville Hicks, Newton Arvin, Harry Levin, Harley Granville-Barker, Kenneth B. Murdock, Caroline Spurgeon, Perry Miller, Constance

---

[4] Marx, "The Teacher," p. 208.

Rourke, Theodore Spencer, H. L. Mencken, L. C. Knights, Hardin Craig, Paul Rosenfeld, V. L. Parrington, John Livingston Lowes, George Lyman Kittredge, William Crary Brownell, Lewis Mumford, Joseph Warren Beach, M. H. Abrams, Morris W. Croll, Cleanth Brooks, and of course Henry James. Short of a full review of modern criticism, one can merely suggest certain basic allegiances to show how Matthiessen drew upon these various resources in constructing his own mode of approach as literary critic and historian.

Perhaps chief among Matthiessen's critical allegiances is the view he shared with all those who have been disposed to follow Francis Bacon in the *De Augmentis Scientiarum,* where Bacon contends that literature represents what might be described as "communalized experience" and that the business of literary history is to transmit the record that literature provides of such experience.[5] That Bacon himself exerted no noticeable influence upon the subsequent development of literary historiography in America is not to the point. As Howard Mumford Jones has argued,[6] Bacon's theory of literary history made its way to America, albeit in a somewhat different form, in the work of Madame de Staël, Simonde de Sismondi, Friedrich Schlegel, Victor Cousin, and Abel François Villemain. These five figures, exhibiting a common indebtedness to the Germany of Lessing, Herder, Goethe, and Schiller, worked from the shared assumption that the history of literary development must be seen in relation to its social and cultural background. Schlegel, whose *Lectures on the History of Literature, Ancient and Modern* was translated and published in America in 1818, and Madame de Staël, whose *The Influence of Literature upon Society* received American publication even earlier, in 1813, further shared the belief that literature is, or should be, an expression of the national spirit and that the health of the one depends upon the health of the other. In fact, Madame de Staël actually equated the health of a nation's literature with the extent of its political freedom, thus providing a strong incentive during the national period to those

[5] The phrase is actually Holbrook Jackson's, though it is used in reference to Francis Bacon by Howard Mumford Jones in *The Theory of American Literature* (rev. ed.; Ithaca: Cornell University Press, 1965), p. 14.

[6] *Ibid.,* pp. 58–71.

who wanted to see America develop a culture commensurate with its political destiny.

But it was not until half a century later, under the influence of Charles Augustin Sainte-Beuve—that "naturalist of minds," as he called himself, who sought to connect literary works with their authors and the authors with their particular periods, places, and nationalities—that these assumptions were to produce native results by encouraging the writing of literary histories by Americans devoted to the development of a distinctively American tradition. In spite of Barrett Wendell's rapid Anglophilism, his *Literary History of America* (1900) might be regarded as the firstfruits of this influence had it not been overshadowed by Moses Coit Tyler's two distinguished works, *A History of American Literature, 1607–1765* (1878) and *The Literary History of the American Revolution* (1897). Tyler, as Matthiessen himself later pointed out,[7] was in complete sympathy with Sainte-Beuve's principle that knowledge of the author is necessary to evaluate the author's work; consequently Tyler fully supported the great French critic's belief that literary study leads, through examination of a writer's life and times, to what might be termed moral study. Sharing these convictions, Tyler could utilize Sainte-Beuve's method to clear advantage by connecting criticism with biography and thus turning literary history into a study not only of specific works but also of the personality that gave them shape and substance.

Yet, despite the rash of histories that followed *A History of American Literature, 1607–1765,* from such popular books as Donald Grant Mitchell's *American Lands and Letters* (1897) and its sequel, M. A. DeWolfe Howe's *American Bookmen* (1898), to serious efforts like William Crary Brownell's *American Prose Masters* (1901) and John Macy's *Spirit of American Literature* (1913), Tyler's achievement remained without equal until Vernon Louis Parrington published *Main Currents in American Thought* (3 vols.; 1927–30). Parrington was clearly more of an intellectual than a literary historian and, like many of the "new historians" who preceded him (James Harvey Robinson, Charles A. Beard, Carl Becker), tended to focus more on selected ideas in history than

[7] See Matthiessen's review of Howard Mumford Jones, *The Life of Moses Coit Tyler* (1933), reprinted in *RC,* 147–55.

on the actual history of selected ideas. Parrington's *Main Currents* was to exert an enormous influence upon the study of American literature. Inspired by Taine as well as by Beard, Parrington was able to synthesize the different strands of American progressivism in constructing a liberal reading of the entire American past; further, he released one of the dominant critical tendencies of the thirties by tending to regard literature as but a reflection of its environment, especially when that environment is reduced to its social and economic components.

There can be no question that Matthiessen owed a good deal to the work of both Tyler and Parrington, though Parrington's influence was much more direct and pervasive. Despite their differing views of the past, particularly the colonial past, Parrington and Tyler displayed a marked similarity of method. They agreed on the necessity of viewing all works of literature in an ever-expanding context of relationships which would enable the critic to take into account not only the factors responsible for their production but also the conditions determining their reception and acceptance. Yet both resisted the temptation to turn the process of accounting into a dull exercise in the history of taste, largely by seeking, as Sainte-Beuve and Taine had urged, to dramatize a writer's *qualité maîtresse*.

The most important differences between Tyler and Parrington grew out of the opposing motives of their interest in the past. Tyler was writing at a time when American intellectuals still felt reasonably confident about the future of American culture. His own interest in the past, like that of many of his contemporaries, resulted from a desire to show how America's earliest republican institutions had in time produced a relatively stable and humane culture. Parrington, on the other hand, was writing nearly half a century later, when confidence in American culture had given way to increasing apprehension and dismay. Having become thoroughly disillusioned with the growing collectivism and commercialization of American society, Parrington could no longer share Tyler's view that the present consists of little more than the continuous evolution of the past; instead he began to view it as an unfortunate departure. So far as Parrington was concerned, the historian should look for moments in the past when Americans still exhibited consciousness of their native traditions, not so much to rescue those moments from passing into oblivion as to uncover the intellectual assumptions that lay back of them; such an effort would define, it was hoped, a series of core ideas which might yet prove serviceable in helping the ship of culture to navigate the treacherous waters of the present and the future.

The desire to find, and if possible to repossess, a "usable past" owed its popular expression to Van Wyck Brooks, whose *America's Coming-of-Age* (1915) probably did more than any other single book to encourage the rediscovery of American literature in the early part of the twentieth century. With only slight exaggeration, one could maintain that Brooks's early work, from *The Wine of the Puritans* (1909) to *Letters and Leadership* (1918), was the most influential factor in the subsequent appearance of such disparate studies as H. L. Mencken's *The American Language* (1919), Harold E. Stearn's anthology entitled *Civilization in the United States* (1922), Stuart P. Sherman's *Americans* (1922) and *The Genius of America* (1923), Lewis Mumford's *Sticks and Stones* (1924) and *The Golden Day* (1926), Parrington's *Main Currents,* Constance Rourke's *American Humor* (1931), Ludwig Lewishohn's *Expression in America* (1932), V. F. Calverton's *The Liberation of American Literature* (1932), Granville Hick's *The Great Tradition* (1934), Perry Miller's *The New England Mind: The Seventeenth Century* (1939), Matthiessen's *American Renaissance* (1941), Alfred Kazin's *On Native Grounds* (1942), and countless others. However diverse the mode of approach or the point of view, it is in these works that the view of literature as an expression of the national experience gained its most secure foothold in modern American criticism; and it is to them, as a consequence, that one must turn for an understanding of the changing images of the past which modern Americans have found most usable.[8]

Yet the second cultural renaissance in American history, which such works as these reflected, was not produced by critics and historians alone. They were themselves responding to a host of other factors which contributed to making the second and third decades of the twentieth century a time of unusual creative ferment. As Matthiessen pointed out, the ground for

[8] For a full discussion of this subject, see Richard Ruland, *The Rediscovery of American Literature* (Cambridge: Harvard University Press, 1967).

a new outbreak of interest in native cultural traditions had really been prepared a good decade earlier in the writing of the muckrakers and their allies, a diverse group of artists, journalists, and historians whose penchant for protest and reform could also be viewed as an expression of nostalgia and hope. Dreiser's *Sister Carrie,* which had initiated the decade of transition, had appeared in 1900; Lincoln Steffens's *The Shame of the Cities* and Thorstein Veblen's *The Theory of Business Enterprise* (a sequel to his *The Theory of the Leisure Class* [1899]), in 1904; Upton Sinclair's *The Jungle,* in 1906; Henry Adams's *Education* and William Graham Sumner's *Folkways,* in 1907; Gertrude Stein's *Three Lives,* in 1908; and Herbert Croly's *The Promise of American Life,* in 1909. The real breakthrough, however, came in the next decade with the founding of Harriet Monroe's *Poetry: A Magazine of Verse* in Chicago in 1912 and the arrival of the Armory Show in New York in 1913. These two events quickened interest in the arts and created new audiences for the revolutionary developments that would follow.

Poetry, of course, was only the first in a series of "little magazines" that eventually provided a forum for new writers—T. S. Eliot, Wallace Stevens, Sherwood Anderson, Marianne Moore, William Carlos Williams—as well as for older writers whose talents had long been ripening, such as Robert Frost, Willa Cather, and Edgar Lee Masters. In 1915 *Poetry*'s reputation as a magazine responsive to the experimental and the avant-garde passed to Alfred Kreymborg's short-lived *Others,* founded in New York in 1915; by 1917 Margaret Anderson had turned Chicago's *The Little Review,* started in 1914, into a more radical alternative to *Poetry.* But it was not until the little magazines, designed for the select few, were supplemented by more ambitious and widely circulating monthlies like *The Smart Set,* brilliantly edited by George Jean Nathan and H. L. Mencken from 1914 to 1923, and *The Dial,* founded in 1920, that the enormous range of fresh literary talent, seemingly springing up from everywhere and beginning to revolutionize not only the practice of poetry but also the writing of fiction, was able to find an adequate outlet. This development encouraged a parallel quickening of activity and interest in the little theater movement, jazz music, the graphic arts, and urban architecture.

One of the more important features of this second cultural flowering is that it was stimulated in part by the transmission of influences from abroad. The Armory Show of 1913 symbolizes one aspect of this influence; Ezra Pound's service as foreign editor to both *Poetry* and *The Little Review* could be said to represent another. For my purposes, the chief importance of the European influence is that the cosmopolitanism thereby injected into the resurgence of interest in American writing and American traditions brought with it a new respect for craft and a fresh excitement about form. Moreover, these factors greatly affected the reorientation in critical method soon destined to accompany the creative developments. T. S. Eliot's first book of essays, published in 1920 under the title *The Sacred Wood,* was a kind of turning point. It was the first in a series of books whose strong commitment to technique was to dominate American criticism for an entire generation. F. O. Matthiessen was no exception. If he owed his first allegiance to critics and scholars who stressed the historical character of literature as a record of man's felt experience, he clearly owed his second to critics and poet-critics who insisted that literature is also a record of the way man's felt experience can and must be expressed within the tensions and resistances of form.

Since the specifics of Eliot's influence on Matthiessen are discussed in chapter ii, it is necessary to observe here only that the interest in form which Eliot helped to awaken among Anglo-American critics, though widely accepted, was not consistently interpreted.[9] Beyond acknowledging that form and content are inextricably related in any work of art, critics tended to diverge sharply in how they construed that unity. Eliot's most influential colleague in England at the time, I. A. Richards, whose *Principles of Literary Criticism* (1925) and *Practical Criticism* (1929) were important contributions to a developing formalistic orientation in modern American criticism, actually had little to say about form per se; he was far more absorbed with the question of how poems might be said to resolve conflicting attitudes and impulses. Nor, for that matter, did Eliot himself say much about form. Although Eliot is sometimes compared with Paul Valéry,

[9] René Wellek, "Concepts of Form and Structure in Twentieth-Century Criticism," in *Concepts of Criticism* (New Haven: Yale University Press, 1963), pp. 54–68.

who went so far as to argue that literature is nothing but form and, on that assumption, tried to create a completely autotelic, nonreferential, and atemporal art, Eliot's own concern with technique, and particularly with diction, never diminished his interest in such related issues as the process of artistic creation, the nature of tradition, the problem of effect, and the question of ethical and religious norms. Among other exponents of the importance of form, the same discrepancy of interpretation exists. T. E. Hulme's opposition of romantic formlessness and classical form, of a poetry of imagination and a poetry of fancy, obviously had little to do with Kenneth Burke's later perception of form as a vehicle for arousing and fulfilling desires and thus as a strategy by which writers deal with painful experiences in their own lives. Again, Yvor Winters's insistence that form is essentially moral, a kind of rational order that must be imposed upon the disordered and often subconscious materials of experience, seems to have been clearly at variance with Cleanth Brooks's interpretation of form as a structure of tensions, paradoxes, and ironies. These examples suggest that the new formal orientation that Eliot helped to introduce into modern American criticism, which Matthiessen picked up and reflected, was intended primarily to correct certain critical abuses, and that its most able representatives used it primarily not to further theoretical speculation but rather to develop stricter methodological discipline and greater critical refinement.

Such, at least, was its influence upon F. O. Matthiessen. If others tried to turn the New Criticism into a new orthodoxy, he simply could not. For one thing, he was constitutionally unable to cut himself off from the many other currents of critical activity swirling around him. If the chief function of criticism, as of art and culture generally, is, as he suggested later in life, "to bring man again into communication with man" (*FHE,* 13), then the critic can neither contribute to the discussion nor develop as a result of it without receiving the constant stimulus and challenge of opposing viewpoints. For another, the very thought that literary intellectuals would isolate themselves from controversy in order to keep their commitments and methods pure was abhorrent to him. To close oneself off from other positions in the name of methodological purity was to risk the danger of one's own ideas hardening into a kind of inflexible and intolerant dogma, and he had already seen enough of that in the criticism of Irving Babbitt. The alternative was to subject one's own criticism to the differing opinions of others for correction and revision, and that is what Matthiessen tried to do in all of his writing. Indeed, one probably comes closest to a definition of Matthiessen's critical heritage by examining the series of partial portraits he drew at various times in his life of the literary critics and scholars he most admired.

3

One critic who exerted an early and decisive influence upon Matthiessen's critical development was Van Wyck Brooks. The Brooks that Matthiessen admired was not the culture hero of the literary monthlies who became famous almost overnight for dividing the American cultural past into highbrow and lowbrow components so that he might excoriate both, but the more mature Brooks who sought to define a viable middle ground between extremes and thus contributed so significantly to the revival of American literature and to the development of a tough-minded native criticism. Matthiessen's sharp reaction to the later Brooks is one sure gauge of the enormous impact the earlier Brooks had had upon him. Indeed, Matthiessen was severely disturbed by the volumes that comprised Brook's "Makers and Finders" series precisely because Brooks had grown deaf to his own rigorous earlier standards. Instead of continuing to act on the principle he had first enunciated, that the critic's responsibility is to think as well as to describe, Brooks had eventually succumbed to the sentimental art of nostalgic evocation, where the critic no longer uses the past to measure the present but instead abandons the present altogether in order merely to restore people's confidence in the past. To this betrayal of Brooks's once discerning perspective on the past, Matthiessen could only respond with frustration and dismay.

Nonetheless, in one of those curious accidents of historical influence, Matthiessen may well have been receptive to the early Brooks because some of Brooks's ideas converged with those of Irving Babbitt. At first glance, this suggestion may seem implausible, for Brooks and Babbitt differed over ideas ranging

from the importance of contemporary letters to a correct evaluation of the past, and they made their disagreements public. Yet
on one or two essentials they were in agreement. First, both men
were sharply critical of the starved and distorted quality of contemporary experience, and both believed that the only correc-
tive was the development of wise standards. Second, though
they would have differed over the nature and the appropriate
way of applying those standards, both also assumed that the
culture of the past provided the chief resource for defining
them, and that anyone who took seriously the responsibility for
creating such standards would find himself alienated from many
of his contemporaries. In 1942, for example, when Matthiessen
reviewed a volume of essays and reminiscences devoted to Babbitt for the *New England Quarterly,* he was not content merely to
criticize Babbitt's well-known intellectual dogmatism or his re-
actionary politics or his aristocratic disdain for the new, but he
went on to stress the exemplary importance of Babbitt's effort
to fulfill Emerson's ideal of Man Thinking and to underscore
Babbitt's admirable courage in committing himself to causes he
knew to be futile. However outmoded many of Babbitt's ideas,
and however imperious and repetitive his style, Matthiessen
could still respect his refusal to be swayed by popular opinion
and his perceptive analyses of some of America's most serious
social and cultural ills. Many of Babbitt's standards may have
been too inflexible and too unsympathetic to the needs of the
common man, but Matthiessen nonetheless realized that the
quality of life could not be improved without them and that the
critic discounts their importance only at the expense of forsaking his chief social obligation.

Brooks and Babbitt were not the only critics and near contemporaries who exhibited an interest in the usable past. The same
concern was evident in the work of Stuart P. Sherman, whose
Life and Letters Matthiessen reviewed for the *New Republic* as early
as 1929. What proved to Matthiessen most impressive about
Sherman, especially in contrast with Babbitt, was his ability to
integrate his view of criticism with his belief in democracy, holding "as his central principle 'the duty of bringing the whole body
of the people to the fullest and fairest human life of which they
are capable' " (*RC,* 155). Sherman, however, was no optimist,

and this made all the difference to Matthiessen. What was needed was a sense of the past, which required extraordinary effort and imagination. Yet what could be achieved by scholarship and letters in pursuit of this end—"to connect us with the great traditions and to inspire us with the confidence and power which result from such a connection" (quoted, *RC,* 155)—was nothing less, in Sherman's view, than a contribution to national reintegration and self-fulfillment.

If a sense of the past was not a sufficient reason for Matthiessen's admiration, Sherman provided him with another by describing what could be gained from the attempt to connect the present with the great traditions. In words that might as easily have been written by T. S. Eliot, Sherman defined the resultant effect as "a kind of innermost poise and serenity, tragic in Sophocles, heroic in Michelangelo, skeptical in Montaigne, idyllic in Sidney, ironic in Fielding," and concluded that "this enviable tranquility reigns only in a mind that, looking before and after, feels itself the representative of something outlasting time, some national ideal, some religious faith, some permanent human experience, some endless quest" (quoted, *RC,* 156). Such upwelling expressions of faith, however noble, might still have been just so much puff, as far as Matthiessen was concerned, if Sherman had not known how to apply them, but at least in his essays in *Americans,* Matthiessen was confident that he did. There, more than in any other work, Sherman had provided what Matthiessen could accept as an effective model of critical practice, first by developing a series of perspectives on every subject, then by probing the complexities of each for their particular essence, and finally by indicating in what sense each might still be considered "an unspent force with some vital energy to communicate to the modern spirit" (*RC,* 156).

Yet there was a dangerous tendency inherent in Sherman's commendable desire for relevance. Devoting more and more of his attention in his later years to contemporaries in the belief that a democratic critic's first allegiance is to the present, his standards began to soften and his prose to become flabby; "and by giving a good deal of time to wholly unimportant books, he threaten[ed] to become, in his own words, an efficient 'critical cheer leader,' a kind of Mark Sullivan of literature, with no finely balanced scale of values, but a glowing enthusiasm for everything simply because it exists" (*RC,* 157). Assured that the best service the critic could perform, in behalf of those "who are moving, lies in calling attention to that part of their motion which seems to be forward" (quoted, *RC,* 157), Sherman eventually contented himself with understanding rather than judgment, with appreciation rather than criticism. This same danger was even more apparent in the work of Sherman's contemporary, James Gibbons Huneker, who, like his predecessors, Anatole France and Jules Lemaître in France and Arthur Symons in England, often confused educated enthusiasm for discriminating assessment. Sherman himself finally avoided this fate only because, in addition to Huneker's vitality, he possessed other virtues Matthiessen respected—"a firmer intellectual grasp, a more solid sense of structure, a deeper perception of the relation of art to life in all its phases"—which, on occasion at least, "enabled him not simply to describe the effect made upon his spirit by a work of art, but to illuminate its essential nature" (*RC,* 159).

The tendency toward critical subjectivism in Huneker and even in Sherman stood out more sharply when contrasted with the practice of someone like Edmund Wilson, a critic who made a profound impression upon Matthiessen because he had "slowly and patiently, and with a degree of thoroughness unequaled by anyone else in his generation," set out to equip himself "for the task of interpreting modern literature" (*RC,* 159). Wilson seemed to possess in abundance precisely the qualities that Sherman exhibited only infrequently, with the result that the former had already achieved, in *Axel's Castle* (1931), what the latter had struggled in vain to accomplish all his life, namely, an actual reappropriation of the past for the purpose of understanding the present. It is important to note, however, that Wilson's success was not due solely to the exhaustiveness, but rather to the quality, of his preparation for the task. Not satisfied merely with immersing himself in all aspects of modern letters, Wilson struck Matthiessen as having gradually "extended his mastery of the culture of the past, and still . . . kept his mind in touch with contemporary movements in sciences and metaphysics" (*RC,* 159). As a consequence, he was able to relate present-day writing to the cultural and philosophical roots from which it had sprung and also to raise hard questions about its relevance and its future. Other critics equally as learned as Wilson might merely have described and analyzed the central works of Wilson's six major figures (Yeats, Valéry, Eliot, Proust, Joyce, and Gertrude Stein), but Wilson took the additional critical step of questioning the wisdom of probing any further into the world of inwardness, as all six insisted upon doing, in marked isolation from society. "In asking this question so forcefully," Matthiessen argued, "Mr. Wilson has proved his supreme value as a critic. Absorbed in the present, he is not lost in its flux; he can indicate both its weakness and its grandeur" (*RC*, 161).

The one point to which Matthiessen objected was Wilson's occasional inclination to substitute a discussion of his poets' ideas for a satisfactory assessment of their poetry. This tendency was vexing chiefly because, in an age of awakened social, political, and cultural concern, it was all too easy for critics like Wilson, who viewed themselves as literary and cultural historians, to forsake their obligation to particular literary texts in favor of an interest either in the cultural milieu surrounding them or in the vision of life they expressed. The interest in milieu, fast becoming apparent in the later books of Van Wyck Brooks, revealed a regrettable proclivity to turn literary interpretation into an occasion for gossip about the life of letters. The stress on the view of life had become even more prominent among moral and sociological critics, whose work betrayed a kindred temptation to reduce critical discussion to a debate on competing value systems or possible modes of social reconstruction.

In order to resist these tendencies and thus to restore proper balance, Matthiessen was eager to reassert that the primary business of critics is the analysis and evaluation of individual works of literature, considering them not as tracts for the times or as reflections of their age but rather as special fusions of form and content. Hence it was not inconsistent for him to counterbalance his respect for critics as broadly cultural as Stuart Sherman, Lewis Mumford, and Edmund Wilson with equally strong claims for the importance of a Coleridge, a James, or an Eliot. As artists concerned with the basic principles of their craft, Matthiessen believed they practiced a type of criticism which "is always fertile" (*AR*, xvii). Together with writers and critics like Stéphane Mallarmé and I. A. Richards, they served as a constant reminder that what finally matters is not what poems mean but what they are.

Matthiessen's view of the primary function of criticism may help to explain why he retained so high an estimation of Edgar Allen Poe's value as a critic at a time when many of his contemporaries were prepared to dismiss Poe outright as a simple romantic. In Matthiessen's view, Poe's affiliation with all other romantic theorists was offset by his firm conception of art as "designed effect."[10] Poe may have been susceptible to exaggeration, Matthiessen conceded, but he also shared with some of his greatest predecessors in the history of criticism a genuine "devotion to the first principles of art."[11] Poe could not only appreciate writers far different from himself; he also showed originality as a literary theorist. Because he was inveterately opposed to accepting anything on authority, Poe was committed to the necessity of considering "*de novo* the capabilities of whatever art he examined."[12] What disturbed Poe most about American letters, Matthiessen writes, "was the replacement of our earlier subservience to British standards by a form of provincialism that he deemed even worse, by the blatant determination to like 'a stupid book better, because, sure enough, its stupidity is American.' "[13] Hence in contradistinction to both extremes, Matthiessen notes, "Poe was to take his stand on the proposition that 'the world at large' is 'the only proper stage' for both writer and reader,"[14] and to insist upon "the application of a rigorous *method* in all forms of thought."[15]

In the realm of critical theory, however, it was clearly James and Eliot rather than Poe or even Coleridge who provided the strongest counterweight to Matthiessen's interest in social and cultural criticism. It was not that these artist-critics repudiated the existence of a relationship between literature and history or

---

[10] F. O. Matthiessen, "Edgar Allan Poe," in *Literary History of the United States,* ed. Robert E. Spiller *et al.* (3rd ed. rev.; New York: Macmillan, 1963), p. 338.

[11] *Ibid.,* p. 329.

[12] *Ibid.,* p. 334.

[13] *Ibid.,* p. 328.

[14] *Ibid.*

[15] Poe as cited by Matthiessen (*ibid.,* p. 334).

between literature and society, but that their comprehensive and sympathetic understanding of the problems of craft enabled them to show how writers experienced social and cultural issues as questions of form and technique. Indeed, Matthiessen's association of James and Eliot in this connection was no mere accident. As early as the first edition of *The Achievement of T. S. Eliot,* Matthiessen exhibited an awareness of the close relationship of James and Eliot as critics as well as artists; he frequently used the critical insights of the older writer to illumine and support the theoretical speculations of the younger. Their closeness was natural and even inevitable, because in Matthiessen's reading there was a wide area of agreement between them. Both insisted upon the fusion of form and content in all great art; both held that such a fusion is possible only to an artist whose sensibility is fully unified. As critics, both Eliot and James were inclined to locate the origins of that sensibility in a writer's awareness of the significance of the past for the present and of the present for the past, and each assumed that this awareness is based on a quality that Eliot referred to as "spiritual reality," that is, an imagination of the ineluctable intermixture of good and evil in every human act. Yet if their shared perception of spiritual reality betrayed their affinity with what was left of the tradition of American Puritanism, like Poe before them they were both convinced of the necessity of an international, not merely a national or a provincial, basis for art and culture.

These and other similarities encouraged Matthiessen to view James and Eliot in the same light or to use them to exemplify similar positions. Yet in one or two particulars Matthiessen eventually acquired from James a deepened and more sophisticated sense of the convictions he typically associated with both writers, and beyond them with the best of the critical tradition generally.

First, if James and Eliot shared a belief that aesthetic experience is in some way different in kind as well as in degree from other types of experience, resulting from so intense a unity of means and ends that the two become one in the created object of art, James nonetheless possessed a less complicated sense of the nature of aesthetic experience. He described it simply as an impression of "felt life," meaning life as it is experienced by those who possess the capacity to imagine their living it in all its emotional and sensuous immediacy, and he encouraged Matthiessen in his later criticism to strive for a direct apprehension of this quality.

Second, James also enabled Matthiessen to perceive how art thus conceived can serve as an affirmation of life by providing through the discipline of form an intense and faithful realization of life's felt quality. This perception of art may sound like a critical commonplace, but Matthiessen nonetheless employed it to great advantage when he turned his attention to such writers as Hawthorne, Melville, and even James. It helped to support and amplify the conviction he had first derived from Eliot, that even the most pessimistic and despairing literature still constitutes a mode of actualization and release by serving as a source of emotional renewal as well as of intellectual insight.

Finally, James's constant emphasis upon the sense of life which great art may be said to express, and thereby often to quicken, also emboldened Matthiessen to agree with James as well about "the great question" that the critic must always address to the great artist: What is his "philosophy" or his "total view of the world"? In the main, Matthiessen was no less reluctant than James himself to identify an artist's ultimate view of life with any paraphrasable set of convictions or articles of belief. As James had suggested, a writer's philosophy is like a figure woven into the entire carpet of his work. While the carpet may be said to cohere aesthetically only because of the design its figure lends it, that figure itself becomes incomprehensible and meaningless apart from the materials it unifies and expresses.

4

Observations such as these suggest more concretely many of the new standards in American criticism which Matthiessen had originally called for in 1929. One measure of their influence and importance is that by 1948 and the publication of *The Literary History of the United States,* edited by Robert Spiller and others, most of these same standards had been fully absorbed by American critical practice. In addition, however, Matthiessen's observations about criticism created a kind of composite portrait of his own ideal critic, of the critic he would try to become in the course of his career. Such a critic would possess Edmund Wilson's devotion to craft together with Stuart Sherman's egalitarianism, V. L. Parrington's historical breadth together with T. S. Eliot's understanding of structure and technique. He would eschew the subjectivism of the later Van Wyck Brooks as vigorously as he repudiated the dogmatism of Irving Babbitt, but he would need to possess that sense of intellectual and moral complexity which permitted him to see, as Matthiessen could, the enduring importance of both. For as Brooks began to forsake the wise standards of his early work in his later criticism, he was nevertheless correct in his initial insistence "on the value of a deeply individual approach to life in opposition to all standardization" (*RC,* 207). And if Babbitt eventually permitted his own standards to harden into inflexible doctrine, he still "demonstrated in his own practice the cardinal importance for any civilization of a man's retaining his hold 'on the truths of the inner life' " (*RC,* 165).

Matthiessen's ideal critic would possess de Tocqueville's genius for "penetrating generalization" which "can serve to light up anew the problems that continue to threaten any democracy" (*RC,* 141), as well as Moses Coit Tyler's desire, in echoing Sainte-Beuve, to "connect criticism with biography" and thus "make the study of letters a study of human nature" (quoted *RC,* 151). He would share T. K. Whipple's "devotion to the equalitarian strain in our democracy" (*RC,* 166), together with Paul Rosenfeld's conviction that "the best attack on the bad is the loving understanding and exposition of the good" (quoted, *RC,* 176). He would appreciate Allen Tate's observation that the business of criticism is not so much to answer questions as to ask them again, as well as Poe's stress upon the necessity of taking each work of art on its own terms. He would exhibit Emerson's belief that the critic's chief instrument is the whole of himself, together with Paul Elmer More's realization that the self attains completion only through the acknowledgment of that which transcends it.

If this were to place an impossible series of demands upon anyone who would become a critic, Matthiessen had no illusions about the likelihood of ever completely fulfilling them. Like Arnold and Eliot before him, he was convinced that the critic's goal is never fully reached; but like them, too, he could find, at least until close to the end of his life, a certain satisfaction which sufficed in the very aspiration toward it. As Arnold once remarked in a similar connection, "That promised land it will not be ours to enter, and we shall die in the wilderness; but to have desired to enter it, to have saluted it from afar, is already, perhaps, the best distinction among contemporaries; it will certainly be the best title to esteem with posterity" (quoted, *ATSE*, 6).

CHAPTER TWO

From the Art of Translation to
the Achievement of Criticism

One cannot be seriously interested in literature and remain purely
literary in interests.

F. R. LEAVIS
How to Teach Reading

F. O. MATTHIESSEN did not exhibit at the outset of his career
the mature critical grasp he was later to display in *American
Renaissance: Art and Expression in the Age of Emerson and Whitman*
(1941), *Henry James: The Major Phase* (1944), *The James Family*
(1947), or even *Theodore Dreiser* (1951). Although he established
his critical positions early and applied them with unusual consistency throughout his life, there was an early time of testing
and development. The three books produced at the beginning
of his career all bear the marks of his critical apprenticeship.
Sarah Orne Jewett (1929), for example, reflects the same nostalgia
for the past and the same traditional sentiment which suffused
a major part of Miss Jewett's work and constitutes one of its chief
deficiencies; *Translation: An Elizabethan Art* (1931), for all its
liveliness and interest, is in the main a derivative study based
heavily, as Matthiessen was the first to admit, on Charles Whi-
bley's pioneering analysis of Elizabethan translations in *The
Cambridge History of English Literature*. Matthiessen's *The Achievement of T. S. Eliot: An Essay on the Nature of Poetry* (1935) is so
dependent upon Eliot's own standards for a critical evaluation
of his poetry that it never quite escapes from the shadow cast
by its subject or attains a genuine authority of its own. Despite
these shortcomings, however, each study possesses real interest,
not only in its own right, but as a record of Matthiessen's early
development as scholar and critic. Taken together, these three

31

books define the crucial period of maturation when Matthiessen consolidated the concerns, refined the methods, and clarified the aims that would remain characteristic of him throughout his life.

1

Although Matthiessen's study of the art of four Elizabethan translators was not published until two years after his biography of Sarah Orne Jewett, it was actually completed almost two years earlier. In substance, *Translation: An Elizabethan Art* was Matthiessen's doctoral dissertation at Harvard. Written under the direction of John Livingston Lowes, author of *Road to Xanadu* (1927), the monumental study of Coleridge's composition of "Kubla Khan" and "The Ancient Mariner," with considerable advice from George Lyman Kittredge and Hyder Rollins, *Translation* exhibits in full measure an exacting attention to philological detail and a comprehensive historical scope. Even so, the book might have become just another scholarly exercise in philology and stylistics, lacking all interest for the general reader, had it not been for Matthiessen's already impressive facility for developing the implications of his materials. In *Translation,* he showed how a study of essentially nothing more than language can disclose a good many secrets of personality and history as well as of style.

Matthiessen's achievement, modest as it was, should be adjudged the more remarkable because the project was something of a compromise. Upon returning from England to complete his graduate study at Harvard, Matthiessen's original intention had been to write a dissertation on the poetry of Walt Whitman, but this proposal was summarily rejected on the ground that Whitman had by that time been pretty well exhausted as a subject of literary study. Still flush with the excitement of his new discovery of American literature, this rejection must have been enormously disappointing to Matthiessen, but he seems to have accepted it without complaint. If expression of his newly awakened interest in the American tradition had to be postponed, he would try to make the best of it by turning to his second major field of interest, the English Renaissance.

Matthiessen's choice of the art of Elizabethan translation was unusually fortuitous, for several reasons. First, it gave him excellent firsthand exposure to the best contemporary methods of textual and philological analysis, so that later, when he decided to supplement those methods with fresher, more flexible, modes of approach, he was in a better position to know exactly what to reject as well as to accept. Second, Elizabethan translation forced him to take up a series of issues related to, but not identical with, such questions of style as the nature of language, the purpose of translation, the problems of composition, and the relation between style and vision. Third and most important, his choice forced him to consider the whole vexed question of the relationship between literature and history: Does literature reflect history? Can literature in any sense be said to shape history? Ultimately, Matthiessen's subject compelled him to explore the connection between the art of Elizabethan translators and the age for which they wrote. For these reasons, then, *Translation* is far more than a study of the stylistic qualities of a representative group of Elizabethan translations. In addition to the analysis of such rudiments as diction and syntax, there are extensive comparisons between the translations and the originals, careful evaluations of faults and virtues in each translation, consideration of the translators' preparation for their task, and even excursions beyond textual and biographical matters into the ethos of the age and the way in which the age was expressed by the art of translation.

In retrospect, it seems clear that Matthiessen was drawn to Elizabethan translators because of the strong patriotic quality of their intentions, their deep commitment to enhancing the life of their country, and the enormous historical impact they achieved in realizing them. This theme Matthiessen sounds over and over again in his book. The Elizabethan translators' distinction lay in the fact that, unlike present-day classical translators who, aiming at a mirrorlike imitation of the original, write almost exclusively for other scholars, they wrote for the nation as a whole; they were more than willing to sacrifice meticulous accuracy for the sake of producing books that would touch the hearts of all. As Matthiessen puts it, their entire effort was directed solely to "naturalizing the quality of the originals, and bringing them out to the full for the English reader" (*T*, 6–7).

To this end they saturated their language with the distinctive spirit of the times and drew upon the talent they shared with dramatists, an "extraordinary eye for specific detail." "Whenever possible," Matthiessen says, the Elizabethan translator "substituted a concrete image for an abstraction, a verb that carried the picture of an action for a general statement." And the result of such practice was "an increased liveliness, a heightened dramatic pitch that often carried . . . [the translator's] words into a realm of imagination and feeling unsuggested by the original" (*T*, 4).

Matthiessen was quick to concede the hazards in this kind of translation. The Elizabethan translator, instead of rendering a faithful copy of the original, was likely to produce a wholly different work of art altogether. His real aim, however, was to create an imitation based on the less crucial distinction between, for example, photography and painting. Instead of striving for an exact copy of the work before him, the translator hoped to create something with "an independent life of its own" (*T*, 90). Only in this way could he make "the foreign classics rich with English associations" and carry "Plutarch and Montaigne deep into the national consciousness" (*T*, 4). The real test of the method, however, lay in its results. Whether or not it could be fully justified in theory, there was no question about its success. By adopting means (however unconventional by modern standards) in perfect accord with his aims, the Elizabethan translator contributed to a radical alteration in English history. Though he sought to do no more than enhance his nation's culture, he in fact assisted in bringing the Renaissance to England.

In Matthiessen's hands, then, the Elizabethan translator became something of a heroic figure. Citizen and patriot as well as scholar and craftsman, he seemed cut from the same cloth as the Renaissance voyager who extended the horizons of his nation's governance and the Renaissance merchant who extended the boundaries of his nation's commerce. And when one compares the products of the translator's labors with the originals that inspired them, one gains insight into the mind of the educated Elizabethan, discovering "what learning meant to him, and why he was so fired with enthusiasm to attain it; what is more significant, you understand the forces which actuated the development of language in the sixteenth century, the qualities its writers strove to express, the difficulties they had to compass, and the ends they achieved" (*T*, 3).

These observations signify rather large ambitions, but Matthiessen's study was admirably designed to fulfill them. For purposes of economy as well as intensity, he limited his study to five of the most important Elizabethan prose translations: Sir Thomas Hoby's translation of Castiglione's *The Courtier* (1561), Sir Thomas North's translation of Plutarch's *Lives* (1579), John Florio's translation of Montaigne's *Essays* (1603), and Philemon Holland's translations of Livy's *Roman History* (1600) and Suetonius (1606). Matthiessen's selections were carefully chosen not only to extend throughout the reign of Elizabeth but also to illumine important elements in the process of cultural transformation. Castiglione's *Courtier,* for example, represented the Italian contribution and Montaigne's *Essays* the French, while the works by Plutarch, Livy, and Suetonius indicated the complementary role played by elements of Greek and Roman culture. But Matthiessen also selected his translators for their representative stature. Whereas Hoby's work epitomized the earliest phases of English Renaissance style, Florio's translation was characteristic of later Renaissance prose. North was important by contrast because, in avoiding the crudeness of Hoby and the occasional affectations of Florio, he attained the directness of expression to which they all aspired. North's was a style in which language fused almost perfectly with experience. Instead of resurrecting a dead Plutarch, North remade him in the image of an English sea captain.

Yet Matthiessen reserved his highest praise for Philemon Holland, calling him "the Translator General." Like the others, Holland wrote with the twofold purpose of making his work as readable as possible and of bringing out the distinguishing characteristics of its model. He was so thoroughly both a master of his craft and a man of his own age that he was able to surpass even North in giving his translations the drama and force of the original. The secret of his achievement, according to Matthiessen, lay in his desire to make his reading a part of his life: "Livy and Suetonius were not ancient classics, but men with something to say that might be vital to England's destiny. They were not to be laid up on shelves and studied, but to be read as eagerly as one would talk on matters of importance with one's fellow townsmen" (*T,* 181). To Holland, as Matthiessen later pointed out in regard to T. S. Eliot, the past was not dead but living, and thus "it was natural for Holland to speak of these books as though they were flesh and blood, since they contained for him an essence as rich as life itself" (*T,* 181). But the affinity with Eliot was stronger still, for Holland's capacity for feeling the vitality and significance of what he read could be attributed only to his possession of a unified sensibility. Hence Matthiessen could conclude, utilizing another insight borrowed from Eliot, that "because Holland's thoughts came to him with the same immediacy as the odor of a rose, he could conceive of his vast labor of translation as a long journey abroad" (*T,* 226).

Of particular significance to Matthiessen was the effect of scholarship undertaken with such motives. If Holland's intention was to share with others what he found on his journeys abroad, he ultimately succeeded in bringing some of the greatest works of classical antiquity into the mainstream of English literature and experience and in that way altered the course of English life and history. Philemon Holland thus provided an early example of the kind of scholar-critic that Matthiessen himself would try to become, one who, though "every inch a scholar," conceives of the whole society as his proper audience and the revitalization of national culture as his proper function.

There was a strong hint of Van Wyck Brooks's notion of a usable past in Matthiessen's remarks on Renaissance translators,[1] but Matthiessen was careful not to overplay it. Though clearly interested in recovering a significant portion of the translators' achievement, he successfully resisted the temptation to do so at the expense of distorting the materials in and through which that achievement was expressed. Hence his analysis of the art of Elizabethan translation could become a study of the history that art reflects and in part created without turning into something other than a work of literary scholarship.

Judged in the light of Matthiessen's later work, *Translation: An Elizabethan Art* displays interests and tendencies that eventually

---

[1] Bernard Bowron, "The Making of an American Scholar," *Monthly Review* 2 (1950): 214.

became highly typical. Not only does Matthiessen ally himself with the public-spirited sentiments of his citizen-translators and forcefully underline the cultural significance of their achievement, but he moves back and forth from literature to history in order to examine the translations against the broadest possible background. Equally as characteristic are his tentative attempts to treat style as an index to vision and thus to regard a study of the translator's art as an examination of the mind of an age. At more than one point Matthiessen acknowledged the inevitable perils attending the rather romantic desire to discuss the man within the work and behind him the mind of his era, but it was altogether characteristic of Matthiessen's humanism that he would view works of art, even those as derivative as translations, as forms of personal and historical expression. Nevertheless, what kept him from writing pure biography or intellectual history, even when focusing on the translator and his age rather than on the translation, was the conviction (not formulated until he wrote *American Renaissance*) that the best approach to such matters must be through attention to a writer's tools and materials and to what he can make of them.

Matthiessen did not always hold as fast to that conviction as he does in *Translation.* There would be times, in his later criticism, when many of his frequently brilliant explications of various texts would be performed merely as a kind of preliminary *rite de passage* before taking up what one occasionally senses to have been his more compelling interests in intellectual and cultural history. In *Translation: An Elizabethan Art,* however, his forays into such areas occur largely as an extension of the critical process itself, an inevitable consequence of the scrutiny of specific literary details, which, when probed with rigor and intelligence, have a way of casting light both backward on the author and forward on emerging patterns of experience. In *Translation,* Matthiessen was thus able to explore some of the relations of art and culture, of literature and life, without oversimplifying or falsifying the distinctions between them.

2

In writing his second book, *Sarah Orne Jewett,* Matthiessen had much the same purpose as in writing his first: to show how a study of literary art discloses important insights into the kind of personal and cultural history which that art might be said both to mirror and to help us repossess. Nonetheless, the result was vastly different and inferior. Perhaps it was only a matter of giving way too easily to that temptation to relax standards which so often accompanies release from the regimen of graduate study. Or perhaps, when turning his attention to more contemporary material which was also more directly related to his own life (Miss Jewett was a relative on his mother's side), Matthiessen could not retain that sense of appropriate complexity which, as he would later insist, should always attend one's image of the past. Whatever the cause, *Sarah Orne Jewett* reveals a marked slackening of critical tension, a serious reduction of intellectual pressure. Forsaking both the rigors of scholarship and the discriminations of criticism, Matthiessen gave full play to the promptings of something closer to mere sentiment. As a consequence, *Sarah Orne Jewett* reveals at least as much about Matthiessen himself and the rare moment of emotional and spiritual composure when he wrote it as it does either about Miss Jewett's life or about her artistic achievement.

Matthiessen once described to his friend Bernard Bowron his great pleasure in writing *Sarah Orne Jewett*. He spoke fondly of leisurely excursions into the countryside surrounding South Berwick, Maine, where Miss Jewett had lived, and of pleasant summer afternoons going through papers and collections in the small but attractive Bullfinch Library in Portsmouth, only 12 miles down the Piscataqua River from Miss Jewett's home. During the relaxed and happy summer he spent working on the book, Matthiessen rented a house at nearby Kittery Point with his friend Russell Cheney, who subsequently lent him some of his paintings to use as illustrations. Shortly thereafter, he and Cheney bought a cottage overlooking the bay at Kittery; it soon became Matthiessen's second home with which many of his friends associated their happiest memories of him. It was a handsome old cottage to which, according to Bowron, "Matthiessen frequently referred, and only half-humorously, as 'the most beautiful house in America.' "[2] Even more important than the house, however, was the region surrounding it. The lovely Kittery landscapes, with fine old houses and weatherworn outbuildings set against a background of seacoast, salt marshes, and woods, were a never-ending source of replenishment and delight. Though Matthiessen never regarded Kittery simply as a pastoral retreat where he might assume the role of a latter-day naturalist, it permitted him to go about, as one friend later remarked, "unarmed,"[3] disencumbered of that attitude of aggressive combativeness which, as the years wore on, frequently made his life in Cambridge strenuous for everyone. At Kittery, particularly with the help of Russell Cheney's gracious ways and undefensive manner, Matthiessen was committed chiefly to enjoying himself and to sharing his sense of enjoyment with those who visited him.

It was in this mood of relaxed and easy communion with himself and others that Matthiessen undertook his biography of Sarah Orne Jewett. Bernard Bowron is surely correct in suggesting that Matthiessen was as strongly motivated by a desire to share Kittery with his friends as by any commitment to the intrinsic value of Miss Jewett's art. Though he insisted upon ranking Miss Jewett second only to Emily Dickinson among America's principal women writers, his primary aim was not evaluation but evocation, and thus he permitted the spirit of the place and his somewhat idealized version of its past to dominate the book from the very first page. The opening paragraph constitutes a gesture of identification which Matthiessen does not wholly overcome until his final chapter:

The first thing she could remember was a world bounded by the white paling fences around her house. There were wide green yards and tall elms to shade them. There was a long line of barns and sheds, one of which had a large room upstairs with an old ship's foresail spread over the floor and made a wonderful play-room in wet weather. Apples were laid out to dry there in the fall, and there were some old chests and discarded pieces of furniture to keep house with. (*SOJ,* 1)

The most striking image in this paragraph is one that remains prominent almost throughout the book. It is the image of the white paling fence by which, to extend the spatial figure, Miss Jewett was able to preserve intact the solid and pristine virtues

[3] C. L. Barber, in *Monthly Review* 2 (1950): 267.

of the past against the approach of such modern elements as
heavy industry and the city. It is often difficult to know exactly
what those virtues were, however, for Matthiessen constantly
uses natural imagery not only to suggest the influence of her
surroundings on her development but also to define the essence
of her art. There are frequent references to flowers which used
to grow in her grandmother's front yard and which keep reap-
pearing throughout the book as devices of evocation—white and
yellow daffodils in early spring, then larkspur and honeysuckle,
Canterbury bells and London pride, ladies'-delight, lilacs,
French pinks, tiger lilies, cinnamon roses, tea roses—all of them
meant to suggest beneficent influences upon Miss Jewett's
maturing spirit. When Matthiessen describes the quality of some
of her most vivid and successful pages, he again turns to nature
by likening their directness to the sun's rays and their freshness
to a breeze blowing across the water. Even when he tries to sum
up some of her most complicated effects, he refers to the sea-
sons and their cycles: "They envelop the mingled charm and
sadness of the countryside just as you feel it on the summer day
that brings the first hint of autumn, when, in the midst of the
wild roses along the dusty road, you are suddenly aware of the
first fateful spray of goldenrod" (*SOJ,* 101–2).

Aside from their occasionally mawkish tone, some of these
passages leave one with the impression that Matthiessen is giving way to a sentimental, if also typically American, attitude
toward nature, one that affects not only his feelings about Miss
Jewett's fiction but also his interpretation of the elements of
modern life which threaten to violate her privileged sanctuary.
Throughout the book, for example, he draws contrasts between
the direct, crisp, ripe tenderness of her best stories, expressive
of a sense of the sanctity of the past, and the defilements of an
encroaching urban and industrial civilization. The invigorating
New England air, which had earlier quickened the artistic impulses of Emerson and Thoreau, is now "clogged with smoke"
(*SOJ,* 20). And worse, the Matthiessen who was later to make
so much of the egalitarian strain in American democracy here
writes almost bitterly of the arrival of Irish immigrants who
crowded out the native village folk and defaced the landscape
with their "rows of drab rickety houses . . . growing like mush-

rooms overnight" (*SOJ*, 20). Before the Civil War, Berwick had been an active inland port which opened a healthy provincial community to currents of influence originating from as far away as London and Santo Domingo. But now it had become merely "an upcountry station on a branch railway line, grappled by bonds of steel and wire to Lawrence and Lynn" (*SOJ*, 19–20).

This striking image of entanglement, even imprisonment, creates a context in which Matthiessen can, by contrast, effectively highlight Miss Jewett's limited but significant achievement. With the world about her becoming more enthralled, and thereby depleted, through its bondage to the historically inevitable, Matthiessen tends to argue that Miss Jewett had little choice but to shut herself off from the turbulent world outside and cultivate the garden of her own private but historically valuable sensibility. He quotes, with apparent approval, her least attractive statement regarding the necessity of this stratagem:

People do not know what they lose when they make away with the reserve, the separateness, the sanctity of the front yard of their grandmothers. It is like writing down the family secrets for any one to read; it is like having everybody call you by your first name and sitting in any pew in church, and like having your house in the middle of a road, to take away the fence which, slight as it may be, is a fortification round your home. More things than one may come in without being asked; we Americans had better build more fences than take any away from our lives. (*SOJ*, 31)

How different this approach is, as Matthiessen himself would later have been the first to perceive, from, say, Robert Frost's feeling about fences. Frost, in asserting that "good fences make good neighbors," expresses the profound moral paradox that separateness and a respect for individual differences are necessary to the establishment of any genuine sense of community; Miss Jewett, on the other hand, is recommending the construction of fences strictly for purposes of defense, to set apart in order to preserve small enclaves of genteel privilege.

It is probably unfair to imply that Matthiessen's tacit endorsement of these self-protective gestures was anything but unconscious, just as it would be misleading to suggest that they are representative of more than a tiny segment of Miss Jewett's art. In fact, if anyone had bothered to bring the idea of protected privilege to Matthiessen's attention, he would surely have denied that either he or Miss Jewett was in any way implicated in it. The only convergence between his motives and Miss Jewett's occurred not as the result of a desire to protect the pristine values of the past from corruption by modern influences, but rather as a consequence of their shared concern to rescue a poignant moment in American life and history from oblivion. His was the task of describing and analyzing or sometimes, regrettably, merely evoking a sense of the life and achievement of a writer who gave that moment enduring artistic dignity.

Although Matthiessen largely failed in this effort, in one sense his method was both appropriate and necessary. The problem of Miss Jewett's art was definitely posed by the nature of her life and her environment, and one could hardly do justice to the first without coming to terms with the second. Growing up in South Berwick, Maine, only to experience a mode of life already on the wane, Miss Jewett wanted to capture in her writing the complex set of feelings associated with its passing and a sense of what would be lost in the process. Her problem was to discover suitable means for expressing the felt quality and significance of her experience in all its sad but noble complexity. Yet without a strong literary tradition to fall back on, she had no resource but the environment itself. Accordingly, when Matthiessen finally got around to considering the actual elements of her art, he was fully justified in asking how she was able to transform her memories and impressions of the life around her into an experience of its inmost qualities. The answer was to be found in a comparison of Miss Jewett's accurate reporting in the stories collected in *Deephaven* (1877) with her more sophisticated artistry in some of the stories published in *The Country of the Pointed Firs* (1896). The difference was that between the faithful transcription of one's experience and an imaginative translation of it. What Miss Jewett had seemed to learn in the interim is that mere description is not enough, that the aim of all good writing must be to turn one's impression of something into a reexperience of it. The first merely yields the truth of observation; the second issues in the life of art.

Matthiessen would return again and again to this point in the course of his career, finally grounding his discussion of it in the fully developed aesthetic that emerges from the pages of *Ameri-*

can Renaissance. In *Sarah Orne Jewett,* however, he was content merely to point out several important implications. At one level, he maintained, a writer's capacity to transform what is seen into what is felt requires the ability to put technique at the service of material; without a union of form and content in this basic sense, his work simply cannot attain an integral life of its own. At a deeper and more characteristic level, however, Matthiessen believed that the capacity to turn a visualization of what is observed into an actual experience of it required the fusion of both technique and material with the distinctive qualities of a writer's own personality, with all that he could bring from his own life. The result of this more complex and important fusion is what Matthiessen here denominated style, and style, as he was later to remark, "has not been such a common phenomenon in America that its possessor can ever be ignored" (*SOJ,* 148). Indeed, just because no art can long survive without style, Matthiessen was obliged to conclude:

If the material is crude, the work will continue to have historical value, such as even the clumsiest of Dreiser's novels will have in throwing light upon their time, but they are not works of art. If the technique is skillful but the personality hollow, the product will fade like that of the poetasters of every generation. Without style Sarah Jewett's material would be too slight to attract a second glance. With it . . . she created—not a world, but a township in the State of Maine. (*SOJ,* 145–46)

With this modulated statement of Miss Jewett's achievement, Matthiessen began to regain the critical control he had all but relinquished to the spirit of her region and her life. But not until the closing chapter, when he finally decided to come to terms with Miss Jewett's limitations, did the rigorous, demanding, searching voice of the mature critic really take over. When Matthiessen ultimately criticized Miss Jewett for evading the central facts of experience and for playing down the sordid, bleak, and tragic dimensions of New England life, brought out much more vividly by Hawthorne and Melville, his interpretation began to exhibit a more fertile balance between appreciation and critical assessment. The Sarah Orne Jewett who emerges at the end of the book is therefore a far more realistic and believable, if also more limited, figure than the person who dominates the beginning. In temperament, ambition, and achievement, she bears an almost identical likeness to her own portrait of the Russian novelist Turgenev:

> . . . there was in him such a love of light, sunshine, and living human poetry, such an organic aversion to all that is ugly, or coarse, or discordant, that he made himself almost exclusively the poet of the gentler side of human nature. On the fringe of his pictures, or in their background, just for the sake of contrast, he will show us the vices, the cruelties, even the mire of life. But he cannot stay in these gloomy regions, and he hastens back to the realms of the sun and the flowers, or to the poetical moonlight of melancholy, which he loves best because in it he can find expression for his own great sorrowing heart. (Quoted, *SOJ*, 133–34)

It is odd that Matthiessen took so long to attain as circumspect a view of Miss Jewett's limitations and virtues as she had acquired of Turgenev's. The reason, I think, is to be attributed to his uncritical willingness to be dominated by her personality and milieu, which brought out all the worst aspects of his own tendency to empathize, to write from the inside. In later books and essays this same inclination, when coupled with a firmer grasp of form and a stronger desire to differentiate weakness from strength, would give his criticism the qualities of toughness and sympathy which became its distinctive hallmark. Early in his career, however, his capacity for subjective identification led all too often to evasion rather than to genuine fulfillment of the critic's responsibilities.

If the writing of *Sarah Orne Jewett* accomplished nothing more, it gave Matthiessen the opportunity to pay his debt to a relative and to the region she helped make so vivid and sustaining a presence to him. He always retained a deep affection for that part of the country, particularly for the dignity of its ways, and the book on Miss Jewett permitted him to record it. But the writing of *Sarah Orne Jewett* did more. It enabled Matthiessen for the first time to direct his attention to the New England tradition of letters, especially to the darker aspects of New England experience which Miss Jewett frequently passed over, elements that were soon to become his touchstones in assessing any serious artistic rendering of experience. Finally, it raised anew the nagging questions as to the nature and the function of art, many of which had been tentatively raised in Matthiessen's study of Elizabethan translators.

In that earlier essay Matthiessen had perceived that literature often reflects or illumines the past and also helps to determine its shape and form. In his book on Sarah Orne Jewett, he had, though with considerably less adroitness, supplemented this perception with the notion that literature also constitutes a source of pleasure and satisfaction in its own right. One issue both books left unresolved is the question of precisely how literature performs each of these functions, and whether, if it does, they may in any sense be conceived of as integrally related to one another. Is the pleasure to be derived from literature solely a result of the fusion between form and content, or of a larger unity between the work itself and the artist's own experience? What is the connection between these several kinds of unity and a work's relation to its age? How is one to conceive of any work of literature both as a reflection of its age and as an instrument for expressing and realizing the qualities of that age? Another issue both books raised without really addressing was the question of aesthetic norms and their relation to a given view of life. In what sense is the ideal of textual unity a norm for aesthetic judgment? How does the ideal of textual unity affect a work's relation to its own age? What bearing does the aesthetic unity of a work have on its expression of a fixed view of life? If literature is a product as well as an expression of historical forces, is it possible or even advisable to look for permanent values by which to judge its constantly evolving and always relative forms?

These were the kinds of critical questions which, more than any others, Matthiessen brought to his work on T. S. Eliot. At the time they may not have possessed in his own mind quite the clarity they exhibit here, but in a few years they would, for one could hardly work on a writer and theorist like Eliot and be unmindful of them. The difference in Eliot's case is that these questions had been asked by someone who had fully exposed himself to the problems and dangers of modern experience. Indeed, this was the reason for Eliot's overriding importance to Matthiessen. However widely the two men might later differ over political and religious, as well as critical, matters, Eliot gave Matthiessen his first real taste of a literary and critical method that had been tested in the crucible of contemporary experience, which had confronted the disintegration of all inherited systems of thought. If Eliot finally could not supply all the right answers, he at least had asked many of the right questions, questions that Matthiessen would go on trying to resolve until the very end of his career.

3

Though Matthiessen had been reading Eliot's poetry for some years, he did not begin to work intensively on Eliot until 1932–33, when Eliot assumed the Norton lectureship at Harvard. Apart from the excitement of witnessing a distinguished literary career in the making and the undoubted stimulation of personal contacts with Eliot during his stay in Cambridge, Matthiessen's interest was specifically aroused by the way in which Eliot's criticism illuminated his poetry and his poetry opened up fresh perspectives on his criticism. For here was a poet-critic in the line running from Jonson and Dryden through Coleridge and Arnold who, as Matthiessen was later to remark, was talking about what he knew at first hand. A major writer was in the process of establishing the theoretical foundations of a new and vital kind of poetry, and, as C. L. Barber suggests in his sensitive preface to the third edition of Matthiessen's book, "the whole landscape [was] being reordered in the process" (*ATSE*, xi). Not only was Eliot forging a whole new literary tradition; he was also reformulating the critical principles necessary to interpret and assess it. The result was a revolution both in theory and in practice which seemed to assure a much-needed alternative to contemporary critical perspectives.[4] Matthiessen therefore

---

[4] There is another, more personal reason for Eliot's importance to Matthiessen, both as poet and as critic. Matthiessen referred to it obliquely in a statement he made about Eliot's relation to the American tradition and in particular to its Puritan strain. The point is that Matthiessen's characterization of the mind that produced that strain bears at least as close a resemblance to himself as it does to Eliot:

"Its special mixture of passion overweighted by thought (as well as the less attractive combination of high moral idealism restrained by practical prudence that was probed by Santayana in 'The Genteel Tradition'); its absorption in the problem of belief and its trust in moments of vision; its dry, unexpected wit; its dread of vulgarity, as perplexing to the creator of 'Sweeney Erect' as to Henry James; its consciousness of the nature of evil, as acute in 'The Turn of the Screw' as in 'Ethan Brand' or 'Gerontion'; its full understanding of the dark consequences of loneliness and repression which are expressed in 'The Love Song of J. Alfred Prufrock' as well as in *The Scarlet Letter;* its severe self-discipline and sudden poignant tenderness, to be found alike in Jonathan Edwards

claimed for his book not a single but a double purpose, "to evaluate Eliot's method and achievement as an artist" and "to emphasize certain of the fundamental elements in the nature of poetry which are in danger of being obscured by the increasing tendency to treat poetry as a social document and to forget that it is an art" (*ATSE,* vii).

In referring to the dangerous tendency of some modern critics to obscure certain of the fundamental qualities of literature as art, Matthiessen was thinking in particular of the way many neohumanist and sociological critics were tempted to value literature chiefly for its ideas and thus to base their evaluations of any given work almost solely on whether those ideas corresponded to their own view of life. Matthiessen's object was not, of course, to suggest that literature is lacking in ideas or to imply that ideas play no part in determining a writer's relation to life or to currents of thought and feeling in his own time. His sole intention was to restore the necessary balance by insisting that a writer's ideas cannot be dissociated from his individual manner of expressing them, which alone gives them value. Believing that "the most fatal approach to a poem is to focus merely on what it seems to state, to try to isolate its ideas from their context in order to approve or disapprove of them before having really grasped their full implications in the poem itself" (*ATSE,* vii), he was concerned to assert that a writer's chief interest for a critic must always reside in his qualities as an artist and not in his qualifications as moralist, social historian, political critic, or theologian. Eliot had begun to popularize this view as early as his first book of essays, *The Sacred Wood* (1920, 1928), and Matthiessen himself would never again swerve from it.

---

and in the author of 'Ash Wednesday'—such attributes and preoccupations are common to the whole strain to which Eliot inextricably belongs" (ATSE, 9–10).

This passage does more than suggest a similarity between Matthiessen's mind and Eliot's; it also serves as an excellent description of the tradition with which Matthiessen was chiefly preoccupied for the rest of his career, the tradition flowing from Edward Taylor and Jonathan Edwards through Ralph Waldo Emerson, Nathaniel Hawthorne, and Herman Melville to Henry James, Henry Adams, and Eliot. It is little wonder that Matthiessen found a literary theory like Eliot's, designed in no small part to explain the nature and effect of this kind of literature, to be at once congenial to his own sensibility and relevant to his own critical purposes. He therefore proceeded without the slightest hesitation to borrow some of Eliot's most representative insights not only to interpret Eliot's poetry but also to fashion the outlines of his own working critical theory.

This commitment is a clear indication of just how far Matthiessen had moved since completing the biography of Sarah Orne Jewett. Much of his progress was no doubt attributable to the influence of Eliot, but there is also evidence that the critical orientation Matthiessen found in Eliot merely confirmed discoveries he had already made on his own, not only in writing on artists as widely different as Michael Wigglesworth and William Vaughn Moody, but also in reviewing the work of critics and historians as various as Moses Coit Tyler, Van Wyck Brooks, Irving Babbitt, Edmund Wilson, and Granville Hicks. Indeed, Matthiessen quickly recovered the critical balance he had temporarily lost in writing *Sarah Orne Jewett* by using these occasions to sort out his own position, and the book on Eliot then provided him with an opportunity to give that position its first tentative expression.

Yet Matthiessen's method of approach in the Eliot book raised serious questions about the critical perspective he wanted to advance. No one would dispute the fact that much of Eliot's criticism was designed to explain his own kind of poetry and that his poetry, in turn, often demonstrated many of the effects he discussed in his criticism. But was there not still a basic contradiction between Matthiessen's efforts to employ Eliot's criticism as a key to Eliot's poetry and the assumption implicit in much of Eliot's early criticism that poetry is essentially an autotelic art which can be understood only in terms of itself?[5] Matthiessen seemed to be using Eliot's criticism almost as a kind of "pony" to interpret his verse, and when his attention focused more directly on critical propositions, the poetry tended to become merely an illustration of certain qualities Matthiessen deemed important.

The flaw in this line of argument is that from the outset Matthiessen never intended to provide a running commentary on Eliot's poetry. His aim rather was to examine Eliot's method as a whole, and so he designed his book "as one connected essay" which would strive "for a sustained condensed effect," his chapter divisions serving "simply as a convenience, in order,

---

[5] In contrast, Stanley Edgar Hyman believed that Matthiessen's mode of approach was fully justified (*The Armed Vision: A Study in the Methods of Modern Literary Criticism* [rev. ed. abr.; New York: Vintage Books, 1955], p. 87).

through their titles, to stress some of the points that I am most interested in establishing" (*ATSE,* viii). Admittedly, this method was experimental, but, Matthiessen felt, it was also necessary if he was to comprehend the unity of Eliot's achievement and define its contemporary value. *The Achievement of T. S. Eliot* was thus a series of extended reflections on six interrelated ideas which Matthiessen used as chapter titles: "Tradition and the Individual Talent," "The Problem of the Contemporary Artist," "The 'Objective Correlative,' " "The Way a Poet Communicates His Meaning: The Auditory Imagination," "The Integrity of a Work of Art," and "The Sense of His Own Age." In the second edition of the book, which appeared in 1947, Matthiessen added two chapters, "The Plays" and "The Quartets," but the original six chapters described what he regarded as the central elements of Eliot's critical theory. To define Eliot's contribution to Matthiessen's own development as a literary theorist and critic, one can do no better than to turn to these controlling ideas.

It was altogether appropriate that Matthiessen began his study of Eliot with a chapter entitled, after Eliot's famous essay of 1919, "Tradition and the Individual Talent." Not only did he share Eliot's sense of the importance of a writer's relation to the past; he also perceived that Eliot's notion of tradition provided the key to his entire critical theory. Thus from the beginning Matthiessen was interested, first, in determining Eliot's relation to the traditions that had shaped him, and second, in showing how Eliot's conception of tradition afforded a way of understanding the relationship of all the other elements of his critical and poetic method.

Eliot's relation to Arnold, whom Matthiessen later acknowledged as his own first critical enthusiasm, offered a logical point of departure, since both men belonged to a distinguished tradition of English critic-writers whose analysis of the problems of art was enriched by their own experience of their craft. This, in fact, made the critical values Eliot and Arnold shared all the more important; one had the sense that where the Victorian and the modern could agree, there was hardly room for dispute. Hence when Matthiessen turned to the qualities of mind revered by both Arnold and Eliot—an awareness of the critic's primary obligation to see the literary object as it really is; a conviction that mature art requires a society hospitable to the influx of new ideas; respect for French intelligence; a tendency to score "not by logic but by flexibility, resilience, and an intuitive precision" (*ATSE*, 6); and a perception of the thinker's inevitable isolation from society—it was almost as though he was defining qualities that were basic to the fully developed critical intelligence.

In citing obvious points of similarity between Eliot and Arnold, Matthiessen was not seeking to blur their differences. The marked discrepancy between the ages in which they lived made it inevitable that there were as many points of contrast as of comparison, but for Matthiessen's purposes they seemed to boil down to one. Arnold stressed substance or content; Eliot put equal emphasis on form, which lent to his criticism as well as to his poetry a far deeper concern for technical details. Where Arnold expounded, Eliot examined; where Arnold declaimed, Eliot dissected. The result was a new kind of criticism in which the mastery of technique afforded an entirely fresh grasp of the whole. Speaking of some of Eliot's essays on various Elizabethan dramatists, Matthiessen defined the method he himself raised to the level of an art in much of his later criticism: "He watches with the trained eye of the hawk, and then swoops on the one point that will illustrate the quality of the whole. His brief essays present in clearest outline the segment of the curve from which the complete circle can be constructed" (*ATSE*, 7).

The questions to be asked were: Where had Eliot acquired his new preoccupation with craft? How had he turned it to account in his own revaluation of poetic and critical method? Eliot's appreciation of Dryden might be cited as one source, but the effect of Dryden's work was really incidental. The chief sources of Eliot's ideas and method lay elsewhere, in Dante, in Donne and the English metaphysical poets, in the French symbolists, and, finally, in Baudelaire. From the first three sources Eliot derived a feeling and a method for the kind of poetry he would himself try to write, a poetry seeking, insofar as possible, to convert thought into its sensuous equivalent and therefore characterized by clear visual images, precise diction, extreme compression, a conversational tone, rapid alterations in mood and feeling, the use of sound and rhythm to convey sense, and the disruption of conventional syntactical arrangements in order to reproduce the arbitrariness of intellectual processes of association. In the fourth source, Baudelaire, Eliot found some of the essential criteria for evaluating the achievements of other poets, notably the conviction that being contemporary entails being traditional as well, and that being both requires perception not only of what is temporal and finite but also of what is constant and unchanging.

In discussing what Eliot gained from each of these four sources, Matthiessen very nearly summed up his entire book on Eliot. Of more pertinence here, however, are the questions of how Eliot's utilization of these strands of the literary heritage shaped his conception of tradition, and of how tradition then became the axis around which all the other elements of his critical theory turned. To put it simply, Eliot's notion of tradition provided a way of understanding how organic unity could be interpreted as at once aesthetic and historical, as expressing not only the unity of content and form or of matter and means, but also the unity of what is relative to the present with what is continuous with the past. Eliot's concept of tradition, presupposing as it did the possession of a unified sensibility, enabled one to see how the unity of an individual work, its fusion of means and ends, reflected in turn whatever unity could be said to typify the entire created order, by bearing within itself the same mixture of the temporal and the timeless which is inherent in all human experience. In short, Eliot's notion of tradition, with its view of the organic relation among the past, the present, and the perennial, made possible an almost religious understanding of literature. At least, this is the way Matthiessen seemed to regard Eliot's concept of tradition, and this is why it had so strong an impact on him. Eliot's theory of literature seemed perfectly designed to overcome the spiritual problem of the contemporary artist—in Eliot's words, "the dissociation of sensibility"—by suggesting how an individual work, in its unity not only with itself but also with tradition, could effect as intense and complete a sense of wholeness, of integration, as men can experience in an age so deracinated as our own. Indeed, by accepting Eliot's insistence that every literary work, no matter how contemporary, should be traditional in his sense,

Matthiessen was implying that all great literature serves a function at least analogous to, even if not identical with, religion, by providing us in a dissociated age such as the modern one with virtually the only occasion when life can be experienced as a vital unity.

Yet it is noteworthy that for all his reliance upon Eliot's view of tradition, Matthiessen never once questioned the assumptions behind it, assumptions that, as several critics have noted, were paradoxical if not downright contradictory.[6] In asserting that a sense of tradition presupposes the historical sense—in Eliot's meaning, a sense of the temporal and the timeless or the relative and the continuous—and that the historical sense, in turn, issues in a twofold perception both of the pastness of the past and also of its presence, Eliot was not only deriving his view of tradition from two different conceptions of reality but also suggesting by it two divergent conceptions of literature.[7] In terms of the first, literature is seen within a developing chronological tradition in which individual works are separated from one another by the influence of time and changing circumstance, as these factors affect their genesis, formation, and eventual acceptance. In terms of the second, literature is set within a static, atemporal dimension, individual works constituting "a simultaneous order" which in some way or other mirrors the order of All Things. The first concept tends to measure the

[6] For an unusually perceptive discussion of the inconsistencies in Eliot's entire theory of literature, see Murray Kreiger, *The New Apologists for Poetry* (Minneapolis: University of Minnesota Press, 1956), pp. 46–56.

[7] Eliot's earliest and most influential statement about tradition, which Matthiessen quotes in full, is as follows:

"Yet if the only form of tradition, of handing down, consisted in following the ways of the immediate generation before us in a blind or timid adherence to its successes, 'tradition' should positively be discouraged. We have seen many such simple currents soon lost in the sand; and novelty is better than repetition. Tradition is a matter of much wider significance. It cannot be inherited, and if you want it you must obtain it by great labour. It involves, in the first place, the historical sense, which we may call nearly indispensable to anyone who would continue to be a poet beyond his twenty-fifth year; and the historical sense involves a perception, not only of the pastness of the past, but of its presence; the historical sense compels a man to write not merely with his own generation in his bones, but with a feeling that the whole of the literature of Europe from Homer and within it the whole of the literature of his own country has a simultaneous existence and composes a simultaneous order. This historical sense, which is a sense of the timeless as well as of the temporal and of the timeless and the temporal together, is what makes a writer traditional. And it is at the same time what makes a writer most acutely conscious of his place in time, of his contemporaneity" (*ATSE*, 26).

value of individual works by standards that take into account something of what is possible to a given writer living at a particular historical time. The second tends to measure the value of individual works by universal norms that are applicable to any age, since each individual work shares with all others "a simultaneous existence" which is relatively impervious to time.

The brilliance of Eliot's statement on tradition (even if he eventually abandoned it in his later criticism) stemmed from his shrewd understanding that neither way of conceiving literature is adequate in itself. The first tends to reduce literature to a product of the times; the second tends to divorce it from history altogether. The one obviates the possibility of achieving critical perspective on the tradition to which a work belongs. The other, by putting the notion of tradition completely at the service of a fixed perspective, destroys the possibility of historical or traditional criticism in the first place.

So long as both conceptions implicit in Eliot's statement on tradition were held together, any criticism seeking to relate an individual writer to his tradition could appeal to standards without becoming either wholly relativist or wholly doctrinaire. Further, Eliot's view of tradition possessed the additional advantage, exploited by Matthiessen in his later criticism, of permitting one not only to see literature in history but also to see history in literature. From this perspective a work of literature was more than a result of the combined historical influences that had shaped it; as an expression of the attempt to revitalize and renew those influences for continued life in the present, it could justly be considered a historical force in its own right.

But what would happen if a critic opted for one of the conceptions rather than the other? For example, what if one were to subordinate the view of tradition as temporal to the view of tradition as timeless and were thus to measure all individual works of literature by standards that were universal and fixed rather than relative and flexible? Hypothetically, this position would pose no insoluble problems. Difficulties would arise only if the standards in question turned out to be based on an insufficiently capacious view of life. Yet that is precisely what had already happened to Eliot. One can trace the narrowing and hardening of Eliot's view of tradition, and consequently of his standards, from "Tradition and the Individual Talent" (1919) through "The Function of Criticism" (1923) to "The Humanism of Irving Babbitt" (1927).[8] By 1928 and the publication of the famous preface to *For Lancelot Andrewes,* Eliot's conversion to classicism in literature, royalism in politics, and Anglo-Catholicism in religion was known. Yet Matthiessen waited until publication of the second edition of *The Achievement of T. S. Eliot* (1947) to respond to Eliot's critical about-face.

By 1932 the confusion about Eliot's new position was widespread enough to evoke a comment even from the potentially sympathetic Paul Elmer More. Reviewing Eliot's *Selected Essays* (1932) for the *Saturday Review of Literature,* More suggested that Eliot was leading critics in two opposite directions. He pointed out that the poet who wrote *The Waste Land* and other early poems "appeals to us as one struck to the heart by the confusion and purposelessness and wastefulness of the world about him, and as dismayed by the impoverishment of our human emotions and imagination in a life so divested of meaning and so dull of conscience."[9] But More was compelled to set "against this lyric prophet of chaos . . . the critic who will judge the world from the creed of the classicist, the royalist, and the Anglo-Catholic, who will see behind the clouds of illusion the steady decrees of a divine purpose, and who has gone so far at least in that program as to compose a long pamphlet (included in the *Selected Essays*) of 'Thoughts after Lambeth.' "[10] As More correctly perceived, the real problem was not to square "the young rebel who rejoices in the disillusion of the 'Waste Land' " with "the Bishops of the Church assembled in solemn conclave to unravel the purposes of Deity"[11]—after all, conversions did occur, and no one would eventually explain the logic of Eliot's conversion better than Matthiessen himself—but rather to reconcile the older poet who kept writing verse in the former skeptical manner with the newer critic who had now taken his position within the secure walls of the Church and would, by 1935, be prepared

[8] See John D. Margolis, *T. S. Eliot's Intellectual Development, 1922–1939* (Chicago: University of Chicago Press, 1972).

[9] Paul Elmer More's review of Eliot's *Selected Essays* is reprinted in *T. S. Eliot: A Selected Critique,* ed. Leonard Unger (New York: Rinehart, 1948), pp. 24–29.

[10] *Ibid.,* p. 27.

[11] *Ibid.*

to argue that literary criticism must be written from a definite ethical and theological standpoint. To the author of *The Sacred Wood* (1920), tradition had been a way of talking about how the past continually revitalizes the present; to the author of *After Strange Gods* (1934) it had become a touchstone for determining the orthodoxy of sensibility. To the critic of "Tradition and the Individual Talent," standards were a means of distinguishing between the authentic and the spurious, but to the critic of "Religion and Literature" they had become a way of protecting the faithful from the harm done by contemporary literature.

Matthiessen had surprisingly little to say about these shifts in Eliot's viewpoints, and what he did say was generally unsatisfactory. The fact that Eliot had changed could hardly be denied; it was simply a matter of deciding whether these changes were for the better or for the worse. Matthiessen assumed they were for the better because Eliot's new interest in religion and politics had merely widened his conception of the nature of tradition. Earlier in Eliot's career, tradition had been restricted largely to the problem of contemporary writing, especially to an explanation of the way the poet, in realizing his individual talent, needed something more valuable than his own personality to which to surrender himself; now, according to Matthiessen, tradition had been broadened to include that part of the inherited wisdom of the race which is somehow carried in the blood, and thus it revealed Eliot's greater sophistication about the complex interplay of various elements in the process of cultural transmission and development. This explanation, however, said very little, or at least it said no more than was absolutely necessary to answer those who found Eliot's latest critical formulations discontinuous with his earlier ones. In any event, Matthiessen admitted that he simply could not understand More's charge that a cleavage existed between the qualities of Eliot's later verse and the aims of his later criticism—"the only relevant distinction that can be made between them is one [Eliot] himself has suggested: 'In one's prose reflexions one may be legitimately occupied with ideals, whereas in the writing of verse one can only deal with actuality' " (*ATSE,* 99)—and so he returned to a subject more congenial to him: What did Eliot mean by the idea, oddly parallel to the idea of tradition, of a writer's "sense of his own age"?

This sense is not easy to analyze, but, for Matthiessen as well as for Eliot, it clearly was one of the essential criteria for great literature. As Matthiessen saw it, a writer's sense of his own age referred neither to a journalistic awareness of the life of the times nor to what the French imply in the phrase "au courant."[12] Instead, the phrase referred to what Matthiessen described, in thinking of Eliot's reflections on poets so diverse as Blake and Villon, as "a condensed, bare honesty that can strike beneath the appearance of life to reality, that can grasp so strongly the instrinsic elements of life in the poet's own day that it likewise penetrates beneath the apparent variations of men from one epoch to another to his essential sameness" (*ATSE,* 19). It was, of course, as apparent to Matthiessen as it had been to Eliot that artists have possessed such a sense in differing degrees in different ages, and that different artists in the same age have expressed it in different ways. It was also apparent, however, that every great artist seeks to express a sense of his own age simply because he cannot, "if he possesses that rare unyielding honesty which alone will give his work depth" (*ATSE,* 19), possibly avoid involvement in his own period. For this reason, Matthiessen could quote Eliot with full approval when the latter remarked: "The great poet, in writing himself, writes his time" (quoted, *ATSE,* 19).

[12] Speaking in another context about what be believed to be "one of the perennial fallacies of American criticism," Matthiessen argued that an authentic sense of one's own age has nothing whatsoever to do with a grasp of its gross realistic details:

"Only the narrowest conception of realism can hold that an author necessarily acquires any sovereign virtue by recording the surface details of a middle-western city instead of those of eighteenth-century Peru. Shakespeare's Roman generals are no less 'timeless Englishmen' than his inhabitants of the forest of Arden. The characters in Cooper's historical novels are not as wooden as those in his satires of contemporary life: his one living figure, the Leatherstocking, owes whatever vitality he possesses to the fact that he is the imaginative symbol for a whole stage of American life and aspiration, a stage which Cooper knew only in memory. Goethe's Faust is as entirely a nineteenth-century German as Marlowe's is an Elizabethan.

"To be sure, the author of a poem or novel dealing with another period or place than that in which he lives runs greater danger of tripping over properties, of mistaking costumes for people, of producing a *tour de force* or a mere museum piece. It is probably more rewarding as a rule for a writer to try to strike to the heart of life by the gradual difficult mastery of his own immediate surroundings. But it is an entire misconception of the way that the shaping imagination works to assume that a man's observation is limited to what is before his eyes; or that, once having observed, he cannot cast his findings into a transmuted guise with an enhancement rather than a loss of their energy; or that he cannot discover his symbols of living reality in memory and myth as well as in the headlines" (*ATSE,* 95–96).

Matthiessen came closest to a precise definition of this sense in his discussion of Eliot's debt to Baudelaire. The chief point about Baudelaire's sense of his own age is that it had nothing to do with his ability to record mere surface details. Though he possessed an extraordinary gift for expressing "the torturing impact of the great modern city upon the lonely individual," his sense of his own age really derived from his capacity to penetrate beneath superficial appearances to a perception of the pervasive and abiding elements underlying them, to what Matthiessen described as "a real perception of good and evil" (*ATSE*, 20). Such a perception, Matthiessen added, is precisely what Eliot had defined as "the first requisite of spiritual life" (quoted, *ATSE*, 20), and it was also close to what Yeats must have meant when he declared that "we begin to live only 'when we have conceived life as tragedy' " (*ATSE*, 20). Indeed, in Matthiessen's mind there was almost no difference between the perceptions of Eliot and Yeats, for they both recognized that "there can be no significance to life, and hence no tragedy in the account of man's conflicts and his inevitable final defeat by death, unless it is fully realized that there is no such thing as good unless there is also evil, or evil unless there is good; that until this double nature of life is understood by a man, he is doomed to waver between a groundless, optimistic hopefulness and an equally chaotic, pointless despair" (*ATSE*, 20).

This statement is unusually revealing. It clearly illustrates how, from this point on in his career, Matthiessen was tempted to relate historical issues to ethical issues and ethical issues to spiritual issues. In several bold strokes he had followed Eliot, first, in suggesting that a writer's sense of his own age depends upon his ability to penetrate beneath the appearances of life to its reality; second, in claiming that an apprehension of reality is predicated on an understanding of the inextricable mixture of good and evil which characterizes all ages, even though it may take different forms in each; and, third, in maintaining that genuine appreciation of life's tragic significance depends upon a conscious acknowledgment of the eternal opposition of good and evil. Matthiessen was then able to bring the discussion back to Eliot himself, and in particular to the several traditions that had influenced him, by concluding that "it is their penetration

to the heart of this struggle between the mixed good and evil
in man's very being, and thus to the central factors in human
nature, which forms a common element between the three
strains of poetry that have affected Eliot most deeply, between
such writers as Dante, Webster, and Baudelaire" (*ATSE*, 21).

Despite their marked influence on Matthiessen's criticism, Eliot's conceptions of tradition and of a writer's sense of his own
age would require less attention if they did not reveal, as Matthiessen explicated them, so much that was characteristic of
Matthiessen himself. Apart from their substantive contribution
to his developing theory of literature, they demonstrate Matthiessen's inclination to move in his criticism from one category
of analysis to another in an effort to get at what was, for him,
the heart of the matter—a writer's intuition of the nature of life
itself. Hence in his attempt to discover what Eliot had absorbed
from the several strands of the tradition that had shaped his
talent—from Dante, the metaphysicals, and the symbolists—
Matthiessen sought to explain why Eliot had turned to these
sources in the first place. Ostensibly, Eliot had found in them
a kind of poetry which, in fusing together intellect and emotion,
could assist a writer in overcoming the serious problem confronting moderns, the problem of the dissociation of sensibility.
But Matthiessen was convinced that such poetry could serve this
purpose only because, in effecting a reassociation of sensibility,
it enabled both writer and reader to get beyond what is simply
temporal and contingent to what is timeless and eternal by discerning beneath the surface aspects of any age the recurrent
conflict between good and evil which characterizes all ages.

As with Coleridge's revealing tendency as a Romantic critic
to turn the question about the nature of poetry into a question
about the nature of the poet, so Matthiessen's revealing tendency as a modern critic was to turn the question about the nature
of poetry ultimately into a question about the nature of the real.
Like Coleridge, Matthiessen ran the risk of obliterating the distinction between literature and other forms of expression by
claiming for the artist a special faculty which he could nevertheless be said to share with other kinds of men—not the ability
to reconcile opposite and discordant qualities, as with Coleridge, but rather the ability to express what is at once temporal

and timeless, unique and yet universal, as with Eliot. But, again like Coleridge, Matthiessen was able, at least at his best, to preserve the distinction between imaginative literature and other modes of discourse by insisting that a writer's poem, novel, or play differs from a moralist's essay or a historian's monograph because of its unique manner of expression—not in a medium which exists merely to please where others serve to instruct, as with one half of Coleridge's distinction, but rather, as with the other half of Coleridge's distinction, in a medium in which form and content are so completely interfused by means of a sustained vision of life that any individual component of the work may serve to illustrate the design of the whole work.

Yet at no point in his career was Matthiessen so systematic or so consistent a critic as Coleridge. Hence, much as he aspired to hold these several ideas together, they occasionally seemed to get away from him. His problem no doubt stemmed in part from his use of someone else's terms to express his own views, but at more than one point in *The Achievement,* Matthiessen revealed his own confusion as to just what some of Eliot's terms really meant. His difficulty was especially apparent when he turned from the larger issues—the idea of tradition and a writer's sense of his own age—to more concrete questions, such as the way a poet shapes his material into communicable form and then expresses his meaning.

In an effort to defend Eliot from the charge of overintellectualization, Matthiessen observed that Eliot had never supposed that the poet's proper business was with thought alone but rather with finding the emotional equivalent of thought. Without pausing to note the problematic character of this assertion, which Eliot had created himself by declaring that there are no substitutes either for thought or for emotion, Matthiessen proceeded to a discussion of the way Eliot had resolved the problem of expressing emotion in a form of art which was supposed to be impersonal, which aimed, as Hulme maintained and Eliot echoed, at "accurate, precise, and definite description" (quoted, *ATSE,* 57). The solution was to be found in Eliot's theory of the objective correlative, a theory Matthiessen already regarded as "a locus classicus of criticism" (*ATSE,* 58).

Matthiessen admitted that Eliot's theory would not disclose its full significance without careful study, but he failed to perceive the inherent problems that careful study should have revealed to him. For one thing, he never noticed the discrepancy between the theory, which assumes a radical difference between the man who suffers and the mind that creates, and Eliot's insistence that the best poetry expresses the experience of the whole man in a medium so intensely unified by the artist's personality that thought and emotion, content and form, are inseparable. For another, he neglected to point out the contradiction between the theory's crude formula of poetic conception, in which means were subordinated to ends, and the intense unity and integrity of expression in which it was supposed to issue.

Even more serious, however, is Matthiessen's failure to realize that Eliot's theory was based upon a clear misreading of *Hamlet.* Eliot had designed his theory of the objective correlative as a way of avoiding what he took to be not only Hamlet's problem but also Shakespeare's problem in creating Hamlet: both were dominated by an emotion that is inexpressible, so the argument went, because it goes beyond the facts responsible for it. Though Hamlet's mother was chiefly responsible for Hamlet's emotions throughout the play, Shakespeare was unable to invest her with sufficient force and power of being so that she might serve as an objective equivalent for the alternating feelings of disgust and guilt which her behavior aroused in her son. Hence Hamlet's predicament and Shakespeare's dilemma: how to express in action a series of feelings that had no apparent basis in fact? The answer, as Eliot perceived it, was clear: "the only way of expressing emotion in the form of art is by finding an 'objective correlative'; in other words, a set of objects, a situation, a chain of events which shall be the formula of that *particular* emotion; such that when the external facts, which must terminate in sensory experience are given, the emotion is immediately evoked" (quoted, *ATSE,* 58). What Eliot failed to comprehend is that Hamlet was not Gertrude, and that therefore Hamlet's emotions of disgust and guilt, though perhaps in excess of anything Gertrude in herself could arouse, were not in excess of the feelings Gertrude could arouse in a man like

Hamlet who possessed the genius to see that the disease infecting his mother had poisoned the whole state of Denmark. Far from exhibiting, as Eliot put it, "the buffoonery of an emotion which can find no outlet in action," Hamlet's behavior revealed the tragic situation of a man whose world provides no alternatives for action because of the range and depth of its moral corruption.

It is difficult to imagine the author of *American Renaissance* glossing over these issues, but in *The Achievement* Matthiessen seemed hardly aware of their existence. Instead of putting Eliot's theory of the objective correlative under critical pressure, he simply used it to try to explain the dramatic quality of Eliot's verse and thereby to show how Eliot had overcome the problem of the contemporary artist. It is interesting to observe that Matthiessen was compelled to define the dramatic quality of Eliot's best verse in terms of its power to communicate what he described as "a sense of real life, a sense of the *immediate present* —that is, of the full quality of a moment as it is actually felt to consist" (*ATSE,* 67). The parallel with what Matthiessen, following Eliot, had earlier described as a writer's sense of his own age is unmistakable. And, as if to substantiate the parallel, Matthiessen immediately went on to explain that the ability to convey a sense of real life, of the immediate present, derived on the one hand from "a unified sensibility, a capacity of feeling that can closely interweave thought and emotion," and on the other from "a mature realization of the existence of both good and evil, an understanding that life takes on dramatic significance only when perceived as a struggle between these forces" (*ATSE,* 68).

One of the chief questions left unanswered by Matthiessen's discussion of the dramatic element in Eliot's verse is how Eliot was able to resolve or unify dramatic qualities in the very act of poetic utterance, and Matthiessen turned to this question in his next chapter. His main interest was to explain how Eliot's poetry could communicate its meaning almost before the reader could articulate what he felt; he found the key in what Eliot described, in referring to the same effect in Dante, as "the auditory imagination," the feeling for syllable and rhythm, penetrating far below the conscious levels of thought and feeling, invigorating every word; sinking to the most primitive and forgotten, returning to the origin and bringing something back, seeking the beginning and the end. It works through meanings, certainly, or not without meanings in the ordinary sense, and fuses the old and obliterated and the trite, the current, and the new and surprising, the most ancient and the most civilized mentality. (Quoted, *ATSE*, 81)

Eliot's meaning in this passage rested upon his assumption that the best way of judging a new poet is to test his sense of rhythm which, to be significant, must arise from the necessity of producing a new form for a new content. And rhythm, in turn, should indicate, Matthiessen contended, the poet's "particular union of past and present, his double possession of 'the most ancient and the most civilized mentality' in his awareness of the primitive magic of sound joined with his quickening sense of the new manifestations of life in his own day" (*ATSE*, 82).

Matthiessen was careful not to extend the significance of rhythm to the point of turning it into something else. Rhythm is preeminently a literary quality which "cannot be faked; it can arise only from the poet's own response to physical and emotional movement" (*ATSE*, 110). Thus Matthiessen firmly insisted upon the modern contextualist insight that "one test of a poet's skill lies in the degree of his awareness of what effects he has caused in his lines, of what forces the flow of his rhythm has made his words release" (*ATSE*, 84). Indeed, "only by releasing the magical possibilities in words," Matthiessen suggested in echoing Eliot, "can the poet impart the feeling that he has sunk 'to the most primitive and forgotten,' that his thought and emotions have returned 'to the origin' and have brought back a deeper sense of life" (*ATSE*, 86).

It was the marvelous efficacy of words which enabled the poet to fulfill what Matthiessen considered one of the poet's most primitive functions, a function that originated in the ancient art of the charm whereby primitive man sought through careful manipulation of words to communicate with the spirits, exorcising evil ones and propitiating good ones. In modern times, of course, a belief in the miraculous potency of language can exist only as a metaphor. But Matthiessen was still convinced, and rightly so, "that the most moving poetry performs a kindred service by the fullness with which it wins for us a vision of liveliness, or with which, in describing ugliness and horror, it thereby lifts us from their burden. And the secret of this power remains the same: it lies in the accuracy by which the poet, utilizing every resource lurking in word and rhythm, manages to convey a heightened sensation of the object itself" (*ATSE*, 98–99).

This passage reveals that Matthiessen was never really interested in the kind of verse T. E. Hulme wanted to champion, verse that is merely descriptive. He was interested instead in poetry that, by conveying the full complexity of the writer's experience, impresses readers, as Eliot's best poetry surely does, with its authenticity. By authenticity Matthiessen did not mean sincerity in the narrow sense. He meant rather that the work of any genuine artist must result from what he called a psychological necessity. If the poet's innovations, to say nothing of his total achievement, are to gain lasting value, they must spring from an inner inevitability, Matthiessen believed, as though the poet were writing not the way he should but the way he must.

Convictions such as these enabled Matthiessen to extend the implications of what Eliot meant by a writer's sense of his own age. Again, he was content in the main to let Eliot do the talking, but it is clear that he intended for Eliot to speak in behalf of himself as well:

> Eliot knows that no experiment in art is valuable unless it is psychologically necessary, that no great innovator has cared for novelty for its own sake, but like Shakespeare, "has been driven on, step by step, in his innovations, by an inner necessity, and that the novelty of form has been rather forced upon him by his material than deliberately sought." This intimate inner necessity is bound up with the history of the age in which the poet lives, with its main movements of thought and feeling. For, as Eliot has noted of Wordsworth's revolution in poetry, "Any radical change in poetic form is likely to be the symptom of some very much deeper change in society and in the individual." (*ATSE*, 86)

This kind of reasoning, seeking to locate a writer's most authentic qualities in his sense of his own age, not only revealed the propulsion toward unity in much of Matthiessen's thinking about literature, but also indicated his already well-developed facility for probing the social and cultural implications of literary and aesthetic categories. Without an appreciation of these two characteristics, it is impossible to understand how Matthiessen could conclude that "the most important value of the artist to society, and the one element that lends his work enduring significance, is to give expression to the most pervading qualities of life *as he has actually known it*" (*ATSE*, 43).

From what has been said thus far, it should be clear that the quality of authenticity was not to be confused with the virtue of sincerity, of attempting to tell the truth about one's feelings. However valuable and difficult of attainment the virtue of sincerity might be, requiring as it does that a poet be fully alive to his own sensations, intensely honest about their implications, and technically expert in transmitting them, Matthiessen was still compelled to agree with Eliot that something more is necessary. For sincerity to issue in truly meaningful expression, expression that rings with the note of authenticity, Matthiessen insisted that "the feelings themselves should be part of a balanced pattern of life" (*ATSE*, 98). If the poet lacked a sustained vision of experience, his feelings would lack unity and his work would fail to cohere. Conversely, if a critic were to try to test any given work for its authenticity, he could not rest content until he had related the feelings evoked by individual lines or passages to whatever balanced pattern of life or sustained vision of experience from which they had proceeded.

But what would happen if a poet's readers could not accept his view of life? Would they then be justified in dismissing the poetry in and through which he tried to articulate it? These were not idle questions to Matthiessen. By 1935, in fact, they had been raised time and again in connection with Eliot, as Matthiessen knew only too well, "by those critics who welcomed the poet of *The Waste Land* as a modern prophet for having voiced our disillusionment, and now damn him because he moves toward faith; as well as by those more traditionally faithful souls, largely academic, who deplored his earlier work as dangerously radical, and now welcome him with hosannas" (*ATSE*, 98).

Thinking chiefly of Eliot's identity as an artist, Matthiessen correctly found both criticisms wide of the mark. While it was true that Eliot's move toward faith could not have been foreseen before it actually occurred, this development appeared in retrospect to follow with perfect consistency from the view of life which preceded it. In his earliest work, from "The Love Song of J. Alfred Prufrock" through *The Waste Land* and "Gerontion" to "The Hollow Men," Eliot's "prevailing theme," as Matthiessen called it, had been "the emptiness of life without belief" (*ATSE*, 99). Accordingly, in the later poems, Matthiessen argued, Eliot simply retained his "persistent absorption in the nature of spiritual reality" and then followed out the logic of his exploration. But the religious poems that resulted, whatever Eliot might say in his prose, were no more complacent in their faith than the earlier poems had been in their skepticism and doubt. If Eliot's later poetry reflected a heightened desire to find "the peace which passeth understanding," he still realized as few other moderns have, either before or since, "that the primary thing for the poet 'is not to have a beautiful world with which to deal: it is to be able to see beneath both the beauty and ugliness; to see the boredom, and the horror, and the glory' " (*ATSE*, 102). Further, Matthiessen was convinced that Eliot's sense of religious assurance developed only from "his growing comprehension of what, encountering it in Baudelaire, he . . . called 'the greatest, the most difficult of the Christian virtues, the virtue of humility' " (*ATSE*, 99–100). Thus Matthiessen could describe the later Eliot in the terms Eliot had used in reference to Pascal:

"I can think of no Christian writer, not Newman even, more to be commended . . . to those who doubt, but who have the mind to conceive, and the sensibility to feel, the disorder, the futility, the meaninglessness, the mystery of life and suffering, and who can only find peace through satisfaction of the whole being." Such satisfaction for Eliot could not lie in Hawthorne's or Henry James's "awareness of spiritual reality" with an indifference to dogma. He needed to find something in which his mind as well as his emotions could rest. (*ATSE*, 100)

If the point in question here was the problem of poetry and belief, the real issue was not a matter of accepting the poet's beliefs but rather of sympathizing with his reasons for holding them, and then the burden of responsibility would be on the poet himself. For example, "the fact that 'Tintern Abbey' is a great poem does not depend on the question of whether or not we agree with Wordsworth's views, but on the realization that these lines beat with the convincing note which only a rarely sincere and original rhythm can communicate, and thus persuade of the genuineness of their vision as they make us share it" (*ATSE,* 133). Indeed, this quality is precisely what impressed Matthiessen most strongly about Eliot. As an individual faced with the twentieth-century problem of finding any absolutes in a world of relativity, Eliot clearly wanted to believe with more certitude than the age would permit. Yet as a poet obliged to express to the full the complexity of his own experience as a contemporary man, Eliot wrote not as he would like to feel, nor even as he may have thought he ought to feel, but only as he obviously did feel. In such poems as *Ash Wednesday* and *The Waste Land,* for example, Eliot was able, according to Matthiessen, not merely to evoke a whole complex state of mind but also to compel others to share and absorb it.

The final impression created in Eliot's own verse was one of integrity. Applied to Eliot's poetry, Matthiessen used this favorite word of both Pound's and Eliot's to refer to a definite wholeness within certain limits. The limits of Eliot's verse derived from his conception that poetry arose out of personal suffering, while its wholeness stemmed from an essentially tragic, though redemptive, view of life. But because Matthiessen also employed this quality, or one of its equivalents, as a criterion for aesthetic judgment in other contexts, it possessed a wider reference for him. The essential meaning of the quality of integrity rested upon Matthiessen's basic assumption, with all its Puritan overtones, "that one of the fundamental secrets of art as of life is that the mature artist finds his strength partly by coming to recognize and reckon with his limitations" (*ATSE,* 41–42).

In *The Achievement of T. S. Eliot,* Matthiessen was attempting to do just that: to measure his own strength by determining his own limitations. The strength of Matthiessen's book is manifest in the very mode of his argument, where he moves from the center of an idea out to its expanding perimeter and then back to the center in a constant effort to widen its implications without losing touch with its central core of meaning. Its limitations are attributable to the fact that many of Matthiessen's ideas or, better, the ideas he borrowed from Eliot possessed more implications than he could adequately account for. The result is not a confusing book, but rather an unsystematic one.

Matthiessen knew exactly what he wanted to do in *The Achievement of T. S. Eliot.* By analyzing Eliot's poetry and criticism, he wanted to adumbrate an organic, or at least a unified, theory of literature which conceives of the individual work of art as a special fusion of form and content exhibiting the capacity not merely to reflect and illumine the past but also to revitalize it and give it fresh life in the present. The key to such a theory lay in Eliot's notion of the inner necessity from which every great work of literature springs. This necessity, which is bound up with the age in which the poet lives, assures his relation to the traditions that have preceded him, enables him to understand reality as he has actually experienced it, and accounts for all the departures in form and substance which make his work unique. But it would take Matthiessen another six years, until the completion of his great study of America's mid-nineteenth-century cultural renaissance, to formulate his theory and to write a book fully expressive of it. By the time Matthiessen finally articulated the theory in *American Renaissance,* he had discovered that the only firm foundations for a truly organic theory of literature are democratic and, in the largest sense, Christian in character.

CHAPTER THREE

"American Renaissance"
and the Theory of Organic Form

Criticism in America is implicitly an attempt by each critic to make of America that kind of country he would like, which in every case is a better country than it is today. . . . As he achieves a sense of values he adopts them, and declares them, and tries to make them prevail.

PERCY BOYNTON
More Contemporary Americans

LOOKING back over Matthiessen's first three books and many of the essays and reviews he published before the outbreak of World War II, one is impressed all the more by the astonishing achievement of *American Renaissance.* Although there is abundant evidence of the genuine promise of such a study in Matthiessen's earlier criticism, the scope and brilliance of the book so exceeded the reach of Matthiessen's previous writing that, like Parrington's *Main Currents,* it seems almost to have erupted de novo. Yet Matthiessen had been hard at work on *American Renaissance* for about ten years and had voiced his own sense of the need for it as early as 1929. Further, many of Matthiessen's essays and reviews during the 1930s on such figures as William Dean Howells, Van Wyck Brooks, Irving Babbitt, Bernard De Voto, Newton Arvin, Edmund Wilson, Granville Hicks, Stuart Pratt Sherman, and others afforded him an opportunity to try out ideas that later gave *American Renaissance* its intellectual force and resilience.

It would no doubt be plausible to suppose that much of the success of *American Renaissance* depended on the material it canvassed so exhaustively. The novels of Hawthorne and Melville, the poetry of Whitman, the essays of Emerson, and the prose writings of Thoreau comprised a glittering series of artistic achievements which now, for the first time, received the close attention they deserved. But *American Renaissance* had more than great material; it also had a great theme whose profound meaning for American life and letters called forth all Matthiessen's potential genius for grasping the essential without blurring details. In setting out to explain, as he said in his "New Standards" review of 1929, what it means to believe that "great literature must be an organic expression of its age and nation," Matthiessen, like Whitman and the others before him, had found it necessary to define "what he conceived to be the fundamental implications of a democratic nation" (*RC,* 182) and to describe the art in which those implications had achieved their richest cultural expression. Almost in spite of himself, Matthiessen was beginning to create, even as he unearthed it, something like a new mythography of the American experience; and the result was a book that, for all its amplitude and complexity, possessed the immediacy, the excitement, and the novelty of an original discovery.

Yet one cannot finally appreciate the impact of *American Renaissance* on many of its first readers—if Matthiessen's book was not the single most important factor in launching the American Studies movement, it at least strongly affected many scholars and critics who subsequently made distinguished contributions to that movement—without taking into account the state of mind that prevailed among many liberal intellectuals at the time of its publication. The late 1930s and early 1940s were an era of considerable disillusionment in which the generous hopes first awakened by the uneasy peace following World War I and then by Roosevelt's first term following the Great Depression had slowly eroded, leaving in their place a sense of confusion and defeat. The rise of fascism in Europe, Stalin's purges in Russia, the massacre of the Republicans in Spain, the collapse of the Popular Front in America, Stalin's nonaggression pact with Hitler, the German blitz into Poland—these were only a few of the blows suffered by the cause of democratic liberalism during those years. Many people, of course, were quickly caught up again in war fever, once America declared war against the Axis powers, and thus found their faith restored as the Allies united to stem the spread of tyranny. But others remained badly shaken at the roots and would not soon recover until they had found some tradition, some defining intellectual and spiritual heritage, to which they could appeal for explanation of the present state of crisis. And that is exactly what Matthiessen's book provided them: a distinctively American tradition founded upon liberal and democratic impulses which at the same time explained how those impulses could go awry and why they were so vulnerable in the first place. As a genuinely native tradition, therefore, it was all the more valuable and all the more usable, just because it carried within itself its own elements of self-criticism. In the novels of Hawthorne and Melville, democratic humanism was tempered by what Melville called "the fine hammered steel of woe" and emerged perhaps no less vigorous but considerably tougher, soberer, and more tragic.

The quickening effect of *American Renaissance* was also heightened by what might be called the politics of its method. The book seemed to unite the two chief strains characterizing the best American criticism of the past without falling victim either to the ideological posturing that had come to possess the one or to the elitist formalism that had eventually captured the other. Like critics of the generation of H. L. Mencken, Ludwig Lewisohn, Van Wyck Brooks, the Lewis Mumford of *The Golden Day,* and V. L. Parrington, Matthiessen believed that all great literature serves as a kind of ice ax to break up the frozen sea of sentiment and yearning within us, or, in other words, that its critical function is frequently identical with its creative function, enabling us to recover contact with our deepest sense of ourselves. Like conservative critics such as Babbitt, More, Sherman, Gorham B. Munson, and Norman Foerster, Matthiessen also accepted the need for standards that would reconnect us with something larger than ourselves, something representative of the collective wisdom of mankind. He differed with conservatives in insisting that the standards must be aesthetic as well as moral; he differed with liberals in believing that literary values cannot be reduced to their social and political equivalents. While the art of literary criticism in *American Renaissance* maintained its high liberal office as the search for a compelling order of belief and value which might release the unspent potential of individuals and thus be conducive to social well-being, it proposed to do so only by showing how the liberating energies of mid-nineteenth-century American literature were expressed within the exigencies and complications of form.

That Matthiessen could unify what was valuable in these two disparate strains of the American critical tradition and thus point the way toward a new kind of literary criticism, at once social and historical, ethical and cultural, indicates just how thoroughly he had become the master of his craft in six short years. The question this raises, of course, is how to account for this process of critical maturation, how to explain the differences in tone, in method of approach, in firmness of grasp, in clarity of judgment, in breadth of vision, between *The Achievement of T. S. Eliot* and *American Renaissance.* Had he made the discovery of some new critical model during these years, say a figure like Henry James or Edmund Wilson, who suddenly united in one person many of the procedures and perspectives toward which Matthiessen had been groping in his earlier work? Or had some mysterious process of inner development taken place, as Matthiessen found himself writing on a subject that engaged his whole being? If Matthiessen's decisive maturation during this period involved something of both, it was still owing chiefly to what he had perceived, and in perceiving had to absorb, in coming to terms with the five writers to whom his book is largely devoted. Indeed, as much as *American Renaissance* deserves recognition as the most detailed, energetic, and comprehensive study of the major writers of the mid-nineteenth century, it also invites examination as a record of Matthiessen's self-education as a literary critic. This process of self-education was set against a very broad background, for Matthiessen's intention was to place the work of his five writers in the context of virtually all the influences they could be said to have assimilated as well as released. Yet throughout the book one can discern the telltale signs of Matthiessen's own involvement. In clarifying the complex achievement of Emerson, Thoreau, and Whitman, as well as of Hawthorne and Melville, Matthiessen sought to measure their accomplishments in terms of their aims in order to estimate the value their different views of organicism might still possess as a working theory of literature and culture. Hence there is nothing coincidental about turning to *American Renaissance* for clarification of Matthiessen's own critical theory; the very nature of the book demands it.

1

Matthiessen was first drawn to his subject by a desire to explain why many of America's literary masterpieces had been produced within a five-year period in the middle of the nineteenth century. The years 1850–1855 had seen the publication of Emerson's *Representative Men* (1850), Hawthorne's *The Scarlet Letter* (1850) and *The House of Seven Gables* (1852), Melville's *Moby-Dick* (1851) and *Pierre* (1852), Thoreau's *Walden* (1854), and Whitman's *Leaves of Grass* (1855). This remarkable outburst of creative activity, almost without parallel in American literary history, deserved to be called a renaissance if only because the writers themselves so thought of it—"not as a re-birth of values that had existed previously in America, but as America's way of producing a renaissance, by coming to its first maturity and affirming its rightful heritage in the whole expanse of art and culture" (*AR*, vii).

Matthiessen conceded that an unprecedented eruption of creativity within a compressed period of time might lead to several different kinds of investigation. First, one could try to explain how the flowering actually came to pass by detailing its antecedents in literary history and its process of historical evolution. Second, one might explore the myriad social, political, economic, and religious reasons for its occurrence at that particular moment in nineteenth-century American life. Matthiessen, however, wanted to pursue a third alternative, related to the other two but also distinct, of judging these literary expressions as works of art by "evaluating their fusions of form and content" (*AR*, vii).

In choosing this course, Matthiessen was not trying to beg the difficult questions as to how or why the renaissance took place; he was merely reaffirming the bias he had acquired from Eliot and had found confirmed in the work of everyone from I. A. Richards to Allen Tate: that the most valuable approach to all such issues is to determine what individual works of literature are in and of themselves. In this instance, however, the issue was complicated because each of his five writers was directly in-debted to Emerson and his theory of organic expression: Tho-reau had built the whole theory and practice of his own work upon it; Whitman had extended its implications in *Leaves of Grass;* and Hawthorne and Melville had then drastically revised without entirely abandoning it by reacting vigorously to its an-thropological and metaphysical assumptions. Hence Mat-thiessen, in stating that his "main subject" had become "the conceptions held by five of our major writers concerning the nature and function of literature, and the degree to which their practice bore out their theories," was projecting something sub-stantially more ambitious than a study of selected literary texts. His foremost intention was better expressed when he added, "It has seemed to me that the literary accomplishment of those years could be judged most adequately if approached both in the light of its authors' purposes and in that of our own develop-ing conceptions of literature" (*AR*, vii).

Matthiessen's double aim was still consonant with the meth-odological assumptions he had earlier elaborated in *The Achieve-ment of T. S. Eliot.* He was interested in aesthetics and not in history, in critical analysis and not in biography. His primary concern was the published work of his five subjects, particularly an evaluation of it as it was realized in specific literary forms. If the relationship among the five writers stemmed from a com-mon conception of the nature and function of literature, their own theories might serve as an appropriate norm for measuring their respective achievements. An examination of the relation-ship between theory and practice might illuminate the particular problems of their age, but Matthiessen still believed with Eliot that real historical insight could be gained only through a close reading of the literary texts themselves.

As before, then, Matthiessen was convinced that the work of every serious writer bears an integral relation not only to the present but also to the past and the future. Each writer is related to the past by conscious or unconscious participation in a liter-ary and cultural tradition which he must revise in the light of his own needs; each writer is related to the future because in revising that tradition he helps transmit it to subsequent genera-tions of readers and writers. Assuming that the critic must always seek to connect writers both with the past they have absorbed and with the future they help to shape, Matthiessen felt compelled in *American Renaissance* not only to relate Melville to Shakespeare, Hawthorne to Milton, Emerson to Coleridge, and Thoreau to Thomas Browne and Robert Burton, but also to use Henry James and T. S. Eliot to shed fresh light on Hawthorne, to employ the forgotten sculptor, Horatio Greenough, to suggest and clarify the functionalism of Thoreau, and to utilize the poetry of Gerard Manley Hopkins to illumine by contrast the poetics of Whitman.

By means of these lengthy forays both backward and forward in time, Matthiessen sought to place the major works of his five writers both in their age and in our own. He knew this ambition would seem unorthodox in a literary historian, but it expressed one of his deepest convictions about his craft, that "works of art can be best perceived if we do not approach them only through the influences that shaped them, but if we also make use of what we inevitably bring from our own lives" (*AR*, xii). In the hands of a critic less sure of his grasp, this conviction might have given way to an irresponsible impressionism, but in Matthiessen's criticism it was balanced by an equally strong commitment to the integrity of every individual work of art. Matthiessen summarized his purpose in words that might equally suffice as a description of the literary theory he first formulated in his book on Eliot:

> My aim has been to follow these books through their implications, to observe them as the culmination of their author's talents, to assess them in relation to one another and to the drift of our literature since, and, so far as possible, to evaluate them in accordance with the enduring requirements for great art. That last aim will seem to many only a pious phrase, but it describes the critic's chief responsibility. His obligation is to examine an author's resources of language and of genres, in a word, to be preoccupied with form. This means nothing rarefied, as Croce's description of De Sanctis' great *History of Italian Literature* can testify: form for De Sanctis "was not the 'form' pathologically felt by aesthetics and decadents: it was nothing else than the entire resolution of the intellectual, sentimental, and emotional material into the concrete reality of the poetic image and word, which alone has aesthetic value." (*AR*, xi)

This aim was characteristically deepened and complicated by the dimensions of Matthiessen's subject matter and its implications for the fundamental problem of literary theory. His ultimate intent was to pass beyond assessment to basic formulations about the nature and function of literature. For instance, he explained that the section "Allegory and Symbolism" was designed not only as a summary of the literary theory to which his five writers were indebted, but also as a definition of "these two fundamental modes of apprehending reality" (*AR,* xiii). Similarly, he hoped that his concluding section, "Man in the Open Air," might draw a circle around the one subject to which all five of his writers reacted in common, the nature of democracy. And, finally, he admitted that the two central books on Hawthorne and Melville were to be read "as a single unit in which the chief value would be the aspects of tragedy that could be discerned through its representative practice by these two writers" (*AR,* xiii).

It should be noted, however, that Matthiessen's concerns were by no means isolated from one another, either in the writings of the five authors or in his treatment of their achievement. The unity among them derived essentially from their shared devotion to democracy, to what Matthiessen called the myth of the common man; this in turn helped to explain both their attraction to organicism, with its impulse toward unity of thought and action, of culture and work, and their susceptibility to tragedy, with its perception of the terrible discrepancy between man's soaring ideals and his limited achievement. Matthiessen believed that all five wrote literature for democracy, as he put it, in a double sense:

> They felt that it was incumbent upon their generation to give fulfillment to the potentialities freed by the Revolution, to provide a culture commensurate with America's political opportunity. Their tones were sometimes optimistic, sometimes blatantly, even dangerously expansive, sometimes disillusioned, even despairing, but what emerges from the total pattern of their achievement —if we will make the effort to repossess it—is literature for our democracy. In reading the lyric, heroic, and tragic expression of our first great age, we can feel the challenge of our still undiminished resources. (*AR,* xv)

This passage provides the clue to Matthiessen's basic angle of perspective in *American Renaissance.* Believing that his five writers had tried to explore, indeed to realize in form, the new human possibilities released by the American Revolution, he wanted to show how this literature *of* our democracy could become a literature *for* our democracy. It could be done only through an act of "repossession," meaning the effort to grasp "the total pattern of their achievement," or what Henry James would have called "the figure in the carpet" of their entire accomplishment. Matthiessen was under no illusions about the best method of procedure. Because literature is made with words, Matthiessen asserted that the only mode of approach to such issues was "through attention to the writers' use of their own tools, their diction and rhetoric, and to what they could make with them" (*AR*, xv). Matthiessen was not talking about semantics. Assuming that "an artist's use of language is the most sensitive index to cultural history, since a man can articulate only what he is, and what he has been made by the society of which he is a willing or an unwilling part" (*AR*, xv), Matthiessen believed that scholarship might itself provide a way of meeting "the challenge of our still undiminished resources" and thus inspire us to fulfill their latent potentiality.

These aims might seem extraordinary for a work of scholarship in American literary history, but for Matthiessen they followed with perfect consistency from his sense of the responsibilities of scholarship in a democracy. Hardly more than an extension of the demands Emerson had laid down for the American scholar nearly a hundred years earlier, they reflected Matthiessen's own commitments as a scholar-citizen. Thus he selected Louis Sullivan's restatement of the Emersonian ideal as a fitting conclusion to his discussion in the section "Method and Scope":

If, as I hold, true scholarship is of the highest usefulness because it implies the possession and application of the highest type of thought, imagination, and sympathy, his [the scholar's] works must so reflect his scholarship as to prove that it has drawn him toward his people, not away from them; that his scholarship has been used as a means toward attaining their end, hence his. That his scholarship has been applied for the good and enlightenment of all the people, not for the pampering of a class. His works must prove, in short (and the burden of proof is on him), that he is a citizen, not a lackey, a true exponent of democracy, not a tool of the most insidious form of anarchy. . . . In a democracy there can be but one fundamental test of citizenship, namely: Are you using such gifts as you possess for or against the people? (*AR*, xv–xvi)

2

The difficulty in speaking this way about scholarship, especially about scholarship directed toward the literature of the past, is that it can open the door to critical subjectivism of the very worst sort. A critic too vigorously concerned with demonstrating how the literature of the past helps one to understand the present and the future can easily misuse and distort it if he does his reading chiefly in terms of contemporary needs and aspirations. Matthiessen was clearly aware of this possibility and took pains to point out its dangerous consequences wherever he encountered them.

As early as 1932, for example, in a review of Van Wyck Brooks's *The Life of Emerson* (1931), Matthiessen pointed to the dangers of distorting the past in an effort to determine its usable component. Brooks's vices, according to Matthiessen, both here and in such earlier books as *The Ordeal of Mark Twain* (1920) and *The Pilgrimage of Henry James* (1925), were but a defect of his virtues. At his best, Matthiessen believed, Brooks exemplified the values of breadth, vision, and penetration; at his worst, he became a poet manqué of his own disillusion and yearning. Although one might have hoped in *The Life of Emerson* "for a book in which Emerson's ideas were probed to their very center and related to the intricate pattern of the thought of their time, and in particular, a book in which their still unspent force and their potential service to contemporary civilization would be trenchantly revealed,"[1] one found instead a book in which Brooks had substituted evocation for analysis and description for judgment. Swayed by personal feeling rather than by intellectual discrimination, Brooks had allowed himself to be tempted "into loose generalizations that, when probed, seemed to force the complexity of American life into too rigid a mold, and to deduce too much from the special case."[2]

Matthiessen knew, however, that it was possible to distort the literature of the past not only by overcoloring it with personal emotion but also by oversimplifying it in the interests of ideo-

[1] F. O. Matthiessen, review of *The Life of Emerson*, by Van Wyck Brooks, *New England Quarterly* 5 (1932): 819.
[2] *Ibid.*, pp. 821–22.

logical relevance. For this reason he was also forced to take exception both to a Marxist like V. F. Calverton, who distorted the literature of the past to make it fit his own political and economic theories, and to a socialist like Newton Arvin, who, as revealed in his book on Whitman, was inclined to assess a writer's significance too narrowly in terms of his supposed appeal to a radical political perspective. Calverton's misuse of literature was by far the more serious, because he was obviously interested merely in saying the timely thing rather than in trying, at least within the limits of his perspective, to make certain that what he said was true. If others had hailed Calverton's *The Liberation of American Literature* (1932) as a pioneer achievement deserving to be ranked with V. L. Parrington's *Main Currents,* Matthiessen found it little more than a simplistic, cliché-ridden, historically inaccurate essay written by "an excited debater" who forces his dubious theses "to interlock with the mechanical rigidity of an intricate system of cogwheels" (*RC,* 185). It was not that Matthiessen was out of sympathy with Calverton's aims, only that Calverton had fallen far short of honestly realizing them. Though Matthiessen was prepared to welcome a Marxist interpretation of American literature, he knew that "the service of the Marxian critic could [only] lie not in the constant repetition of the catchwords, bourgeois and proletarian, but in some at least tentative definition of the meaning of these terms in relation to American society; not in emotional proclamations of an unexamined faith, but in coming to grips with the problem of what the virtues and defects of a proletarian culture in America might really be" (*RC,* 189). And despite the value of the idea that literature and society are organically related, Matthiessen felt constrained to add that "it has been apparent for some time to others than Marxians that the movement of our culture has been from the center outwards, that our most powerful individuals have again and again been dangerously isolated from or opposed to society as a whole, and that the construction of a society in which both the individual and the group can have some measure of full development is the gravest problem with which we are faced" (*RC,* 188–89).

These strictures could in no way be applied to Newton Arvin's more sensible and balanced book on Whitman. Even where

Arvin's exposition was determined solely by the question of Whitman's socialism, his book was designed to provide as thorough and intelligent an answer as possible. Doubts arose only as to the way Arvin chose to use Whitman, for he argued that Whitman had a special claim upon socialists, as, for instance, Poe and Melville could not, because he was forward-looking and optimistic whereas they were the opposite. The questions elicited by this kind of argument suggested answers already characteristic of Matthiessen's assumptions about the artist's relation to society:

> Is the availability of a poet to be made to correspond to the degree in which his opinions chime in with our hopes? Is it not rather the function of the artist to bring to concentrated expression every major phase of human experience, its doubts and anguish and tortured defeats as well as its cheerful confidence? Indeed, is not one measure of the great artist his refusal to yield us any innocent simplification, his presentation of an account of life as intricate in its harsh tragic matching of good and evil, as complex in its necessities of constant struggle as the life that we ourselves know? Will any less dense past correspond to our usages as mature human beings? (*RC,* 217)

Matthiessen was convinced that the problem of misusing the past stemmed most frequently not from a misconception of what literature is but from a misunderstanding about what literature does; before writing *American Renaissance* he confronted this issue in a lengthy review of Granville Hick's *The Great Tradition: An Interpretation of American Literature since the Civil War* (1933). What Matthiessen liked about *The Great Tradition* was its unequivocal commitment to the idea that, as Hicks put it, "art not only expresses something, but also does something" (quoted, *RC,* 192). The chief problem with the book was that Hicks placed too limited an interpretation upon what might be taken as literature's most characteristic mode of action. Whereas Hicks wanted to restrict literature's scope of action to the explicit righting of wrongs, Matthiessen felt obliged to argue to the contrary that the greatest literature "performs its most characteristic action in more subtle ways; it does something in the novels of Fielding or Proust, by bringing its reader a new understanding or a fresh insight into the full meaning of existence. It thus acts on life by giving it release and fulfillment" (*RC,* 193).

It was here that Matthiessen and Hicks really parted company.

From his rather narrow ideological point of view, Hicks assumed that literature can give life release and fulfillment only if it arises from an awareness of man's material conditions and seeks effectively to deal with them. He further believed that literature must be optimistic in tone if it is to assist man to do more than merely accept those conditions, if it is to enable him to cope with them by changing them. Hicks could therefore agree with the later Van Wyck Brooks, and with public taste in general, that skepticism and pessimism must always be avoided because they enfeeble the creative imagination and thus deprive it of the confidence it must exhibit if it is to challenge men to constructive social action and reform.

To Matthiessen, however, these assumptions conveyed a serious misunderstanding of the nature of literary art. For one thing, they denied to tragic as well as to satiric art the unquestioned vitality and the underlying love of life which ultimately characterize a play like *Hamlet* or a work like Swift's *Modest Proposal*. For another, they overlooked the fact that doubt and bitterness and dismay, far from remaining beside the point, are an ineluctable part of life itself. What Hicks failed to comprehend is that the poet's chief service to society frequently lies not in avoiding such feelings but rather in giving them full expression. Hence Matthiessen could conclude:

> Mr. Hicks's limitations as a critic are owing to his lack of understanding not only that art is a richer experience, but also that it possesses more varied uses than he perceives. Its role is not only that of revolt, but the counterbalancing one of realization. And owing to the very roots of American life having sprung from the forces of the Reformation, so much emphasis has been thrown on the protesting strain that it is doubly important that whatever full-created affirmation there has been, not of life as a future dream, but of life itself as it has been lived, should not be allowed to be lost sight of. Consequently for any American future it is essential to preserve by wise evaluation far more elements than Mr. Hicks stresses, since only thus can an individual find revealed in the past of our country the complexity that he knows to compose life. (*RC*, 198–99)

Matthiessen was suggesting more than a criticism of Granville Hicks. He was also articulating a series of ideas that would eventually control much of his own exposition in *American Renaissance*. His chief purpose was to elucidate a sense of the very "complexity" which he himself knew "to compose life" and which he believed had been revealed in the literature of the mid-nineteenth century. And because he further believed that Emerson, Thoreau, Melville, and the others had acquired that sense not from the life they had merely dreamed but rather from the life they had actually lived, he was convinced that their realization of it through the enabling vitalities of art, no less than his own recovery of it through the repossessive stratagems of criticism, might constitute an act of "full-created affirmation."

Yet when one looks at *American Renaissance* in its entirety, one cannot help feeling bewildered by its staggering complexity. It really consists of four separate volumes, each one of which could almost stand alone, the first entitled "From Emerson to Thoreau" and the second, third, and fourth devoted to Hawthorne, Melville, and Whitman, respectively. These four volumes, or books, are broken down into fourteen sections whose titles suggest Matthiessen's controlling ideas:

Book One
    I. In the Optative Mood
    II. The Actual Glory
    III. The Metaphysical Strain
    IV. The Organic Principle
Book Two
    V. The Vision of Evil
    VI. The Problem of the Artist as New Englander
    VII. Allegory and Symbolism
    VIII. A Dark Necessity
Book Three
    IX. Moment of Transition
    X. The Revenger's Tragedy
    XI. The Troubled Mind
    XII. Reassertion of the Heart
Book Four
    XIII. Only a Language Experiment
    XIV. Man in the Open Air

The fourteen sections are further subdivided into some sixty individual essays.

Matthiessen defended the structure of his book by saying that it enabled him to provide full-length portraits of the five greatest writers of the pre–Civil War period in America and at the same time to treat in detail selected, interrelated aspects of their work. Rather than publish a separate volume on each individual writer, Matthiessen chose to present his material as a single comprehensive volume so that the writers might cast as many reflections as possible on one another. Through this complex series of crosslights, then, Matthiessen hoped to present a picture not so much of individual writers as of their entire age. But this, in turn, tends to blur the outlines of his interpretations. Indeed, the various contexts Matthiessen developed for placing the five writers in their own age as well as in ours, the multiple perspectives he brought to bear upon each, his numerous ways of relating one writer to the others, and the many sides he sees in all of them, while giving *American Renaissance* the density, variety, and originality of a critical masterwork, simply defy summarization. Further, within these interpretations there are sorties into everything from economic theory, political philosophy, epistemology, and metaphysics to open-air painting, the opera, ethics, oratory, psychology, music, folklore, myth, epic tradition, and the Bible. There are excursions into Manichaeanism, Zoroastrianism, Puritanism, Quakerism, Calvinism, classicism, and transcendentalism; there are discussions of Plato, Shakespeare, Spenser, Bunyan, Milton, Rabelais, Donne, Blake, Coleridge, Wordsworth, Carlyle, Byron, James, Eliot, Mann, Lawrence, and Pound. At times, therefore, it seems that the only cohesive element in *American Renaissance* is the presence of Matthiessen himself, as he moves tirelessly back and forth over a vast expanse of tradition, here to liken, there to differentiate, next to amplify, then to qualify, but always probing deeper by constantly making comparisons and contrasts, associations and distinctions, until the book begins to resemble what Melville described in *The Confidence-Man* as a "revolving Drummond light, raying away from itself all around it."

Yet amid this great welter of material one can find an ordering thread of meaning. Therefore I will risk separating what Matthiessen himself took such pains to integrate by attempting to show how the complex unity of Matthiessen's main argument leads from his discussion of the organic principle, which occupies the remainder of this chapter, to his interpretation of life's inmost complexity, which constitutes the subject of the next. Central to Matthiessen's discussion of the organic principle was the literary theory first advanced by Emerson and later revised by Thoreau and the others in an attempt to resolve the problems Emerson had initially created for it. Central to Matthiessen's interpretation of life's inmost complexity was the tragic vision of both Hawthorne and Melville, who in their greatest works gave it the fullest expression.

3

Matthiessen makes clear from the outset that the organic theory of expression reflected the chief concerns of an age that was highly ambiguous. For the transcendental era, if so it may be called, was at once an era of boundless optimism and deepseated anxiety, and the anxiety was the negative side of the optimism. It was an age everywhere characterized by an overwhelming impulse to achieve unity of being not only in literature and culture but in life generally. Yet this preoccupation with unity was the natural reaction to a pervasive fear that existence was coming apart at the seams. The dogmatism of faith had long since started to give way before the skepticism of reason, and the deep wellsprings of feeling and sentiment were drying up in the process. A reality once unified in the uneasy synthesis of Puritan culture and religion was rapidly disintegrating, separating subjects from objects, words from meanings, minds from experience, individuals from community, men from God. Some representatives of nineteenth-century American thought and culture faced the crisis with equanimity and even anticipation, finding in nature or in man himself a new source for reuniting the fragments. Others, however, felt anxiety and even trepidation, doubting that any source of unity could be found save in God alone, who seemed to have all but disappeared. Yet both groups perceived the need to find a basis for a unified view of life. Hence no matter what hopes they held for its realization, most representative thinkers of the period tended to be obsessed with the problem of reconciliation—of the one with the many, the individual with society, appearance with reality, fact with ideals. In this, of course, they were all incipient organicists, and Emerson was chief among them.

Emerson belonged to what he called the Party of Hope,[3] a loose designation referring to all those who believed that man is but a reflection of God, nature but a symbol for spirit, history but a synonym for biography. The confidence he derived from his convictions, according to Matthiessen, led him to stress with Coleridge " 'the *all in each* of human nature,'—how a single man contains within himself, through his intuition, the whole range of experience" (*AR,* 7). Emerson was to state this point of view in many different ways—"the individual is the world," "the highest revelation is that God is in every man," "there is One Mind, and . . . all the powers and privileges which lie in any, lie in all"—but Matthiessen makes clear that Emerson's conviction, however abstract his expression of it, sprang from his own experience. Having discovered for himself how the sublime reveals itself in the commonplace, how the infinite suffuses the finite, Emerson wanted to develop a theory of expression which would reunite the appearances of reality with whatever lies behind them, so that the word could become one with the thing.

Like so many of Emerson's recurrent themes, this one also derived from Coleridge. Its origin, as Matthiessen brings out, lay in Coleridge's attempt to revive in his criticism the Christian doctrine of the Word made flesh, of the Logos incarnate, and it issued directly in Coleridge's assertion that "the truth is universally placed in the coincidence of the thought with the thing, of the representation with the object represented" (quoted, *AR,* 31). Emerson, accepting this assumption in its entirety, attempted to build on it an organic theory of art which, in reuniting the human subject not merely with the objects of his perception, but also with whatever those objects represented beyond themselves, might serve as a theory of culture as well as of literature, of religion as well as of art.[4]

A crucial problem in connection with Emerson's theory of expression was reflected in the discrepancy between his statement of it and his own literary practice. Based upon an eccentric but nonetheless recognizable version of the incarnational view

---

[3] For a full discussion of this term, see R. W. B. Lewis, *The American Adam: Innocence, Tragedy, and Tradition in the Nineteenth Century* (Phoenix Books; Chicago: University of Chicago Press, 1961), pp. 7, 13–53.

[4] See *American Renaissance,* p. 31.

of life, Emerson's organic theory should have produced a poetry which took the finite and the concrete with full seriousness as realms in and through which the universal and the infinite reveal themselves. Instead, however, it produced a poetry always veering away from the concrete and the finite in an effort to get beyond them to whatever they symbolized of a larger spiritual significance. If Emerson's problem had been merely the technical one of failing to practice what he preached, it would have had only passing relevance to a discussion of the organic principle. Matthiessen was convinced, however, that Emerson's problem was theoretical as well as practical, that it stemmed as much from the weakness of his basic critical assumptions as from his inability to fulfill the requirements they set for him.

Emerson's chief difficulty was his susceptibility to influence not only by a master theorist such as Coleridge, who believed in the materiality of language and the limitations of poetic statement, but also by a Swedenborgian like Samson Reed, who argued that language is essentially an illusion that seeks to become one not with the thing at all but rather with being itself. Emerson apparently wanted it both ways. Though Matthiessen's careful reading of the *Journal* proves the extent to which Emerson tried to resist the seductions of the airily abstract, Emerson's insistence that language is both material and spiritual nonetheless perpetuated the problem. Hence of the three propositions Emerson offered about language in *Nature* (1836)—"Words are signs of natural facts"; "Particular natural facts are symbols of particular spiritual facts"; "Nature is a symbol of spirit"—he tended to emphasize the latter two at the expense of the former. His resulting theory of literature revealed little respect for the sheer intractability of matter, for the hard stuff of reality. Emerson's deepest inclinations, in fact, all went the other way, issuing in a literary theory where, as in Plato's *Ion,* art is not conceived of as the product of craftsmanship and technique but is based, finally, on inspiration, and where, as a consequence, content is stressed at the expense of form. Indeed, Emerson made no bones about it. If Emerson had to have form in literature at all, he wanted a form without limits, a form commensurate with the unlimited potentiality of pure spirit.

Such assumptions as these encouraged Emerson to believe

"that in order to poetize anything, 'its feet must be just lifted from the ground' " (*AR*, 53). Emerson could therefore take Bacon's formula for poetry as "our best definition" and paraphrase it to say: "Poetry, not finding the actual world exactly conformed to its idea of good and fair, seeks to accommodate the shows of things to the desires of the mind, and to create an ideal world better than the world of experience" (quoted, *AR*, 52).[5] Matthiessen was quick to point out the deficiencies of this formula by contrasting it with the definition he felt to be more adequate: "Emerson's view is in fundamental opposition to the view that holds that the greatest art comes from immersion in the complexities of experience. This latter view, which prevails in major tragedy, maintains that the potential world that art can envisage must be sought by wrestling with the actual, and not by evading it" (*AR*, 52). By accepting Bacon's definition, Emerson was able to ignore aspects of experience which conflicted with his own generous hopes. Believing with Swedenborg that "the soul makes its own world," Emerson refused to be restrained by "the hard actuality of experience" (*AR*, 54). Hence it was inevitable that Emerson should believe "that the deeper insight of the poet, 'who re-attaches things to nature and the whole . . . disposes very easily of the most disagreeable facts' " (*AR*, 54).

4

Matthiessen found that the best way to criticize Emerson's theory was to contrast it with the practice Thoreau built upon it. In Emerson's thinking, the organic principle led to a vision of the poet "Without halting, without rest, / Lifting better up to best" (quoted, *AR*, 55). In Thoreau's hands, the principle provided the challenge to other poets to "settle ourselves, and work and wedge our feet downward through the mud and slush of opinion, prejudice, and tradition, and delusion, and appearance . . . till we come to a hard bottom and rocks in place, which we can call *reality,* and say, This is, and no mistake" (quoted, *AR*, 165).

---

[5] Matthiessen gives Bacon's actual statement in a footnote in *AR*, p. 52: "And therefore it [poesy] was ever thought to have some participation of divineness, because it doth raise and erect the mind, by submitting the shows of things to the desires of the mind; whereas reason doth buckle and bow the mind into the nature of things."

The difference in direction implied in these two passages was no mere accident. Employing imagery that suggests a lifting upward, Emerson wanted a poetry that would regain contact with the infinite by transcending the finite. Employing imagery that suggests, on the other hand, a penetration downward, Thoreau wanted a literature that would also regain contact with the infinite but would do so by sinking down to and through the concrete and the finite. Emerson and Thoreau shared the organic impulse to reunite appearance with reality, the word with the thing, the symbol with the idea, yet each perceived a different way of achieving it. For a critic like Matthiessen, who believed with Thoreau that the approach to truth, whether in literature or in life, requires immersion within the complexities of experience rather than an attempt to escape them, Emerson's way was bound to fail and Thoreau's was more likely to succeed. The effort to transcend matter was certain to separate the writer from the vital currents of reality; the attempt to descend into matter was more likely to put a writer in touch with those currents and enable him to tap them.

This lesson was not lost on Thoreau. Unlike Emerson, who "raised himself too early to the perpendicular," Thoreau was content to "lie along the ground long enough to hear the secret whispers of our parent life."[6] Moreover, Thoreau's intuitive awareness of the physical basis of both language and rhythm gave him a dogged respect for things in all their wonderful specificity and sheer thereness. Finally, his keen appreciation of the importance of all the senses restrained his organic view of reality from gliding away from the thickness of life as experienced into romantic reveries about its meaning. Thoreau may have been a man of his own age in regarding the material world as a symbol of the spiritual world and in desiring to think in images that represented more than they stated, but he still believed that those images must emerge organically out of the very processes of thought, when those processes are understood to have their basis in feeling.

Matthiessen took as the paradigmatic statement of Thoreau's craft his famous declaration of purpose in *Walden:*

[6] Margaret Fuller, *The Writings*, sel. and ed. Mason Wade (New York: Viking, 1941), p. 393.

I went to the woods because I wished to live deliberately, to front only the essential facts of life, and see if I could not learn what it had to teach, and not, when I came to die, discover that I had not lived. I did not wish to live what was not life, living is so dear; nor did I wish to practice resignation, unless it was quite necessary. I wanted to live deep and suck out all the marrow of life, to live so sturdily and Spartan-like as to put to rout all that was not life, to cut a broad swath and shave close, to drive life into a corner, and reduce it to its lowest terms, and, if it proved to be mean, why then to get the whole and genuine meanness of it, and publish its meanness to the world; or if it were sublime, to know it by experience, and be able to give a true account of it in my next excursion. (Quoted, *AR*, 95)

Nothing indicates Matthiessen's special empathy for Thoreau and his ability to get inside the actual workings of Thoreau's mind simply through an analysis of his rhetoric and diction as well as Matthiessen's brilliant response to this passage. It is worth quoting entire, not least because it demonstrates what Matthiessen meant by the organic method of "presenting an experience instead of stating an abstraction" (*AR*, 96):

The measured pace seems in exact correspondence with his carefully measured thoughts, and serves, as effective rhythm always does, to direct the fullest attention to the most important words. The satisfaction that we have seen him taking in the feel of syllables in the muscles of his mouth and throat is carried across to us by the placing of "deliberately": as the first long word in the sentence, followed by a marked pause, it compels us to speak it as slowly as possible, and thus to take in its full weight: deliberate = *de-librare*, to weigh. A kindred desire to bring out the closest possible relation between the sense of a word and its sound seems to operate in his placing of "resignation," for again the pause emphasizes its heavy finality. . . .

But the chief source of power here seems to lie in the verbs of action: "front," barer than the more usual "confront," is also more muscular. Behind Thoreau's use of it is his conviction that the only frontier is where a man fronts a fact. The extension of its range is reserved for the third sentence, where his metaphors shift rapidly but not in a way to interfere with one another, not until each has released its condensed charge. For the primitive act of sucking out the marrow is not incompatible with the military image, appropriate to this Spartan intensity, of putting to rout life's adversaries. And as the campaign returns from the enemy to the pursuit of the essence, both the range and pressure of Thoreau's desire are given fuller statement by the widened image of harvesting and the contracted image of closing in on a hunted quarry. With that final dramatic concentration, we are able to feel what it would really mean to reduce life to its lowest terms. The phrase is no longer a conventional counter since we have arrived at it through a succession of severe and exhilarating kinesthetic tensions. After which a characteristic turn for Thoreau is not to leave the impression of anything grim, but, by mentioning his "next excursion," to suggest its relaxed pressure. (*AR*, 95–96)

According to Matthiessen, Thoreau could practice the organicism he preached because he shared what Eliot called a unified sensibility with the metaphysical poets to whom he, like several of the others, was indebted. Confident that "a man thinks as well through his legs and arms as his brain," the earthy Thoreau could do what the speculative Emerson could not, "unite thought and sense impression, the immediate feeling with the reflection upon it" (*AR*, 98). Hence Thoreau was able to fulfill one of the essential insights that M. W. Croll attributed to the whole metaphysical strain, "that an idea separated from the act of experiencing it is not the idea that was experienced" (quoted, *AR*, 130–31).

Though Matthiessen argued later in the book that Melville possessed a firmer grasp of this insight than either Emerson or Thoreau, he nonetheless believed that some perception of it was absolutely crucial for anyone who subscribed, as all five of his writers did, to Coleridge's conception of the creative process. Coleridge's understanding of the organic principle was founded upon the assumption that genius is "the power of acting creatively under the laws of its own origination." Thus it followed for Coleridge that

the form is mechanic, when on any given material we impress a pre-determined form, not necessarily arising out of the properties of the material;—as when to a mass of wet clay we give whatever shape we wish it to retain when hardened. The organic form, on the other hand, is innate; it shapes, as it develops, itself from within, and the fullness of its development is one and the same with the perfection of its outward form. Such as the life is, such is the form. Nature, the prime genial artist, inexhaustible in diverse powers, is equally inexhaustible in forms. (Quoted, *AR*, 133–34)

As Matthiessen was quick to point out, undue emphasis upon the inner urge instead of the outward form could easily lead to artistic formlessness. But Thoreau, like Melville, was able to avoid this difficulty because, in contrast with Emerson and later with Whitman, he was never tempted to confuse art with nature or nature with himself. Hence, despite his being able to produce a book that, in shaping itself so completely from within, struck

Matthiessen as being almost perfectly organic, Thoreau never lost the sense that he was at once participant in and interpreter of whatever experience he was rendering. To turn an earlier formulation around, Thoreau knew that to experience something required having an idea of it, even though the idea itself could not be dissociated from the experience, and this knowledge prevented him, even as an organicist, from reducing the complex analogies among art, nature, and himself into simple identities. When Thoreau went to the woods to front the facts, he was not content merely to provide an account of the emotions stirred in the process; he sought as well to record the meaning of the entire experience. In this sense, then, Thoreau's conception of the principle of organic form was at the farthest remove from that popular misconception of it which Yvor Winters once aptly termed "the fallacy of imitative form." Rather than suppose that form follows fact, that art imitates nature, Thoreau intuitively sensed, in anticipation of Louis Sullivan's penetrating insight, that form follows function. Yet it was not Thoreau himself but the American sculptor Horatio Greenough who most clearly articulated this principle for mid-nineteenth-century Americans and, by so doing, afforded Matthiessen the opportunity for one of his richest digressions.

Greenough's discovery of this key element in the theory of American organicism occurred upon his return home after a twenty-year absence abroad. In response to the shock of realizing that his country lacked a living cultural tradition to which he could attach himself, Greenough suddenly perceived that the most beautiful aesthetic objects in America had never been those created by professional artists but rather those that had "sprung out of an adaptation of structure to the needs of common life—the New England farmhouse, the trotting-wagon, the clipper ship" (*AR*, 145). Matthiessen found Greenough's new perception expressive of an admirable, an almost heroic, egalitarianism. Because of his faith in democracy, Greenough realized that art must have its sources in the community or it will decay. The task was to reconnect art with action and to reinstate action as an expression of the needs of the heart. Greenough therefore proposed that "instead of forcing the functions of every sort of building into one general form, adopting an outward shape for the sake of the eye or of association, without reference to the inner distribution, let us begin from the heart as a nucleus, and work outwards" (quoted, *AR*, 144).

Greenough's effort was concentrated on resisting any attempts, "whether in the social structure or in art, to divide man's wholeness and so to disperse and drain his vitality" (*AR*, 151). His sole ambition was to achieve a recognition of the unity within art itself and between art and other functions of society. But the unity for which he strove, even if he never achieved it as a sculptor, was always double instead of single, embracing "the subordination [both] of the parts to the whole" and "of the whole to the function" (quoted, *AR*, 151–52).

Greenough's view of function was clearly a social rather than a personal one. The New England farmhouse, the trotting wagon, and the clipper ship were all great works of art not merely because they served the needs of individuals but also because, as "the adaptation of the forms and magnitude of structures to the climate they are exposed to, and the offices for which they are intended" (quoted, *AR*, 149), they served the needs of the community as well. Moreover, Greenough's view of function gained added force because of his conviction that "a healthy society can exist only if the magnificent and terrible energies of man can find through its organization their fulfillment" (*AR*, 151). But from there it was only a short step to complete the circle, to show how an organic theory of literature and of art might assist in promoting the general welfare. The explanation was obvious: when literature and art were truly rooted in the needs of the community, they could be said to contribute to national well-being by providing in their functionally derived forms modes of expression for the release and realization of latent human energies.

Although in *American Renaissance* Matthiessen never fully integrated these scattered reflections from Greenough's pseudonymously published *The Travels, Observations, and Experiences of a Yankee Stonecutter* (1852) into a working theory of art, it would be difficult to overestimate their importance for him. They suggested a way of overcoming one of the chief problems in Emerson's organic theory by grounding art firmly within the concrete and the particular; they also brought out to the full the democratic bias that had been inherent in Matthiessen's discussion of organicism, as well as in its actual historical development, from the very beginning. Further, they supported Matthiessen's conviction that literature must be appreciated in terms intrinsic to its own mode of being and yet corroborated his belief that those terms cannot be fully understood without an awareness of the historical and existential conditions that generated them. Greenough's observations also reinforced Matthiessen's assumption that great art represents a fusion of form and content, of means and ends, and yet reconfirmed his belief that art not only is something but also does something. They supported his perception that every unified work of art is a new creation following laws of its own origination, while upholding his assumption that serious art reflects and discovers even as it creates. And, finally, they served to explain Matthiessen's frequent reiteration of Harley Granville-Barker's famous assertion, that great dramatic art, in its fully developed form, is the working out not merely of the individual alone but of society as a whole.

Yet it was Thoreau in *Walden*—and, even more spectacularly, Melville in *Moby-Dick*—who realized in practice what Greenough could only envisage in theory. "In his full utilization of his immediate resources," Matthiessen writes, "Thoreau was the kind of native craftsman whom Greenough recognized as the harbinger of power for our arts" (*AR*, 172). Thoreau had shown what one could do with Greenough's principles: by starting from the simplest elements of the common life, one could reach the universal; by digging down into the mud and slush of Walden Pond, one could grasp fundamental patterns of human experience. Restricting himself solely to the limitations of life as he had actually known them and to the materials readiest to hand, so to speak, Thoreau was nonetheless able "to create 'a true Homeric or Pathologonian man' in the likeness of the French woodchopper" (*AR*, 175).

Matthiessen regarded this achievement as the more important because it served so eloquently to undercut the popular misconception of Thoreau as an extreme protestant whose value lay chiefly in his gestures of dissent and repudiation. To Matthiessen this impression was grossly distorted. Any political significance Thoreau might be said to have derived hardly at all from his famous act of civil disobedience in refusing to pay the poll tax, but rather from his radical critique of New England industrialism and its tendency to separate the worker both from his work and from himself. The heart of Thoreau's revolt, according to Matthiessen, was his willingness to combat any obstacle that stood in the way of the pursuit of life, and its fruits were the pages of *Walden* whose "structural wholeness makes it stand as the firmest product in our literature of such life-giving analogies between the processes of art and daily work" (*AR*, 173).

In light of this achievement, Matthiessen believed that Thoreau's political as well as his literary significance deserved careful reexamination. If the dominant thrust of our national life ever since the days of restless pioneering had been outward, clearly Thoreau belonged among those who represented a counterthrust toward consolidation and permanence. This was not to deny Thoreau's contributions as a dissenter and an explorer; it was merely to assert that in the final analysis Thoreau's place was among the settlers and the community builders, and Matthiessen made no bones about their crucial importance and continuing relevance: "From such islands of realization and fulfillment within the onrushing torrent have come the objects, the order and balance of which now, when we most need them, we can recognize as among the most valuable possessions of our continent" (*AR*, 172).

Matthiessen might well have used similar words to explain Whitman's achievement in *Leaves of Grass.* Although Matthiessen postponed his treatment of Whitman until the end of his book, it is obvious that he viewed Whitman much as he viewed Thoreau—neither as a protestant nor as merely a pioneer, but also as a colonizer and settler. Indeed, at one point Matthiessen defines Whitman's greatness in terms of his ability to make the modern spirit feel at home in the natural world, and it is apparent that Matthiessen placed such a high value on this achievement because of what Whitman had realized so concretely and so vividly in the lines of his great poem. This is not to suggest that Matthiessen accepted Whitman whole. The Whitman who defined himself as visionary and seer, and whose mystical confidence in his own bardic election encouraged him to espouse the most naïve kind of American romanticism, was for all his Emer-

sonian orthodoxy dangerously deluded about life and was playing false with his own gifts. Though frequently shunning the
local and the particular in order to make his voice one with that
of American democracy, Whitman was at his best not when he
was being expansive but when he was being concrete, "when
contemplating with delicacy and tenderness some object near
at hand" (*AR*, 547). The source of Whitman's real poetry,
Matthiessen believed, "was not in the grandiose or orotund but
in the common and humble" (*AR*, 546). His central symbol—the
single blade of grass—was his most authentic.

Matthiessen attributed Whitman's strength in part to his
Quaker background, particularly to its stress "on social values,
on sympathy and mutual helpfulness" (*AR*, 539). This orientation accentuated his identification with the masses and
grounded it in a "concrete humanism" (*AR*, 539). "But when
Whitman turned from contemplating the transfiguration of
common humanity through sacrifice to celebrating the rare individual, the poet as prophet, he could expand into the pride
that annihilates all valid distinctions between the actual and the
ideal" (*AR*, 545).

By maintaining the actual and the ideal in appropriate tension, Whitman fulfilled the organic principle, but only when
holding to his belief that "actuality and the imagination must
be united." The poetry that resulted from this fusion Matthiessen could refer to, after Whitman himself, as "only a language experiment" which might be studied, at least up to a
point, simply through an examination of its diction. Whitman's
experiments with words, however, acquired cultural as well as
literary significance from his perception "that language was not
'an abstract construction' made by the learned, but that it had
arisen out of the work and needs, the joys and struggles and
desires of long generations of humanity, and that it had 'its
bases broad and low, close to the ground' " (*AR*, 517). By remaining faithful to the concrete materiality of words alone,
Whitman, like Thoreau, could make language release its hidden
potential as an expression of the most fundamental experiences
of the race.

This achievement suggests to what degree both Whitman and
Thoreau were able to surpass Emerson's practice of the organic

principle. Whereas Emerson's interpretation of the Incarnational view of reality led him all too frequently to forsake the flesh of words for the sake of the spirit they were supposed to incarnate, Whitman and Thoreau tended to view words themselves as incarnations, identifying what they embodied with their own dense reality.[7] Even here, however, there were important differences. Thoreau, for example, possessed a much firmer grasp of the physical basis of language and expression; Whitman perceived more clearly their sexual origin. Yet what finally seems to have mattered is that both viewed language as an expression of man's wholeness, and therefore each sought to unite the energies of his art with the primary needs of the community as he saw them.

5

Nonetheless, though Whitman and Thoreau came close to fulfilling the organic ideal, they still fell short of the achievement of Hawthorne and Melville. For one thing, they lacked the mature sense of evil which Matthiessen, like Yeats before him, considered the chief prerequisite of the spiritual life. For another, their writing never quite issued in anything like the fully developed modes of experience and expression produced by the other two. Matthiessen felt he could summarize his discussion of the transcendental theory of literature and culture by examining the two kinds of writing—"Allegory and Symbolism"— which resulted from Hawthorne's and Melville's most characteristic practice of that theory.

Matthiessen's treatment of these two forms of artistic expression is both characteristic and innovative. Others, like Cleanth Brooks, for example,[8] had assumed that allegory and symbolism

[7] For a more detailed discussion of this contrast, see Richard Ruland, *The Rediscovery of American Literature* (Cambridge: Harvard University Press, 1967), p. 250.

[8] Matthiessen was thinking of Cleanth Brooks's observation that allegory "is perhaps the first attempt which man makes to unite the intellect and the emotions when they begin to fall apart—Spenser's *Faerie Queene,* for example" (quoted, *AR,* 246). However symptomatic of the taste of a whole generation, Matthiessen found this remark somewhat misleading. The problem was that it cited as one of the first signs of a process a work that clearly represented a later stage. To locate the origin of the historical process to which Brooks referred, one had to go back at least as far as Saint Augustine, where it became clear that allegory initially arose to serve a somewhat different purpose than that ascribed to it by the New Critics: "His *Confessions* are not allegory, but they show what happened as the classical world yielded to the Christian. His gaze was turned

arise from quite different modes of experience and issue in almost mutually exclusive forms of expression, but Matthiessen believed that they are best understood, at least in the work of Hawthorne and Melville, merely as different species of expression within a single mode of thought. Matthiessen's aim, however, was not to blur the distinctions between these two forms of expression, but rather to seek a fresh understanding of each by determining the common ground they shared.

Despite allegory's obvious tendency to abstraction, for example, Matthiessen was convinced that in selected instances—the one he cites is Hawthorne's description of "the way that 'the mystic symbol' of the scarlet letter had struck him, 'communicating itself to my sensibilities, but evading the analyses of my mind' "—allegory entails as dense a process of creation and issues in as "subtly imaginative" a created object as does symbolism (*AR*, 249). But this rather superficial testimony was immeasurably strengthened by a realization of the common epistemological assumption which lay behind both forms, an assumption Hawthorne had expressed when he permitted one of his characters to remark that "everything, you know, has its spiritual meaning, which to the literal meaning is what the soul is to the body" (quoted, *AR*, 242).

This axiomatic belief in the priority of spirit over matter formed the common bond not only between Hawthorne and Melville but also between both of them and the transcendentalists generally. Yet, as Matthiessen was quick to point out, the idealistic tendency to find traces of spirit in every fact of nature was not confined to transcendentalism: "Loosely Platonic, it came specifically from the common background that lay behind Emerson and Hawthorne, from the Christian habit of mind that saw the hand of God in all manifestations of life, and which, in the intensity of the New England seventeenth century, had gone to the extreme of finding 'remarkable providences' even in the

---

inward. He could not rest content with the level of external appearances, since he was obsessed by the drama of conflicting forces that was going on in his own heart. For the projection of this struggle, for the probing of hidden significances, allegory was to become the prevailing means of expression, as the long popularity of *The Romance of the Rose* and of plays like *Everyman* can attest" (*AR*, 246–47).

smallest phenomena, tokens of divine displeasure in every cap-
sized dory or runaway cow" (*AR,* 243).

There is no doubt that, when applied to literature, this idealistic epistemological assumption produced widely differing results. If, on the one hand, it formed the basis upon which Melville built the "cunningly linked analogies" which eventually
became the scaffolding of *Moby-Dick,* it also did much to help
destroy all four of Hawthorne's unfinished romances. But
Matthiessen was less interested in its effects than in the reasons
for its pervasive influence; what he wanted to know was why, as
he put it, "the mode of symbolizing, whether it remained richly
allusive or whether it froze into a conventional and arbitrary
allegory, was basic to the kind of Christian thought that condi-
tioned Emerson and Thoreau as well as Hawthorne and Melville, and was still latent in Whitman's Quaker strain" (*AR,* 269).
He found the clue to an answer in Hawthorne's reaction to
England's Lichfield Cathedral, as noted in his *Journal.* In observing with "uninstructed vision" what appeared at the moment to
be "the object best worth gazing at in the whole world" (quoted,
AR, 270), Hawthorne recalled his having been doubly struck
with a sense of his own earthly limitations and the infinity of the
Absolute. Having marveled at the intricacy, vastness, and profound simplicity that made of a Gothic cathedral "surely the
most wonderful work which mortal man has yet achieved," Hawthorne added:

> Not that I felt, or was worthy to feel, an unmingled enjoyment in gazing at
> this wonder. I could not elevate myself to its spiritual height . . . Ascending
> but a little way, I continually fell back and lay in a kind of despair, conscious
> that a flood of uncomprehended beauty was pouring down upon me, of which
> I could appropriate only the minutest portion. After a hundred years . . . I
> should still be a gazer from below and at an awful distance, as yet excluded
> from the interior mystery. But it was something to be gained, even to have
> that painful sense of my own limitations, and that half-smothered yearning to
> soar beyond them. The cathedral showed me how earthly I was, but yet whis-
> pered deeply of immortality. (Quoted, *AR,* 270)

This passage brings out, as perhaps nothing else could, the
essentially religious cast of mind which Matthiessen wanted to
ascribe to both allegory and symbolism. Hawthorne's sense of

radical cleavage between the human and the divine was not the result of some "vague desire of the moth for the star" (*AR*, 270), but rather an expression of the deep Christian roots Hawthorne shared with practically everybody else of his time. Like the others, he was obsessed with the problem of reuniting the fact with the symbol and the symbol with whatever lay behind it; and even if he rejected Emerson's method of doing this, by lifting "better up to best," he was clearly willing to acknowledge a transcendent dimension within experience whose ground was quite beyond his powers of comprehension. This religious perception, so like Pascal's earlier recognition of the contrast between the littleness of man and the immensity of the universe, is what Hawthorne acknowledged in his response to Lichfield Cathedral and what he wanted to convey a sense of in his fiction. Yet it was not Hawthorne but rather Melville, according to Matthiessen, who ultimately provided the best formulation of this heightened sense of reality they both wanted to express in their writing. The statment to which Matthiessen referred is Melville's famous remark in *The Confidence-Man,* where he interrupts the flow of his narrative to assert that "it is with fiction as with religion; it should present another world, and yet one to which we feel the tie" (quoted, *AR*, 269).

Matthiessen regarded this religious propensity for imagining worlds elsewhere, as Emerson put it, as an important factor in Hawthorne's development of "the crucial definition of romance." Occupying a middle ground somewhere between mimetic realism on the one hand and pure symbolic expression on the other, Hawthorne conceived of the romance, Matthiessen contended, much as Melville understood his own representative forms, as an attempt to unite inner experience with outer reality by establishing a neutral ground where "the Actual" and "the Imaginary" might meet. What Hawthorne therefore sought was not a realm of pure ideality but rather a realm where reality was purified: "not actuality transformed into an impossible perfection, but actuality disengaged from appearance" (*AR*, 264). His goal, which in Matthiessen's judgment Melville shared, was the creation of a sense of reality so managed by the medium in and through which it was presented that the picture of it, together with the action that unified it, might do the fullest possible justice to "the truth of the human heart" (quoted, *AR*, 268). The main concern of the romance was not with external details but with inner meaning. Like the characteristic forms developed by Matthiessen's other four writers, Hawthorne's "crucial definition of romance" was preoccupied with what Gervayse Hastings in "The Christmas Banquet" had missed in life, "the deep warm secret—the life within the life" (quoted, *AR*, 238).

In seeking reunification of the inner with the outer by grounding his art in the life of the affections, Matthiessen argues, Hawthorne was every bit as much a democrat as any of the others. Hawthorne's severest criticisms of the injustices of early New England life derived from his perception "that its feelings were less developed than its mind" (*AR*, 347), and he always assumed that reliance upon the life of feeling forces a man out of the protected enclosure of his own individuality and into the wider life of society. Matthiessen makes much of the fact that Hawthorne viewed his artistic vocation as an attempt, in his own words, "to open an intercourse with the world" (quoted, *AR*, 222), and that he sought whenever possible to measure the dangerous effects of his characters' frequent alienation from themselves and others against a warmly human and collective norm. Indeed, the one thing that terrified Hawthorne most about the isolated individual, Matthiessen writes, "was the cold inability to respond to ordinary life, whether, as in the case of Gervayse Hastings . . . , it was owing to the fact that since he had never suffered, other people seemed to him only shadows; or whether, as with an unscrupulous scientist like Rappaccini or a self-centered reformer like Hollingsworth, it was because their minds had lost touch with 'the magnetic chain of humanity' " (*AR*, 228).

Yet for all the comparative dignity and importance of his aims, Matthiessen was frank to admit that Hawthorne had his limitations. Of his four mature romances, only *The Scarlet Letter* seemed to attain the imaginative wholeness that Hawthorne sought for it. Not only was his plot in *The Scarlet Letter* most coherently developed and his several types of characters most clearly differentiated; he was also in this novel most nearly successful in establishing "the continual correspondences that his theme allowed him to make between external and inner significance" (*AR*, 276). But even where Hawthorne developed his themes to the utmost, he could never structure his treatment of them so as to negotiate, as Melville could at his best, "a whole extension of consciousness" (*AR*, 284). As Matthiessen later brings out in comparing Hawthorne with Henry James, Hawthorne simply could not imagine anything more dramatic than the caught image or the skillfully constructed tableau, as in the encounters of Hester, Dimmesdale, and Pearl on the scaffold in *The Scarlet Letter*, in Zenobia's confrontation with Hollingsworth at the base of Eliot's pulpit in *The Blithedale Romance*, or in Miriam's and Donatello's acceptance of their unhappy union under the shadow of the statue of Pope Julius in the cathedral square at Perugia in *The Marble Faun*. Such tableaus enabled Hawthorne to achieve "picturesque arrangement," but they did not make for "dynamic composition" (*AR*, 301).

Nonetheless, Hawthorne's severest limitation, according to Matthiessen, was not his lack of a fully developed sense of the dramatic but rather his inability to think in symbols. Though he could use symbols to summarize and express a mind's thoughts, he could not use them, as Melville could, to convey as well the actual experience of a mind thinking, of a mind engaged in the very moment of symbolic discovery, "when the literal details were separating out in . . . consciousness into metaphors and yielding that extension of awareness which is metaphor's most valuable gift" (*AR*, 129). This distinction accounts for the broad difference Matthiessen perceived between Hawthorne's highly suggestive allegorical treatment of the loss of faith in the story "Young Goodman Brown" and the symbolic art which operates "on an entirely different plane" in the chapter "The Mat-Maker" in *Moby-Dick*. When the ball of free will drops from Ishmael's hand as he hears Tashtego's cry of "There she blows!" split the air, Melville creates "a bridge of metaphor" which carries "us across from one mode of existence to another" (*AR*, 284). And lest no one underestimate the scope of this achievement, Matthiessen immediately added that "only by discovering such metaphors can the writer suggest the actual complexity of experience; and consequently, the more of them he is able to perceive, the more comprehensive is his grasp of human life" (*AR*, 284).

Matthiessen was under no illusions as to the intermittency of Melville's realization of the artistic fusion of internal and external. According to his own reckoning, Melville succeeded in uniting his early gifts for historical narrative with his equally strong penchant for allegorical speculation in the creation of a genuinely organic and symbolic art only three times in his entire career: first in selected passages of *Moby-Dick* and then in two shorter works separated by a period of almost thirty years, *Benito Cereno* and *Billy Budd*. But the outcome of Melville's effort was an art that fully satisfied Matthiessen's conception of organicism. By providing the symbol's miraculous extension of unified awareness, Melville's best work performed that function analogous to religion, by presenting us with "another world, and yet one to which we feel the tie."

Observations such as these led Matthiessen to suggest—one feels almost reluctantly—that the distinction between allegory and symbolism, which could also be said to characterize the difference between Hawthorne and Melville at their most typical, was related to Coleridge's famous differentiation between imagination and fancy. Symbolism, Matthiessen conceded, "is esemplastic, since it shapes new wholes; whereas allegory deals with fixities and definites that it does not basically modify" (*AR*, 249–50). And this statment in turn compelled him to conclude that *"Moby-Dick* is, in its main sweep, an example of the reconcilement of the general with the concrete, of the fusion of idea and image; whereas, even in *The Scarlet Letter,* the abstract, the idea, is often of greater interest than its concrete expression" (*AR*, 250).

Matthiessen, however, was not interested solely in isolating the points of similarity and difference between allegory and symbolism; he also sought to account for Melville's success in the symbolic mode. Apart from differences of temperament and ability in Melville and Hawthorne, Melville's greater achievement as a symbolist seemed to derive from two interrelated factors. The first had to do with what Matthiessen referred to as Hawthorne's "lingering attachment to the eighteenth century" (*AR*, 261), an attachment that became manifest both in his use of diction and in his theory of the imagination. Whereas Melville and the other transcendentalists conceived of the imagination as an instrument of projection and illumination, Hawthorne stubbornly persisted in holding to the older view of it primarily as an instrument of reflection. This more classical bias inevitably disposed him to pay stricter attention, just as the Augustans had, to the general than to the concrete, to the abstract than to the particular. As a result, even when Hawthorne could produce living symbols, he could never make his symbols, like Melville's, transcend the allegories on which they depended for their meaning. No matter how hard he worked to make his art appeal at once to the senses and to the intellect, Hawthorne was always tempted to substitute the idea of the thing for the thing itself.

Closely related was the second reason for Melville's having greater success in the symbolic mode than Hawthorne: his capacity to assimilate and express a larger abundance of concrete life. Even more than Thoreau, Melville knew that the body thought, that the feelings should reflect the motions of the mind. Thus he perceived intuitively and directly the principle that Henry James ultimately came to more rationally and obliquely, "the perfect dependence of the 'moral' sense of a work of art on the amount of felt life concerned in producing it" (quoted, *AR,* 304). By contrast, this is where Hawthorne's work was most deficient. In spite of his great moral seriousness, Hawthorne was always gliding away from "the surfaces from which the realistic novelist draws his sustenance" (*AR,* 241). In a word, Hawthorne's fiction lacked the "earth-smell," and without it his symbols could never attain that further reach accomplished by Melville's, where, at their most comprehensive, Melville was able, as no one else in his age, "to elicit 'what remains primeval in our formalized humanity' " (*AR,* 656).

If this encomium signifies little more, it indicates how thoroughly Melville dominated Matthiessen's imagination of the entire era. Even when he could identify with the aims and acknowledge the achievements of the other four, it was Melville who provided the standards of measurement. Melville was the greater writer because, in spite of exposing himself to more disparate and disruptive experiences, he succeeded more completely than any of his contemporaries in making those experiences yield to the organizing, unifying energies of his art. The gauge of Melville's success as an organicist was his ability to incarnate in his forms that intense fusion of inner and outer, of private and public, of "the life within the life," which was the organic ideal of them all.

Matthiessen was not content, however, to drop the discussion of organicism at this point. If Hawthorne's art, like that of all the others, suffered by comparison with Melville's when measured against the organic ideal, Hawthorne still shared with Melville the deeper insight "that there can be no authentic style," no authentic fusion of matter and means, "unless it has been created by a meaning, by a close response to the complexity of existence" (*AR*, 190). By "meaning" Matthiessen referred to something far more subtle, far more complex, than an individual work's paraphrasable content; he referred instead to that essential core of values upon which the work's vision is based and by means of which the work becomes unified as a special fusion of form and substance. The point to be noted is that such assumptions in turn prevented one, indeed, absolutely forbade one, to identify a work of art with any of its distinguishing attributes of style, technique, structure, or theme. The essence of its life for the true organicist, its "life within the life," was rather to be found in its sustained vision of experience, by which it could then be said to lend imaginative shape and realization not merely to itself but also to a significant portion of our actual or potential experience.

These convictions constituted the heart of the literary theory Matthiessen derived from his five writers, a theory he would then turn back upon their own achievement by referring to their work as a mode of realization and renewal in and through which is recreated "the challenge of our still undiminished resources." But in order to release the "unspent potential" of those resources, Matthiessen was required, in fidelity to the organic principle, to pass beyond a discussion of his writers' aims and and the variety of means by which they had sought to achieve those aims to a more concrete analysis of the enabling principle of their art, their vital core of meaning. If Matthiessen was to appropriate what he had learned, an examination of theory and technique had to give way to an interpretation of vision. And thus he turned in the long central sections of his book to Hawthorne and Melville, the two writers of the period who, in their respective treatments of tragedy, made what for Matthiessen was the nineteenth century's most profound "close response to the complexities of existence."

CHAPTER FOUR

"American Renaissance" and the
Possibility of Democratic Christianity

> You have got to pull the democratic and idealistic clothes off Ameri-
> can utterance, and see what you can of the dusky body . . . underneath.
> . . . You must look through the surface of American art, and see the
> inner diabolism of the symbolic meaning. . . . The Americans refuse
> everything explicit and always put up a sort of double meaning.
>
> D. H. LAWRENCE
> *Studies in Classic American Literature*

IN WHAT still remains the best short analysis of Matthiessen's
entire career, Henry Nash Smith says that Matthiessen's "close
response to the complexities of existence" in *American Renaissance* issued in two fundamental preoccupations, with the meaning of tragedy and with the meaning of democracy. "His absorbed meditation upon the workings of these two conceptions
within the American tradition," Smith argues, "gives us at once
his act of possessing the past and his act of self-knowledge."[1]
Professor Smith readily concedes that these two concerns,
"which were respectively the highest values that . . . [Mat-
thiessen] perceived in art and in politics,"[2] have usually been
understood by contemporary thinkers as deriving from different, if not opposing, traditions. Tragedy's emphasis upon the
heroic figure rather than upon the average man, and its perception of the inevitable conflicts and the possible defeat to which
all human aspirations are susceptible, have often seemed to
undercut the egalitarian premises of modern democratic thinking and to question its faith in progress. On the other hand,
much modern democratic thinking has been based upon instru-

---

[1] Henry Nash Smith, "American Renaissance," *Monthly Review* 2 (1950): 225.
[2] *Ibid.*, p. 227.

mental theories of knowledge which have often exhibited a
marked distrust of the imagination and have, further, equated
truth with measurable results. Yet for Matthiessen, according to
Professor Smith, tragedy and democracy were not only compati-
ble; they were almost identical. The key to their unity lay in the
theory of knowledge Matthiessen derived from Coleridge. In
Coleridge's poetic application of the doctrine of the Word made
flesh, Matthiessen discovered a way of bridging the gap between
aesthetics and politics: "The moment in which the artist grasps
truth is also the moment in which he achieves an integration of
his faculties and embodies his insight in words: the imagination
effects a coalescence of objective and subjective in an act of
expression which brings 'the whole soul of man into activity.' "[3]

Professor Smith's argument is correct so far as it goes, and
it helps to clarify and confirm much of what has been said in the
preceding chapter. But in one particular it seems to stop short
of the full truth. Matthiessen, who tended to turn literary questions about form and technique into moral and religious questions about the nature of reality, would never have been content
to secure the unity he sought between these two major preoccupations merely by means of a theory of knowledge, no matter
how inclusive in scope. His own mind was too strongly an-
thropological, too absorbed in the question of man's nature and
destiny, to find in epistemology alone a satisfactory bridge between all that he meant by democratic theory on the one hand
and a tragic view of life on the other. Coleridge's theory of
knowledge and expression might unite these two concerns at the
level of literary theory, but at the level of lived experience their
integration required an apprehension of something still more
central.

In retrospect I think it would be more accurate to say that
Matthiessen's intense interest in the meaning of democracy on
the one hand and in the tragic nature of man's fate on the other
served less to unify the elements of his thought than to mark
its determining boundaries. As the two outermost poles of his
reflection—the limits toward which his characteristic medita-
tions on the nature and function of literature, on the relation

---

[3] *Ibid.,* p. 228.

of the artist to his age, and on the responsibilities of the critic were attracted—they were themselves unified, both in *American Renaissance* and in other works, by the moral and religious anthropology upon which he based them, an anthropology he derived mainly from his study of the American experience. In *American Renaissance* this anthropology received its fullest expression in what Matthiessen made of "that unshackled, democratic spirit of Christianity in all things" which Melville attributed to Hawthorne and Matthiessen in turn applied to Melville. In Matthiessen's highly original interpretation, however, this intimate union of democratic and Christian influences was less the sole possession of either Hawthorne or Melville than of the entire age to which they belonged. As the underlying spirit of their era, the confluence of social and religious impulses held an enormous attraction for Matthiessen, not only drawing him to the culture of mid-nineteenth-century America but also defining what he later referred to as "our still undiminished resources."

1

Matthiessen suggested some of the contours of that anthropology and at the same time indicated its relation to the theory of knowledge adumbrated by Coleridge, in the way he described the alteration of belief which had occurred in nineteenth-century America. Assuming that this alteration was ethical and theological rather than merely aesthetic and that it centered in the Christian doctrine of the Incarnation, Matthiessen defined it in exceedingly bold terms as a movement "from belief in the salvation of man through the mercy and grace of a sovereign God, to belief in the potential divinity in every man" (*AR,* 446). To anyone as "concerned with orthodoxy" as Matthiessen was, this transformation of the nineteenth century's "object of belief from God-Man to Man-God" was cause for real alarm (*AR,* 446). At its very worst, as Matthiessen observed in connection with Whitman, this shift in emphasis could lead to such terrifying lengths as the proclamation of man as his own messiah; at best it meant the loss of "several important attitudes": that individuality is not synonymous with autonomy; that man can find completion only in something greater than himself; and that the real basis for human community lies "not in humanitarianism but in men's common aspiration and fallibility, in their humility before God" (*AR*, 446).

The attitudes whose loss Matthiessen here deplores bear a striking resemblance to the beliefs he expressed many years earlier in one of the first pieces of writing he ever published, the credo he wrote as a "leader" editorial for the *Yale Literary Magazine* during his senior year in college. To be sure, this undergraduate piece, which sought to bring its readers "face to face with the Truth that in order to realize our highest possibilities we must be utterly dominated by an ideal" (*RC*, 252), exhibits all the naïve moral strenuousness one associates with the YMCA movement. But if the credo's youthful ardency of tone and moral buoyancy were qualities that Matthiessen would soon outgrow, the sentiments expressed underneath were not. The credo's assumption that one finds his life only through an act of self-surrender, and its consequent stress on such values as commitment, humility, and selflessness, would remain unshakable tenets of Matthiessen's religious position for the rest of his life—only toughened and tempered, as John Rackliffe perceptively suggested, by the suffering and self-scrutiny elicited by an "often lonely career" (*RC*, xii). The difference between the two documents lies in the fact that the idealistic undergraduate of the credo was concerned largely to criticize his classmates for their impatient and irresponsible contempt for such values; the mature critic of *American Renaissance* was interested more precisely in determining exactly why such a displacement of values had occurred at all.

The roots of this nineteenth-century alteration in belief were not hard to find. Though in part a result of the forces unleashed by the French and American revolutions and the subsequent emergence of the Romantic cult of the individual, this spiritual alteration had distinctively American origins, Matthiessen believed, in the perennial American problem of society versus solitude, or the relation between the community and the individual. Matthiessen first noted the substance of this problem as early as 1930 in a review of Newton Arvin's *Hawthorne* (1929), correctly remarking that "our most characteristic achievements have been those of the isolated spirit: Emily Dickinson in her lonely room, Melville restlessly wandering the seas, the pioneer of a hundred years ago, and the captain of industry today—all have won their victories by turning their backs on society, by denying its claims or escaping from them" (*RC*, 209). When the creative individual was thrown back upon his own resources and forced to alienate himself from society merely in order to survive, it is little wonder that the Christian myth was reinterpreted; "by Melville's time," as Matthiessen later remarked, "and especially in protestant, democratic America, the emphasis was no longer on God become Man, on the unique birth and Divinity of the Christ, who was killed and died back into eternal life; but on the rebel killed by an unworthy society, on Man become the Messiah, become God" (*AR*, 446).

Matthiessen gave Hawthorne full credit for understanding the consequences of this religious transformation. Hawthorne knew, as none of his contemporaries did, the dire effects of this centrifugal movement in American life, which elicited and forced "a constant expansion from the center outwards" (*RC*, 209). In working to separate the individual from everyday life, this alteration determined the tragic destiny of many of Hawthorne's chief characters: "The tragedies of Ethan Brand, Rappaccini, and Roger Chillingworth are all owing to the fact that they have lost their grasp of the central human elements, and have drifted dangerously away from the center. They no longer feel any bond with society, and, as a consequence, they are no longer individuals, but restless burning exaggerations of a single quality" (*RC*, 209).

As Matthiessen noted in *American Renaissance*, Newton Arvin had brought this point out vividly in his biography. All our grand national types, from the best to the worst, have been united in what Arvin described as "their common distrust of centrality, their noble or ignoble lawlessness, their spiritual pride," and have thus emerged from the centrifugal pressures of history as "partial and lopsided personalities, men and women of one dimension, august or vulgar cranks" (*AR*, 343). And the reason Hawthorne could depict their fate so honestly is because in some dark recess of his mind he suspected that it might become his own fate as well, that as a result of his necessary detachment as a novelist, he had lost the ability to participate in life directly. Indeed, it was precisely his fear of alienation from life which enabled Hawthorne to see the damaging consequences of America's expansion from the center outward, which seemed to lead us further and further away from the saving bonds of human fellowship. Even if Hawthorne could not envisage a way of overcoming the difficulty, he had, Matthiessen was convinced, suggested, at least by indirection, what might. By relentlessly dramatizing the distorting effects of our reckless individualism, Hawthorne pointed "to the need for a new ethical and cultural community" (*AR*, 343).

Such observations led Newton Arvin to conclude that Hawthorne's orientation was essentially social, but Matthiessen believed that it was more fundamentally religious. By "religious," however, Matthiessen did not mean that Hawthorne's fiction conformed to the creeds of any particular church or dogma. On the contrary, if there was anything readily obvious about Hawthorne's attitude toward organized religion, it was his marked indifference to all such matters. But whatever his feelings about the dead husks of religious tradition, Hawthorne still retained an ability to perceive the living kernels of truth beneath them, an ability that permitted him to recover for his contemporaries "what [the] Puritans professed but seldom practiced—the spirit of piety, humility and tragedy in the face of the inscrutable ways of God" (quoted, *AR*, 199).

In pursuing this line of argument, Matthiessen was simply following up suggestions that Herbert Schneider had made more than a decade earlier in his pioneering study, *The Puritan Mind* (1930). Yet it is a tribute to Matthiessen's sense of critical tact that he refused to reduce these insights to another set of theological postulates. Unless such suggestions are considered merely a way of dismissing Hawthorne's ideas, of consigning them either to the dustbin of history or to the couch of the psychoanalyst, Matthiessen was convinced that the real value of Hawthorne's spiritual discoveries still had "to be reckoned with" (*AR*, 337). And such reckoning could occur, he insisted, "only if we start from the inside, so to speak, only if, instead of discounting his views as part of a world gone by, we try to experience to the full what he thought and felt about human destiny. For only then will we be in a position to test his interpretation against others, and against what we ourselves may believe to be the primary forces in the universe" (*AR*, 337).

2

It should perhaps cause little surprise that when Matthiessen turned to the task of opening up Hawthorne's fiction "from the inside" to understand what Hawthorne really "thought and felt about human destiny," he received considerable assistance from Melville. The crucial document was Melville's response to Hawthorne's stories in the two volumes of *Mosses from an Old Manse* (1846); Melville's article, "Hawthorne and His Mosses," was published in Evert Duyckinck's *The Literary World.* This review was important to Matthiessen in a double sense. As a brilliant assessment of the work of one writer by another whose own writing would soon begin to eclipse it both in scope and in power, Melville's essay not only provided Matthiessen with many of the terms by which to measure Hawthorne's achievement; it also provided him with a statement of values which would eventually guide his interpretation of Melville as well, and of the whole age to which they both belonged.

In Matthiessen's view, Melville's first encounter with Hawthorne in *Mosses from an Old Manse* precipitated in him one of those remarkable "shocks of recognition" which can sometimes change the course of an entire literary tradition by leading to the discovery of a community of shared interests and sentiments and thus helping to release long pent-up springs of creative vitality. The scope and impact of this recognition was naturally more profound on Melville than on Hawthorne, if only because Melville was a younger and less well-established writer who suffered from a more acute sense of isolation and public neglect. Yet the very force of Melville's recognition also radiated backward on Hawthorne, throwing an entirely new light on a writer who was having public difficulties of his own in shedding a reputation he had acquired in the literary weeklies as no more than a perceptive but congenial New England romancer. The brilliance of Melville's essay derived from his ability to explain the reasons for this kind of response to Hawthorne while at the same time establishing the grounds for a very different interpretation altogether. Melville could appreciate the unobtrusive maturity of Hawthorne's best stories, which gave to almost every page "the mark of unhurried completion," but he also realized that the "Indian-summer mellowness" in which this resulted was owing to something far more significant than mere charm (*AR*, 187). The richness of Hawthorne's surfaces was the result of his willingness to dive, his Shakespearean "probings at the very axis of reality" (quoted, *AR*, 189), which in turn lent to his seemingly placid descriptions a fullness of significance that depended upon his sense of the disturbing depths underneath. Hawthorne's ripeness, Melville realized, was not so much the product of his artifice as of his sensibility, of what Melville described as "a great, deep intellect which drops down into the universe like a plummet" and "which sends few thoughts into circulation, except they be arterialized at his large warm lungs and expanded in his honest heart" (quoted, *AR*, 190).

Yet Melville's analysis of Hawthorne's strength was all the more compelling because it was based upon a clear perception that such strength always derives its moral fiber from personal suffering, the result of which, at least in Hawthorne's art, being what Matthiessen later described in reference to Melville as a balanced "matching of the forces" (*AR*, 442). On the one side, according to Melville, was Hawthorne's "great power of blackness" which derived such "force from its appeals to that Calvinistic sense of Innate Depravity and Original Sin, from whose visitations, in some shape or other, no deeply thinking mind is always and wholly free" (quoted, *AR*, 190). On the other side, Melville insisted, there is "such a depth of tenderness, such a boundless sympathy with all forms of being, such an omnipresent love, that we must needs say that this Hawthorne is here almost alone in his generation—at least, in the artistic manifestation of these things" (quoted, *AR*, 190). This felicitous union of opposites, so close to the one Matthiessen eventually discerned in Melville himself, led Melville to feel that Hawthorne was "deep as Dante" and that America, in producing its first native writer, was at last on the threshold of a new age.

Yet if Hawthorne's achievement left Melville feeling that the world had once again become as young and as fresh as it was on the first day of creation, Matthiessen was convinced that this feeling of invigorating renewal had little to do with the world evoked in Hawthorne's fiction. When Hawthorne looked back over the American past, Matthiessen pointed out, he was struck not by images of regeneration and rebirth but rather by images of decay and impotence, "by the broken ends to which the Puritan effort had finally come, by the rigidity that had been integral to its thought at its best, by modes of life in which nothing beautiful had developed" (*AR,* 322). Hawthorne was not less eager than other writers to overcome the transcendentalist gap between the actual and the ideal, but, because of deeper psychological and religious penetration, he recognized the futility of attempting to bridge that gap through recourse to a belief in man's potential divinity. To exalt the divine in man was to run the risk of obliterating all the distinctions between man and God, between time and eternity. Though Hawthorne was no theologian, he did retain enough of a hold on the central Christian elements to insist that man lives both in time as well as out of it, and that the constant interaction between time and eternity constitutes a portion of his tragic destiny. Because of man's capacity for imagining a perfection that is timeless, Hawthorne seemed to believe, man is always driven to transcend himself in an effort to realize the perfection of which he dreams. Yet because man is finite and limited, he also knows, Hawthorne realized, that nothing perfect can be achieved within time itself. Hence, in contrast with all doctrines of historical progress and all views of individual perfection, Hawthorne's interpretation of human destiny remained closer to the darker view expressed in *The Scarlet Letter* by the heartless but clear-sighted Chillingworth, who rebuked Hester's boldness with the words: "My old faith, long forgotten, comes back to me, and explains all that we do, and all we suffer. By thy first step awry thou didst plant the germ of evil; but since that moment, it has all been a dark necessity" (quoted, *AR,* 316).

For all his undeniable pessimism, however, Matthiessen's Hawthorne was no strict predestinarian. If it was true that Hawthorne, like Jonathan Edwards before him, came closest to universality through his recognition of the bond of human depravity, his dark portraits of New England life still showed an affirming flame. In this way, according to Matthiessen, Hawthorne's fiction retained an essentially tragic balance. Taking as his major theme not so much the nature or the inevitability of sin but rather the inexorable consequences of sin, Hawthorne intended for his art less to depress than to release; his aim was to illustrate the outcome of those first steps taken awry, to which Chillingworth alluded, so that men and women might be fore-warned about the consequences of exchanging "the magnetic chain of humanity" for the imprisoning bond of "a dark necessity."

Matthiessen's insight into Hawthorne's tragic sense led him to center his interpretation of it, and of Melville's as well, on two interrelated questions. Assuming that Hawthorne, like Melville, could sustain "the balance of great tragedy, that he could portray the horror of life" as well as "its moments of trans-figured glory" (*AR*, 344), Matthiessen wanted to know to what extent Hawthorne's treatment of tragedy was democratic and to what extent it was Christian. These two concerns followed logically from Matthiessen's conviction that a mature sense of tragedy, as he stated at the beginning of his discussion of Haw-thorne,[4] requires a firm conception both of man in relation to society and also of the relation between good and evil. If the sociopolitical or democratic component of tragic art depended upon a determination of the degree to which a writer can imag-ine individuals who are representative of a whole interrelated condition of society, the ethicoreligious or Christian compo-nent, on the other hand, was based on the extent to which a writer can accept the intermixture of good and evil which Mat-thiessen believed to be an unavoidable part of life.

Measured against the first of these two standards, it is clear that Hawthorne placed well below Melville on Matthiessen's scale of values. Even though Hawthorne could criticize the quest for utopia in *The Blithedale Romance,* or create characters repre-sentative of an entire social and historical milieu in *The House of Seven Gables,* he failed to perceive what was fundamentally wrong with a society that produced the Brook Farm experiment in the first instance or the Pynchon family in the second. Conse-quently, Hawthorne was always in danger of confounding his

---

[4] See *American Renaissance,* pp. 179–80, for Matthiessen's most compressed but defini-tive statement of the nature of tragic art.

own purposes, even in a novel so acutely conscious of its own age as *The House of Seven Gables.* In analyzing the curse the Pynchons brought upon themselves, "the lust for wealth that . . . held the dominating Pynchons in its inflexible grasp" (*AR,* 326), Hawthorne remained blind to the fact that he was merely "sowing all over again the same seeds of evil" by bestowing economic largess in the end on all those to whom the unscrupulous judge had previously denied it. In this sense Hawthorne's problem always remained the same: "how . . . to bridge the gap between foreground and background, how to suggest the whole scene of which his characters were part" (*AR,* 335).

The reason for Hawthorne's failure to close this gap was not wholly social or political, according to Matthiessen. Although Hawthorne's skepticism about all schemes for human betterment reflected a deep strain of conservatism, his sincere admiration for Andrew Jackson and his willingness to undertake a campaign biography of Franklin Pierce both testified, Matthiessen argued somewhat weakly, to Hawthorne's strong commitments as a democrat. Was this mixture of conservatism and progressivism expressive of a sentimental inconsistency in Hawthorne? Matthiessen did not think so, and here found firmer ground for his argument. Hawthorne's attraction to the party of the common people seemed rooted in precisely the same qualities that impelled him to pay close attention to the private consciousness of individuals: his conservative but no less egalitarian curiosity about and sympathy for what is universal and constant in the humanity of all men. As Hawthorne said himself, his researches were not confined to a study of "human character in its individual developments" but were also directed toward "human nature in the mass" (quoted, *AR,* 239); it was "the depths of our common nature" which Hawthorne wanted to explore, as he remarked in the preface to *The Snow-Image,* and by this means, Matthiessen added, "he hoped to make his art a bridge between man and society" (*AR,* 239).

But why, then, did Hawthorne so often fail to build that bridge? What prevented him from closing the gap between all that Whitman meant by "the single solitary self" and "the democratic en-masse"? Matthiessen's answer was as simple as it was

illuminating. "Although . . . [Hawthorne] could see his characters in a definite environment, he could not give the sense of
their being in continuous contact with that larger world outside"
(*AR*, 335). And when this diagnosis was applied to the realm of
morality, where most of Hawthorne's fiction operates, Hawthorne's lack of a sense of connectedness between the universe
within characters and the universe without meant that, though
he could conceive of evil in the world, he could not conceive
of a world that was truly evil. Hawthorne's problem, therefore,
was metaphysical, and the only writer of his age whose mind was
speculative enough, whose imagination was daring enough, and
whose feelings were primitive enough to attempt to confront it,
Matthiessen insisted, was Melville.

3

In contrast with Hawthorne, Melville exhibited an acute sense
of the social and the political almost from the very beginning.
Though his first two novels, *Typee* and *Omoo*, only hinted at what
he learned on his voyage to the South Seas—"that all the preten-
sions of civilization might be no better grounded than those on
which the French and English missionaries attempted to convert
the Polynesians, while actually preparing their ruin at the hands
of predatory commerce" (*AR*, 376)—Melville's early realization
of the discrepancy between the noble professions of Christianity
and democracy and their shabby practice soon surfaced in some
of the speculative sections of *Mardi*, his third novel, and then
reached center stage in *Redburn*, his fourth. Moreover, once
having appeared in Melville's writing, the economic, political,
and social factors were never again to leave. If *Redburn* was a
study in youthful disillusionment with poverty, Matthiessen believed, *White Jacket* could be viewed as an indictment of criminal
injustices in the American social system; *Moby-Dick*, as a prefigu-
ration of the destructiveness of late nineteenth-century industrial and financial tycoons; *Pierre*, at least in part, as a dramatiza-
tion of the plight of the isolated individual who is finally
overborne by the heartlessness of the modern city; *Israel Potter*,
as a study of the terrible degradation of out-and-out destitution;
"The Tartarus of Maids," as an attack on the inhumanity of the
American factory system; and "the whole bitter sequence of *The*

Confidence Man," as an exposé of "characters who are made fools or knaves by money" (*AR*, 401).

With such strong philosophical and religious biases, however, Melville's sharp awareness of social, economic, and political injustice only drove him deeper into metaphysics, into the problem that was Hamlet's, into "the difference between what seems and what is" (*AR*, 376). Yet, unlike the transcendentalists, Melville realized the danger of trying to negate that difference by reference to Emerson's belief in "the infinitude of the private man." To obliterate all the differences between appearance and reality by relying on some doctrine of man's potential omniscience was to risk ultimate destruction; and in one of the many parablelike vignettes in *Moby-Dick,* Melville exposed the fatal consequences of such an attempt:

Lulled into such an opium-like listlessness of vacant, unconscious revery is this absent-minded youth by the blending cadence of waves with thoughts, that at last he loses his identity; takes the mystic ocean at his feet for the visible image of that deep, blue, bottomless soul, pervading mankind and nature, and every strange, half-seen, gliding, beautiful thing that eludes him; every dimly discovered, uprising fin of some undiscernible form, seems to him the embodiment of those elusive thoughts that only people the soul by continually flitting through it. . . . But while this sleep, this dream is on ye, move your foot or hand an inch; slip your hold at all; and your identity comes back in horror. Over Descartian vortices you hover. And perhaps, at midday, in the fairest weather, with one half-throttled shriek you drop through that transparent air into the summer sea, no more to rise forever. Heed it well, ye Pantheists! (Quoted, *AR*, 405).

Matthiessen attributes Melville's ability to see through the platitudinous assumptions of the transcendentalists to several interrelated factors. For one thing, Melville was instinctively aware "that these beautiful fins were part of cruel forms" (*AR*, 406), that cruelty might inhere in the very nature of life. For another, he realized that, if cruelty was indeed inherent in life, the "infinitude" of Emerson's private man, when unchecked by the demands of love, might well become a howling waste. Melville's twofold insight therefore enabled him to go beyond either Hawthorne or any other contemporary in challenging the nineteenth-century theological "shift of emphasis from Incarnation to Deification" (*AR*, 446) by severely scrutinizing Emerson's heady notion of the individual man as a law sufficient unto himself.

Matthiessen regarded Captain Ahab as Melville's test case, as Melville's "most profound response to the problem of the free individual will *in extremis*" (*AR*, 447), for Ahab was fashioned in the image of the nineteenth century's "Man-God, the self-appointed Messiah" (*AR*, 459), who takes upon himself all the prerogatives usually reserved to God alone. Nevertheless, what most impressed Matthiessen about Ahab was less his presumption of the role of God than the frighteningly ironic consequences of that action: of how this puritanical sea captain, in all the mad righteousness of his hatred of evil, becomes in the course of the narrative an incarnation of the very evil he would destroy. Emerson might well have agreed with Ahab that visible objects are little more than pasteboard masks hiding a reality within, but, he would have "felt none of Ahab's torment at the demonic element in the unseen, at the hidden malignity which caused him to break out: 'That inscrutable thing is chiefly what I hate; and be the White Whale agent, or be the White Whale principal, I will wreak that hate upon him' " (*AR*, 406). This perception raised Ahab above all the members of his crew and earned for him Captain Peleg's description as "a grand ungodly, god-like man"; yet the same perception drove him to put every last vestige of his humanity behind him as he assumed the role of "the Fates' lieutenant" and swept himself and his entire crew, save one, to destruction. Having rejected all influences that might have softened his will and opened his heart, Ahab purchased his monomaniac desire for revenge at the expense of what Matthiessen describes as a Faustian bond with the devil. As a result of his diabolical bondage, Ahab's tragedy could admit of no catharsis because Ahab showed no moral recognition of the evil he alone had released. Thus Matthiessen was forced to conclude that Ahab's final destruction was just, even necessary: "In his death . . . colossal pride meets its rightful end, and there can be no unmixed pity for him as a human being. . . . His tragedy is that of an unregenerate will, which stifles his soul and drives his brain with inescapable fierceness. He suffers, but unlike Hawthorne's Hester or Miriam, he is not purified by his suffering. He remains, like Ethan Brand, damned" (*AR*, 456–57).

Matthiessen's invocation of Hawthorne at this point was no mere coincidence. Hawthorne may have lacked an understanding of the range and depth of evil's governance, but he insisted that his characters face their own evil and accept its consequences; by doing so they could experience at least the first stage of their eventual deliverance from it. For example, as Hester moves toward a state of repentance or Miriam and Donatello express a sense of remorse, Matthiessen could detect the beginning of a rising counteraction in their tragedies which seemed to follow naturally from their recognition of the moral reasons for their suffering. By accepting the evil within themselves, such characters became in a certain measure able to reverse it and thus to participate in what Matthiessen referred to as "the purgatorial movement, the movement towards regeneration" (*AR*, 350).

Matthiessen was under no illusions that this formula could be applied to all tragic writing. If it served to describe the rising inner action at the end of *Samson Agonistes* or *Oedipus at Colonus* or even *Oedipus Rex*, it still failed to describe the ending of a book like *Moby-Dick*. Unlike Lear, who is able, as Matthiessen pointed out, to come to terms with his limitations and in that very act of self-recognition to overcome them, Captain Ahab, who spurns all self-knowledge, is denied the consequent personal enlargement. Hence, as Matthiessen remarked in a footnote,

There is no moment of release comparable, for instance, to one that Melville marked: when, at Anthony's death, Cleopatra sees and feels herself as she is, and answers Iras' "Royal Egypt! Empress!" with

> No more, but e'en a woman, and commanded
> By such poor passion as the maid that milks
> And does the meanest chares.

The effect of that reduction is to magnify. It endows Cleopatra with the "august dignity" of common humanity, which Melville proclaimed in his crew. But he does not portray its full working in Ahab, since, though the captain sees, he does not amply feel. He is not caught out of himself and transfigured by sympathy. As a result, his madness is not divine like Blake's or even like Pip's, since his burning mind is barred out from the exuberance of love. (*AR*, 456–57)

This passage is worth noting because it identifies nobility with common humanity, it stresses the affective character of all tragic knowledge, it assumes that sympathy and love are the keys to tragic enlargement, and it insists that the effect of all great tragic art is less to deflate than to magnify, less to depress than to release and transfigure. But these convictions, characteristic of much of Matthiessen's writing about tragedy, might suggest that he was applying to every kind of tragic writing, from ancient to modern, a series of expectations that could legitimately be applied merely to a few. Was Matthiessen's Christianity getting the best of him by tempting him to suggest, through such statements as the one quoted above, that real tragedy inevitably points beyond itself to a realm of being which remains unscathed by the destructive course of the tragic action? This is the assumption upon which William Butler Yeats grounded one of the most affirmative of tragic theories; and in an essay published the same year as *American Renaissance,* Matthiessen gave his response to Yeats's position and to the question of tragic theory in general.

4

Yeats was convinced that every tragic conflict should result ultimately in a kind of victory, a form of triumph in defeat. Placing his emphasis squarely on the tragic protagonist and the way he virtually overcomes himself in the act of straining against all that obstructs or baffles him, Yeats found the key to the understanding of tragedy not in the mystery of tragic suffering but in the glory of heroic passion, though heroic passion, he conceded, might issue either in despair or in joy. This distinction allowed Yeats to divide tragic poetry into two kinds, both of which, he assumed, are present in the greatest of tragic poems:

The one kind is produced "when the tide of life sinks low," and the poet, like Keats in the "Ode to a Grecian Urn" or Virgil at the plucking of the Golden Bough, makes us "sorrowful," since we share in his "separation from what he describes." "But when Lucifer stands among his friends, when Villon sings his dead ladies to so gallant a rhythm, when Timon makes his epitaph, we feel no sorrow, for life herself has made one of her eternal gestures, has called up into our hearts her energy that is eternal delight." (*RC,* 37)

Without taking Yeats's distinction in an absolute sense, Matthiessen felt that it might help to explain the wide differences in tone and feeling between Yeats's poetry and the poetry of someone like T. S. Eliot. It revealed that each poet stressed a different quality at the heart of the tragic experience, so that "each might well declare of the other that, although he possessed a tragic sense, he had not been able to write full tragedy" (*RC*, 38). Matthiessen surmised, for example, that Yeats would probably have objected to Eliot's emphasis upon the passive role of suffering in "Gerontion" and "The Hollow Men," whereas Eliot expressed his sense of the dangers of trying to create a private mythology. Or, again, Yeats would have found the alternation between doubt and belief in some of Eliot's later poems altogether joyless and depressing, while Eliot would have been repelled by Yeats's occasional Dionysian abandon. Matthiessen was explicit in his judgment as to which of the two writers had the better argument:

Eliot's excruciated awareness of evil has given him a more unerring psychological grasp: his "Portrait of a Lady," as MacNeice suggests, "throws a cold, cruel light on the sort of woman whom Yeats regarded as a masterpiece of civilization." It might be argued that this renewal by Eliot of our sense of evil has brought us back into possession of the element without which no tragedy can be created; and that although Yeats is by no means blind to evil, his most characteristic expression is not tragedy, but a special product of the tragic attitude, the "zest" of the hero, to use another of his favorite words, a zest that could mount in many poems to a final ecstatic frenzy in his exercise of "an old man's eagle mind." (*RC*, 38)

Even though Matthiessen made less of it than he might have, the real point at issue between Yeats and Eliot was the question of temporality. Was the tragic hero able to escape becoming a casualty of the temporal process or not? Could his zest redeem the terrible wreckage of time if it was dissociated from any recognition of his own implication in the disastrous course of events? That Matthiessen would have sided with Eliot and against Yeats at this point is attested by the fact that for him no one could escape the prison of time; no one, not even the Christian, could break the chains of finitude. Speaking in another context, Matthiessen pointed to the contrast in Eliot's "Burnt Norton" between time as mere continuum and time in the paradoxical Christian view that man "is immersed in the flux and yet can penetrate to the eternal by apprehending timeless existence within time and above it" (*ATSE,* 183). Matthiessen went on to say that "even for the Christian the moments of release from the pressures of the flux are rare, though they alone redeem the sad wastage of otherwise unillumined existence" (*ATSE,* 183–84). As Matthiessen frequently commented of writers as various as Hawthorne, James, and Eliot, men and women enter most nearly into a comprehension of what is eternal only as they become aware of their own finite limitations.

These reflections on the nature of tragedy and the relation between temporality and the tragic attitude are important because they show to what extent Matthiessen insisted upon a sense of balance as the sine qua non of all great tragedy. He did not deny that a tragic writer must be able to imagine harmony and wholeness in order to depict distortion, chaos, and defeat, but he was convinced that the affirmative aspects of tragedy should not blur perception of its destructive consequences. The double nature of life—"there is no such thing as good unless there is evil, or of evil unless there is good" (*AR,* 349)—prevented him, as he felt it should also prevent the tragic dramatist, from stressing one at the expense of the other.

Nonetheless, a perception of this duality of life was not sufficient to guarantee fully tragic art. The true tragic attitude was dependent upon something deeper and more illusory and much more difficult to define. It was less a product of the mind's recognition than of the heart's response, or, as Matthiessen suggested in discussing Hawthorne's psychology, of "the depth to which the writer's emotions have been stirred by what he has recognized, from the degree to which he has really been able to comprehend and accept what Edgar meant by saying,

> Men must endure
> their going hence even as their coming hither:
> Ripeness is all. (*AR,* 349)

Ripeness seems to have been the perfect word to express Matthiessen's understanding of the tragic attitude, because he firmly believed that tragedy presupposes both a kind of knowledge and a particular relationship to it. As J. V. Cunningham has argued, by "Ripeness is all" Shakespeare probably meant to suggest that man's death is in the hands of Providence, that the fruit will fall when it is ready; but Matthiessen interpreted the phrase in its more modern sense, as connoting the ultimate worth of mature responsiveness, the possibility that there is a fullness of feeling, an inner emotional and spiritual readiness, of which man is sometimes capable and which alone must, and can, suffice in the face of all his tragedies.[5]

According to Matthiessen, Keats offered the briefest summary of *ripeness* when he described it simply as "the love of good and ill," but its full implications came closer to Keats's own notion of "negative capability," or to what Matthiessen described as a writer's "ability to hold an undismayed control between the pressure of conflicting forces" (*AR*, 349). Though Matthiessen believed that an author's possession of such an attitude could be determined only by experiencing its presence in "one of his whole compositions" (*AR*, 349), he did risk a further elaboration of it in the working definition of tragedy he offered at the beginning of his discussion of Hawthorne and Melville. Claiming first that "the creation of tragedy demands of its author a mature understanding of the relation of the individual to society," he went on to assert that

unless the author also has a profound comprehension of the mixed nature of life, of the fact that even the most perfect man cannot be wholly good, any conflict that he creates will not give the illusion of human reality. Tragedy does not pose the situation of a faultless individual (or class) overwhelmed by an evil world, for it is built on the experienced realization that man is radically imperfect. Confronting this fact, tragedy must likewise contain a recognition that man, pitiful as he may be in his finite weakness, is still capable of apprehending perfection, and of becoming transfigured by that vision. But not only must the author of tragedy have accepted the inevitable coexistence of good and evil in man's nature, he must also possess the power to envisage some reconciliation between such opposites, and the control to hold an inexorable balance. He must be as far from the chaos of despair as he is from ill-founded optimism. (*AR*, 180)

It is worth noting that the emphasis is again upon balance. Believing in the inexorable balance of life, Matthiessen insisted upon a comparable balance in art and found that balance nowhere more fully exemplified than in the true tragic attitude, the

[5] For a fuller discussion of the phrase "Ripeness is all," see the brilliant analysis, to which I am heavily indebted, in J. V. Cunningham, *Woe or Wonder: The Emotional Effect of Shakespearean Tragedy* (Denver: University of Denver Press, 1951), pp. 9–16.

attitude of ripeness. What is particularly interesting, however, is his characteristic anthropological interpretation of this conviction in using it to illumine the nature of the tragic hero. As nature reflects a combination of both good and evil, so must the tragic protagonist. The tragic hero, though radically imperfect in Matthiessen's understanding of him, is never so completely fallen or depraved as to have altogether lost the vision of perfection or the capacity for being transformed by it. Though fallen, one might fairly say that he is still redeemable within the terms of his own destiny. But redemption in this instance never leads to perfection but only to rejuvenation, only, that is, to the kind of quickening that follows inevitably when suffering leads from heroic self-affirmation through confusion and despair to self-knowledge.

To amplify Matthiessen's definition of tragedy by using all his reflections upon the tragic hero and the tragic attitude helps to bring out the theological assumptions that lay behind it. Like neoorthodoxy and classical Protestantism generally, Matthiessen held firmly to the view that man—for him the tragic hero simply represented the most noble of men—is fallen and is thus unable to attain the perfection once vouchsafed to him, the perfection of the God in whose image he was fashioned. Yet in keeping with the Roman Catholic tradition, Matthiessen insisted that man has not fallen so far as to have altogether lost his memory of the original vision of grace; in keeping with radical Protestantism, on the other hand, he assumed that the original vision of grace might still transfigure man. Matthiessen did not, however, permit the basic insight of any one of these traditions to cancel out that of the other two. Only if all three were held in appropriate tension could he do sufficient justice to his own sense "not only of life's inexorability and sordidness, but of its possibilities of beauty and grandeur" (*AR*, 351).

To point to the religious assumptions lying back of Matthiessen's conceptions of tragedy and the tragic hero might seem irrelevant if Matthiessen had not taken pains time and again to be theologically discriminating. Not only did he deplore the critical irresponsibility of all those who hold that religious belief is no more than mere wish fulfillment; he also insisted upon putting the work of such widely different writers as Eliot and

Whitman, James and Dreiser, under the most searching though tactful theological scrutiny. What saved Matthiessen from heavy-handedness was his awareness that religious and meta-physical issues are often raised in other than explicitly theological language. As a literary critic working in the medium of poems and novels rather than of doctrines and theologies, Matthiessen was always careful to respect the original terms in which such issues were expressed in literature, to "hold on hard to the huckleberry bushes," as Emerson put it. Indeed, he seems to have known instinctively that translation of ethical and religious ideas from the language of action, image, and character, in which they are first articulated in literature, into a language more conventionally theological and systematic renders them bloodless and abstract. Furthermore, he seems to have realized almost from the beginning of his career that the most persuasive religious writers are usually those who try to break through the molds of traditional theological formulation in order to put their readers once again in touch with the primordial experiences of need, guilt, terror, and awe which first elicited them.

When Matthiessen finally turned his attention to what he considered the religious center of Hawthorne's and Melville's fiction, he resisted any temptation to translate it into the terms of dogma or creed, restricting himself instead to an elucidation of their own particular way of comprehending and expressing it. This is not to suggest that Matthiessen confined his remarks exclusively to an examination of Hawthorne's and Melville's explicit statements. When the situation warranted it, he was more than willing to use the terms of Milton's theology to illumine the darker lights of *The House of Seven Gables* or to employ the heretical theology of the ancient Manichaeans to gain insight into the ethical oppositions in *Moby-Dick;* but all these tactics were no more than strategies for penetrating beneath the surface of their articulated beliefs to that core of meaning which underlay them, to what Melville described in relation to Hawthorne as "that unshackled democratic spirit of Christianity in all things."

It is difficult to overestimate the importance Matthiessen attached to this last phrase. Not only did he follow Melville in using it to describe the best writing of the period; he also saw it as a description of that felicitous union of head and heart, intellect and emotion, which both Melville and Hawthorne took to be the sign of a fully integrated personality. Moreover, the phrase defined the norm in terms of which Melville criticized the reigning theological and ecclesiastical orthodoxy of his day, and it also epitomized what Hawthorne had learned from his explorations into "the life within the life." Most important, however, Matthiessen seems to have employed this phrase, at least in *American Renaissance,* as the keystone of the arch in his own evolving philosophy of life, an arch that was self-consciously designed to unite his political commitments to democracy with his more broadly existential concerns with tragedy. Serving at once, then, as a summary of what Matthiessen considered the unifying spirit of the age and as an expression of what he himself found to be that age's greatest personal resource, its most usable component, Melville's noble phrase brings us to the spiritual and religious center of *American Renaissance.*

5

Matthiessen found the key to Melville's conception of the spirit of democratic Christianity in the image of man upon which it was based, the image first expressed by Greenough but characteristic of the entire era, "of man in his full revolutionary and democratic splendor as the base and measure of his society" (quoted, *AR,* 151). This image corresponded almost perfectly, Matthiessen believed, with the singer of Whitman's "Song of Myself" and with Thoreau's narrator in *Walden* recollecting his decision to front only the essential facts of life. It was corroborated by Melville's conviction "that men not very much inferior to Shakespeare are this day being born on the banks of the Ohio" (quoted, *AR,* 372), and was then given nearly perfect expression in Emerson's declaration in "The American Scholar" that "not out of those on whom systems of education have exhausted their culture, comes the helpful giant to destroy the old or to build the new, but out of unhandselled savage nature" (quoted, *AR,* 372). It was the same image that Melville had rendered so poignantly in Ishmael's relationship with Queequeg, where the racial suspicion of the one gave way to the primitive goodness of the other, as the Presbyterian Ishmael slowly came to accept the fact that the pagan Queequeg was a human being just as he was and thereupon began to learn the sobering consequences of his own "mortal interdebtedness." But it received its most lyrical expression, Matthiessen believed, in the chapter entitled "Knights and Squires" in *Moby-Dick*, where Melville explains why he could endow his characters with such compelling dignity:

> But this august divinity I treat of, is not the dignity of kings and robes, but that abounding dignity which has no robed investiture. Thou shalt see it shining in the arm that wields a pick or drives a spike; that democratic dignity which, on all hands, radiates without end from God; Himself! The great God absolute! The centre and circumference of all democracy! His omnipresence, our divine equality.
>
> If, then, to meanest mariners, and renegades and castaways I shall hereafter ascribe high qualities, though dark; weave round them tragic graces; if even the most mournful, perchance the most abased, among them all, shall at times left himself to the exalted mounts; . . . then against all mortal critics bear me out in it, thou just Spirit of Equality, which hast spread one royal mantle of humanity over all my kind! Bear me out in it, thou great democratic God! who didst not refuse to the swart convict Bunyan, the pale, poetic pearl: Thou who didst clothe with double hammered leaves of finest gold, the stumped and paupered arm of old Cervantes; Thou who didst pick up Andrew Jackson from the pebbles; who didst hurl him upon a war-horse; who didst thunder him higher than a throne! Thou who, in all thy mighty, earthly marchings, ever cullest thy selected champions from the kingly commons; bear me out in it, O God! (Quoted, *AR,* 444–45)

Matthiessen placed enormous weight upon this passage, which represented "one of the summits of Melville's rhetoric" and completed "his fusion of Christianity and democracy" (*AR,* 445). As the declaration of his purpose in writing *Moby-Dick,* it brought together "Melville's hopes for American democracy, his dread of its lack of humane warmth, his apprehension of the actual privations and defeats of the common man, and his depth of compassion for courageous struggle" (*AR,* 444). Through his use of symbolic figures such as Bunyan, Cervantes, and Andrew Jackson, Melville was able to reveal the "wealth of suffering humanity" engaged "in the dynamic struggle against evil" (*AR,* 445). And by his profound affirmation of "that abounding dignity" which "the great God absolute," who is the "centre and circumference of all democracy," confers upon the "meanest mariners, and renegades and castaways," Matthiessen believed that Melville had also revealed "with what assurance he felt that a great theme could be created from the common stuff of American life" (*AR*, 445).

Matthiessen is very clear, however, that there was another side to the image that inspired Melville's lyrical outburst. This anti-image was made evident to Melville when, in contemplating the actualities of American democratic life, he perceived "the gap between our professions and our practice, as in the great wrong of slavery; in the tendency to sacrifice everything to the grasping individual will; in the difficulty of establishing adequate human contacts in our violently expanding life" (*AR*, 444). When he turned to the writing of *Israel Potter*, Melville could observe in Paul Jones a frightening symbol of the American character: "Intrepid, unprincipled, reckless, predatory, with boundless ambition, civilized in externals but a savage at heart, America is, or may yet be, the Paul Jones of nations" (quoted, *AR*, 444). But it was not in Paul Jones so much as in Captain Ahab that Melville gave complete expression to the underside of the Christian and democratic image of man. By depicting in Ahab the destruction that must inevitably overtake a great individual who, in response to the promptings of the age and his own injured ego, seeks to set aside all human limitations and constraints and to become a divinity in himself, Melville was expressing his own horror of the consequences of naked self-assertion. Indeed, Matthiessen believed that Melville had provided in his portrait of Ahab a frightening glimpse into the future, when the virtues embodied in the phrase "democratic Christianity" were to be utterly betrayed by those who turned the Emersonian belief in man's potential divinity into a conviction that nothing is divine save man's own will to mastery and domination:

The strong-willed individuals who seized the land and gutted the forests and built the railroads were no longer troubled with Ahab's obsessive sense of evil, since theology had receded even farther into their backgrounds. But their drives were as relentless as his, and they were to prove like him in many other ways also, as they went on to become the empire builders of the post-Civil War world. They tended to be as dead to enjoyment as he, as blind to everything but their one pursuit, as unmoved by fear or sympathy, as confident in assuming an identification of their wills with immutable plan or manifest destiny, as liable to regard other men as merely arms and legs for the fulfilment of their purposes, and, finally, as arid and exhausted in their burnt-out souls. Without deliberately intending it, . . . Melville created in Ahab's tragedy a fearful symbol of the self-enclosed individualism that, carried to its furthest extreme, brings disaster both upon itself and upon the group of which it is part. He provided also an ominous glimpse of what was to result when the Emersonian will to virtue became in less innocent natures the will to power and conquest. (*AR*, 459)

Melville's awareness of the double nature of man—his "democratic splendor" as well as his radical imperfection—was, according to Matthiessen, the source of Melville's sense of tragedy. And, as developed by both Hawthorne and Melville, Matthiessen found this tragic sense of life in striking contradiction to the blander optimism of Emerson, Thoreau, and Whitman. Though all five of Matthiessen's writers shared the transcendental impulse to find spiritual significance in every natural fact, they differed widely over the kind of significance they attributed to those facts. Whereas Emerson, Whitman, and even Thoreau found a degree of correspondence between man's heroic aspiration and his uncommon deeds, Hawthorne discovered life everywhere at odds with itself, set in conflict by the divisiveness buried deep within man's own heart which continually tempts him, once he has grasped the uniqueness of his own individual will, to destroy his bond with his fellows by subordinating everything to his own right to self-fulfillment. Yet it was Melville, in Matthiessen's reading of the American tradition, who carried this understanding of life's tragic nature to its absolute limits. Melville differed from Hawthorne in locating tragic conflict not in human nature alone but also in the very nature of life itself. And this awareness drove Melville, as it drove his narrator Ishmael, to the brink of believing that "though in many of its aspects the visible world seems formed in love, the invisible spheres were formed in fright" (quoted, *AR*, 441). What prevented Melville from going over the brink, according to Matthiessen, was his comprehension that the one thing that can redeem an otherwise "wolfish world" (quoted, *AR*, 443) is sympathetic fellowship with another human being. It was this experience that finally dispelled Ishmael's initial siege of melancholia and revived for a brief moment, in Lucy's act of selfishness, Pierre's flagging spirits. The sympathetic bond of human fellowship was also the basis of White Jacket's relationship with Jack Chase and constituted, so we are meant to believe, the secret discovery that Billy Budd made during his closeted interview with Captain Vere. Partaking of that "depth of tenderness" and that "boundless sympathy with all forms of being" which Melville had first recognized in Hawthorne, Matthiessen was convinced that this insight into the salutary power of human brotherhood provided Melville with the resources to invest his story of "the kingly commons" with a dignity at once noble and heroic and, further, that it enabled him to evoke, in a magnificent chapter like "The Pacific," a sense of "the levels beyond," where Melville was able to fulfill Eliot's injunction by "sinking to the most primitive and forgotten, returning to the origin and bringing something back, seeking the beginning and the end" (quoted, *AR,* 466).

To refer to the enormous scope of *Moby-Dick* is to recall that Matthiessen viewed the novel as the literary epic of its age. It expressed to the full, to paraphrase Matthiessen, the nineteenth century's sense of plenitude and variousness, its disastrous glorification of the individual at the expense of the community, its paradoxical belief in the goodness as well as the evil in life, its awareness of the priority of sentiment over reason, and, finally, its effort to comprehend "nothing less than the whole of life," to take "man beyond history to the source of his elemental energies" (*AR,* 466). From its pages emerged two images of man, or rather one image with two sides—the one a bane, the other a blessing—which were united in the figure of the potentially heroic but imperfect American individual. If Captain Ahab revealed that individual's dangerous potentialities, Ishmael in his relationship with Queequeg and then the shadowy figure of Bulkington could be said to reveal his rich possibilities. But Ishmael was no more capable of standing up to Ahab's wrath than the other members of the crew, and Bulkington was buried in his "six-inch chapter" where he was last seen early in the voyage at the *Pequod*'s helm steering the ship straight into the "cold, malicious waves."

The only other individual who might have proved a match for Ahab was the man Melville noticed in Hawthorne's "The Intelligence Office" and took to be an image of Hawthorne himself:

A man now entered, in neglected attire, with the aspect of a thinker but somewhat too rough-hewn and brawny for a scholar. His face was full of sturdy vigor, with some finer and keener attribute beneath. Though harsh at first, it was tempered with the glow of a large, warm heart, which had force enough to heat his powerful intellect through and through. He advanced to the Intelligencer and looked at him with a glance of such stern sincerity that perhaps few secrets were beyond its scope. "I seek for Truth," said he. (Quoted, *AR*, 348)

For Matthiessen this seeker after truth was the nineteenth century's most compelling example of a fully balanced individual. Possessed of a great heart to warm his powerful intellect, he incarnated the possibility of reconciling the two sides of the American image of "man in his full revolutionary splendor as the base and measure of his society." Intrepid in the pursuit of truth, he would no doubt remain sympathetic in the face of need. Little wonder, then, that Matthiessen found in him a striking resemblance to Emerson's American scholar. Embodying the potentiality of a native American culture, "its thought grounded on the heart-felt acceptance of the homely facts and opportunities of our life, and therefore able to make its strength prevail" (*AR*, 349), Hawthorne's noble figure seemed to epitomize what Matthiessen first meant by "our still undiminished resources."

That Hawthorne's noble seeker after truth existed, as it were, only in posse rather than in esse seems not to have troubled Matthiessen very much. The mere fact that we might still feel his "unspent potential" apparently served as sufficient guarantee that we would continue our efforts to realize it. But now, more than thirty years after the publication of *American Renaissance*, we may well ask ourselves if Matthiessen's hopes were not exaggerated, if his optimism was not beyond a certain point illusory. Indeed, if anything, we now seem to have become even more insensible to those "undiminished resources" than we were in 1941, and this is nowhere more vividly exhibited than in the way we have revised Matthiessen's readings of the mid-nineteenth-century writers, substituting for them interpretations that often evince comparatively little feeling for the kind of usable potential Matthiessen found in them.

Where Matthiessen discovered in Melville an artist who believed that, though goodness often goes down to defeat and death, "its radiance can redeem life" (*AR*, 514), we now tend to find in him only a growing epistemological and metaphysical skepticism which finally gives way to the desperate conclusion that life has no meaning at all. Or where Matthiessen perceived in Hawthorne a deeply tormented man who yet believed in the redemptive possibilities of moral recognition and human solidarity, we tend instead to see a neurotic who sought through the art of fiction to lock himself within the prison of his own consciousness rather than face his own worst psychological demons. Or where Matthiessen saw in Thoreau a writer who had sunk to bedrock and beneath in order to reconnect us with what he called "our parent life" and thus to break down all the artificial barriers between art and experience, between work and culture, we tend to discern instead an artist who withdrew from the life around him in order to prove in his one great book that the only real life is the one men create for themselves out of words. Or, again, where Matthiessen found in Whitman a poet who at his best believed in the possibility of transfiguring all of life through a loving vision of its most minute and concrete particulars, we tend to read Whitman more and more as a visionary poet dedicated chiefly to the recreation of himself through the loving practice of his art. Finally, where Matthiessen recognized in Emerson a religious radical (albeit an unsuccessful one, even in his own terms) who sought to release man's divine potential by restoring to him a sense of his integral place within the entire cosmic order, we are still inclined to regard Emerson as our great solipcist, our American Narcissus, whose religious aspirations to become a kind of "transparent eyeball" amounted to nothing more than seeing in the world around him precisely what he put there himself.

Do these reinterpretations mean that contemporary criticism has invalidated much of Matthiessen's work on the writers of the mid-nineteenth century, or merely that we now find in those writers qualities quite different from those Matthiessen perceived? This question probably can be answered only by the history of subsequent scholarship. Certitude in matters of interpretation is more than anything else dependent on which readings gain the broadest assent and hold up over the longest period of time. Many of Matthiessen's readings have been challenged, directly or indirectly, in a variety of ways just because more sophisticated methods of analysis have brought to light fresh issues which Matthiessen was never compelled to consider; but it is not yet clear whether some of these more recent interpretations will prove any more durable than Matthiessen's have. It is clear, however, that whatever the validity of Matthiessen's interpretations in relation to those that have succeeded them, most contemporary readings of his five writers present a more limited, if not diminished, sense of their usability, of their quickening power in the present, than Matthiessen's did; to this extent such revisions seem to indicate just how far removed we have grown from the nexus of values and aspirations which Matthiessen associated with the writers of the 1850s and then tried to make vivid once again for Americans in the 1940s.

Nonetheless, Matthiessen was not without his blind spots, nor was he above stressing certain qualities in a writer and neglecting others. There is little doubt, for example, that he placed too affirmative an interpretation upon *Billy Budd* in an effort to show that Melville had finally found his way to the sunlight again after his long journey through the darkness. So, too, Matthiessen tended to overlook certain disturbing elements which exist on the borders of Thoreau's picture of life at Walden Pond, elements that might well have disrupted Thoreau's experience of spiritual renewal if he had fully realized their implications. Again, Matthiessen seems at times to have been inclined to interpret Hawthorne as a less complex moralist than he actually was, and to have paid too much attention to Whitman's experiments with language and too little to his experiments in extending through language the parameters of conscious experience.

But these are faults that can be rather easily forgiven. Deriving from a basic generosity of spirit which forced Matthiessen to see his subjects, as he said, from the inside, to view them sympathetically, they are balanced, even overbalanced, by Matthiessen's exhaustive efforts to understand and be understood, to make *American Renaissance* both an act of interpretation and a kind of testament. Thus if Matthiessen's own ethical and religious commitments occasionally tempted him to close too quickly the gap between the actual and the ideal, between what was really there in these writers as opposed to what he hoped to find there or could see there as hidden potential, still he at least realized that they had brought to expression something very much worth finding, something that we are still badly in need of rediscovering. And viewing the literature of the American past in this way, as a resource for renewing and extending the energies of the present, Matthiessen in turn invested that literature with a new energy of presence, a new vital immediacy.

In his essay on A. E. Housman's *A Shropshire Lad* (published in *The Triple Thinkers*), Edmund Wilson made an important distinction between works that are "among the jewels of English literature" and works that are "among its great springs of life."[6] While Matthiessen was intensely interested in many of the former, it is clear that his real preference was for the latter. *American Renaissance* remains one of the great books in the American critical heritage not only because it is devoted to a series of works that deserve to be conceived as among "the great springs of life," but also because Matthiessen was willing to conceive them so, as inexhaustible repositories in which "we can feel the challenge of our still undiminished resources." Henry Nash Smith once remarked in private conversation that this ultimately made *American Renaissance* more of a work of art, a poem, a kind of critical "Song of Myself," than a fully realized work of scholarship, and that its conclusions, like its methods of approach, were more a product of will and aspiration and brilliant intuition than of hard evidence and meticulous reasoning. On this point, I am convinced, there is little room for dispute; had Matthiessen tried to write in any other way, he could not have fulfilled Emerson's imperatives in "The American Scholar." As it was, however, he did meet the demands he had set for himself, the same demands he used to gauge Melville's achievement on the last page of his book. Indeed, the words he used in reference to Melville provide a fitting coda to his own achievement in *American Renaissance,* for he, too, strove to give "full expression" to the nineteenth century's sense of possibility and "abundance, to its energetic desire to master history by repossessing all the resources of the hidden past in a timeless

---

[6] Quoted by Alfred Kazin, *On Native Grounds* (Garden City: Doubleday Anchor Books, 1956), p. 349.

and heroic present. But he did not avoid the darkness in that past, the perpetual suffering in the heart of man, the broken arc of his career which inevitably ends in death. He thus fulfilled what Coleridge held to be the major function of the artist: he brought 'the whole soul of man into activity' " (*AR*, 656).

CHAPTER FIVE

From the Ambiguities of James
to the Bare Truths of Dreiser

The great question as to a poet or a novelist is, How does he feel about
life? What, in the last analysis, is his philosophy? When vigorous writers
have reached maturity, we are at liberty to gather from their works
some expression of a total view of the world they have been so actively
observing. This is the most interesting thing their works offer us. Details are interesting in proportion as they contribute to make it clear.
HENRY JAMES
Partial Portraits

THERE can be little doubt that *American Renaissance* overshadows
everything else Matthiessen ever attempted. *Henry James: The
Major Phase* is, for all its breadth of reference and trenchant
observation, a close study of only four novels; *The James Family*,
though larger in bulk, is less a definitive biography than a group
study stitched together for the most part by copious though
judicious selections from the writings of the elder Henry James
and his three illustrious children, William James, Henry James,
and Alice James; and *Theodore Dreiser*, the critical biography
Matthiessen was working on at the time of his death, is an unfinished piece of work, even though the editors of the series for
which it was written felt that it exhibited enough coherence and
consistency to merit publication. *From the Heart of Europe*, an
account of less than a year in Matthiessen's life, is a meditative
journal which he chose not to revise before publication, although subsequent events altered important aspects of the
political situation Matthiessen was describing. *Russell Cheney* is
but a brief introduction to the painting of a beloved friend,
carefully and empathetically wrought but nonetheless an evoca-
tive memorial rather than a major study.

136

Matthiessen, of course, produced other things in the last decade of his life. He supplemented these five book-length studies with two large editing jobs (the first in collaboration with Kenneth Murdock on *The Notebooks of Henry James* [1947], and the second by himself on *The Oxford Book of American Verse* [1950]), two less ambitious anthologies of the fiction of Henry James (*Henry James: Stories of Writers and Artists* [1944] and *The American Novels and Stories of Henry James* [1947]), and a variety of essays, articles, and reviews (the most famous of which are the two pieces he prepared for *The Literary History of the United States* [1948], "Edgar Allen Poe" and "Modern American Poetry"). Yet this striking body of production contains no masterwork of the caliber of *American Renaissance*, perhaps because Matthiessen lacked the energy or the vision to commit himself to another work of creative scholarship, or because he became absorbed with the invitations and opportunities that naturally followed the publication of *American Renaissance*. In any event, Matthiessen was never again to undertake a major project of critical and cultural synthesis.

Still, one cannot say that Matthiessen stopped developing as a critic and scholar after his great book of 1941, or that the work of his final phase is without significance for the history of American criticism. All his remaining books represent further extensions and elaborations of the critical and theoretical assumptions he had sought to define and express in *American Renaissance*. Moreover, each one makes an important contribution to the understanding of its particular subject. *Henry James: The Major Phase*, for example, together with Matthiessen's edition of *The Notebooks* and his group biography of the James family, helped launch the James revival of the 1940s and shifted critical attention from James's early and middle work to the greater novels of his final period. *Theodore Dreiser* extended critical awareness of the affinities between the dark strains of American romanticism and the pessimistic accents of American realism, and it incidentally contributed significantly to the theory of the novel by showing how the awkwardness of Dreiser's style, when not cluttered with literary mannerisms, served as an appropriate vehicle for illuminating the American urban experience. *From the Heart of Europe,* in addition to supplementing the library of personal narratives at which Americans have excelled ever since the time of Samuel Sewall, John Woolman, and Jonathan Edwards, helped to clarify the political and religious grounds of the Christian-democratic humanism Matthiessen had earlier discovered in American writers of the mid-nineteenth century. Matthiessen's two long essays on American poetry (the second being his lengthy preface to *The Oxford Book of American Verse*) quickly came to be esteemed as among the best introductions we have to the American poetic tradition.

These later writings might seem lesser achievements if the circumstances of Matthiessen's personal life had not become so distracting and besetting during these years, eventually wearing him down by the end of the decade to the point where suicide seemed preferable to the prospect of continued existence. The terrible events of the decade preceding Matthiessen's death —Hitler's rise to power, the Spanish Civil War, the Moscow trials, Stalin's pact with Germany, and ultimately World War II—had taken a heavy toll, and then when Matthiessen, like many of his friends and colleagues, finally overcame his pacifist prejudices and decided to enlist, he was summarily turned down for being half an inch too short. Even though he tried to make light of it, the rejection was a bitter disappointment, not only because the original decision to enlist had been so agonizing, but also because he was denied the opportunity to put himself back together again through military service. The only option remaining open to Matthiessen was to stay on at Harvard and attempt to keep alive a sense of the humanities in wartime, but this course was to involve difficulties of its own in a university retooling itself for the war effort and stressing the training of scientific and military personnel. This alteration in the life of the university was only temporary, of course, but when the war ended and the veterans returned, the climate of Harvard Yard had changed drastically. Though many of the returning students, eager to make up the time they had lost overseas, brought back with them a genuine intellectual seriousness, it was no longer coupled with the sense of shared ideals and common political goals which had meant so much to Matthiessen in the years just preceding. It was now more or less every man for himself in a world that bore little resemblance to its prewar counterpart. The heady and exciting atmosphere of the Popular Front days belonged to an era long dead, and in its place was developing an austere ethos of careerism from which Matthiessen came to feel more and more alienated.

Nonetheless, the worst blows were still to come. In addition to the loss of several close personal friends—Russell Cheney died in the summer of 1945, Phelps Putnam three years later, and Theodore Spencer in 1949—there came, in rapid succession the establishment of a loyalty oath for government employees in March, 1947; the beginning of the headhunt for Communists under the Smith Act of 1940; the takeover in Czechoslovakia in February, 1948; only weeks later the heartbreaking news of Jan Masaryk's suicide; soon after that the hostile reactions to *From the Heart of Europe;* and finally the disintegration of Henry Wallace's third-party movement for which Matthiessen had worked hard in the summer and fall of 1948. Each of these events—and there were others both before and after—diminished the number of possible alternatives to an increasingly arid and repressive future. Yet Matthiessen continued to function for several more years, teaching, writing, and lecturing seemingly at his old pace, but with less and less confidence in himself or in the value of his contribution. During the last months of his life, it is certain that the inevitable course before him was becoming clearer, but it is altogether characteristic that he almost never shared his growing sense of desperation with anyone. Refusing to become a burden to others, he resolutely kept his suffering to himself. When the news of his suicide was reported on radio and in newspapers on the morning of April 1, 1950, it caught virtually everyone off guard and struck with the savage, lightning shock of some terrible, tragic reversal. As one commentator wrote so truly, Matthiessen's death was "another demonstration that the people who can best arouse and instruct our sensibilities . . . are by their nature most vulnerable themselves to the tensions which their work may have helped others to understand and endure."[1]

---

[1] Janet Adam Smith, "F. O. Matthiessen," *New Statesman and Nation* 39 (1950): 482.

1   '

It has been suggested that *Henry James: The Major Phase* provides a clear indication of the direction Matthiessen's subsequent writing might well have taken "if he could have rid himself of tautness rather than of life."[2] There is both "a controlled handling of the vigorous words of American colloquial speech, and a welding of easier, looser speech rhythms with the more complex, rich, and exploratory contour of his own thought."[3] Instead of edging toward an idea with little probes and jabs from peripheral points and then developing the idea through associative comparisons and contrasts, Matthiessen attacks the problem more directly and with greater self-confidence, while still maintaining the sense of balance and modulation necessary for comprehending and analyzing complex material. Verbs do more work in shifting attention from one issue to the next; phrases are used less to evoke and expand than to illustrate; and Matthiessen exploits significant images to bind his exposition into a unity. Further, Matthiessen gives evidence of just how far he has moved beyond the early teachings of Van Wyck Brooks and V. L. Parrington. Besides exhibiting a more relaxed and cadenced style and greater directness of approach, *Henry James: The Major Phase* reveals how thoroughly Matthiessen had become his own kind of cultural historian.

Yet the book represents no marked departure from Matthiessen's earlier interests. Though drawn to take a closer look at James out of renewed respect for his extraordinary gifts as a craftsman, Matthiessen still valued James essentially for what he did with those gifts. James was worthy of serious attention because, like Hawthorne and Melville, he understood the dimension of evil in human existence, and, again like the earlier writers, he used his knowledge—though with far greater technical sophistication—to probe issues that arise at what Eliot might have called the point of intersection between the temporal and the timeless. Despite his frequent use of the formal structure of the comedy of manners, then, James's real subject was the ambiguity of being, and Matthiessen believed that James's art in-

[2] John Rackliffe, "Notes for a Character Study, " *Monthly Review* 2 (1950): 251.
[3] *Ibid.*

creased in significance the more he treated that subject in a tragic manner. As Bernard Bowron once noted, it was "as a consummate 'moral romancer' that James spoke most deeply to Matthiessen. In *The Major Phase*, in *The James Family*, and in his editing of James's stories and notebooks, Matthiessen never strayed very far from this major concern of his *American Renaissance*."[4]

Matthiessen's aims for *Henry James: The Major Phase* were on the whole quite modest. He claimed to be writing nothing more ambitious than a work of aesthetic criticism, though, as we shall see, this phrase was considerably amplified in Matthiessen's exposition of it. He had found his subject, he tells us, while examining the 150,000 pages of James's notebooks, where it became obvious that Van Wyck Brooks's "whole thesis of flight, frustration and decline" was thoroughly discredited (*HJ*, xiii). In *The Pilgrimage of Henry James* (1925) Brooks argued that James's career describes the fate of the writer who becomes an expatriate. Having cut himself off from his native material just as he was coming into artistic possession of it, James's later works, Brooks maintained, lost the freshness of his early fiction and eventually declined to the point where they became "hardly more than the frustrated gestures of 'an habitually embarrassed man' " (*HJ*, ix). In refutation of this judgment, which Parrington had reiterated almost verbatim in *Main Currents of American Thought*, the notebooks revealed to Matthiessen that James's final period was in fact his ripest, and that after the failure of *Guy Domville*, James's abortive attempt at playwriting, he became conscious of "hitherto unplumbed powers, as his first anxious and tentative hopes yield[ed] to the finally assured confidence of the master craftsman" (*HJ*, xiii). Indeed, the notebooks made clear that James had discovered the germinal ideas for his last great works—*The Ambassadors* (1903), *The Wings of the Dove* (1902), and *The Golden Bowl* (1904)—some eight to twelve years before he completed them. These ideas provided Matthiessen with his subject. What he hoped to do was to trace them through to their "created embodiment" in a kind of biography of their development toward artistic realization. But because of his assumption

[4] Bernard Bowron, "The Making of an American Scholar," *Monthly Review* 2 (1950): 221.

that "the act of perception extends through the work of art to its milieu," Matthiessen insisted that "aesthetic criticism, if carried far enough, inevitably becomes social criticism." Hence, in studying the genesis and flowering of James's major novels, Matthiessen believed that he was also functioning as a cultural historian "by showing the kind of light that such novels throw back upon their time" (*HJ*, xiv).

Matthiessen's discussion of *The Ambassadors*—James's favorite among his novels not so much for its theme as for its skillfully wrought structure—is confined largely to the development of Lambert Strether as the novel's center of consciousness, which constitutes the book's major contribution to the theory of the novel. Permitting the entire content of the novel to be filtered through Strether's eyes, "James . . . perfected a device both for framing and for interpreting experience" and thus achieved "both 'the large unity' and 'the grace of intensity' which . . . [he] held to be the final criteria for a novel" (*HJ*, 22). This much, of course, had been observed many times before; the only point in any way original was Matthiessen's contention that this method should not be confused with the stream of consciousness novel. Since James's central figure suffered none of the dark threats of the subconscious and was exposed to no sudden upwellings of repressed images out of the past, Matthiessen regarded James's works not as novels of full consciousness but rather as novels of intelligence.

The pertinence of this distinction was fully borne out by the notebooks. The kernel of James's idea had to do with an elderly man who discovers that he has spent nearly his entire life without ever having really lived. "He has never really enjoyed," as James formulates it in his notebook; "he has lived only for duty and conscience . . . for effort, for surrender, abstention, sacrifice" (quoted, *HJ*, 23). Matthiessen's primary interest was James's development of this idea in terms of the basic situation he imagined for it, of the old man's mission of mercy to Europe to bring back a much younger man whose family had grown anxious about him. James's problem, Matthiessen correctly realized, was to express the challenge to live as the older man came to discover it in the circumstances that enmeshed him; by using Strether as his single point of focus, James was able to concentrate fully on the challenge. Through this rigorous principle of selection, James demonstrated to what extent "he had mastered 'the art of reflection' in both senses of that phrase—both as a projector of the luminous surfaces of life, and as an interpreter of their significance" (*HJ*, 35).

Matthiessen was fully aware of what James lost as well as of what he gained through this method. By framing the entire experience of the novel in terms of Strether's vision, he had to omit everything that Strether could be counted on to overlook in life, such as the terrible suffering and the economic exploitation that had made his privileged way of life possible. Further, there was something inherently wrong with Strether himself. Even though he becomes conscious of a wholly new sense of life, he does almost nothing to fulfill it. Matthiessen therefore was obliged to concede that Strether conveyed an impression of "relative emptiness" which betrayed "a certain soft fussiness" in his creator as well (*HJ*, 39). James was at his best, on the other hand, when he was able "to endow some of his characters [e.g., Madame de Vionnet] with such vitality that they seem to take the plot into their own hands, or rather, to continue to live beyond its exigencies" (*HJ*, 39). This ability, which James found so admirable in Turgenev, eventually made his own novel "survive the dated flavor of Strether's liberation" (*HJ*, 39).

Despite James's own preference for *The Ambassadors*, Matthiessen felt that *The Wings of the Dove* was James's real masterpiece. Matthiessen's reasons had to do with the character of Milly Theale, whom he considered James's richest symbol of the human condition. Following James's own prescription to explore an image by recovering its context, Matthiessen wisely began his discussion of Milly's significance by trying to recapture all that Minny Temple, James's cousin who died of tuberculosis at the age of twenty-four, once meant to him. That James based his portrait of Milly Theale on Minny Temple was amply borne out by his own testimony, even though he gave Milly a sense of completion which Minny failed to achieve in her life. Indeed, Minny Temple's lack of fulfillment was part of her tragedy; she died long before she had really finished living and thus suffered what James regarded as the most tragic aspect of life.

While observing that Minny's death had struck to the core of James's sympathies, Matthiessen was quick to point out that James was hardly alone in finding rich artistic material in the untimely death of a beautiful woman. Such an event, for example, had seemed to Edgar Allan Poe to be of the very essence of the poetic, but Poe's treatment differed markedly from James's. Whereas Poe sought to exploit the feelings evoked by the spectacle of dying, James tried to make his characters appeal through their resistance to death, even though he knew that such appeals are immeasurably heightened "as the conditions plot against them and prescribe the battle" (quoted, *HJ*, 66). The idea that finally prevailed for James was one that played down the pathos of death in order to play up the passion for life. A fabulously wealthy New York heiress with all the world before her was to be pitted against an inexorable fate, but the drama of her situation was to arise not merely from the doomed quality of her existence but also from her eager and courageous, if ultimately futile, opposition to it.

The question Matthiessen faced was whether a novel written in this spirit, in a mood of affectionate and devoted tribute, could meet the requirements of real tragedy. On the whole his answer had to be negative. Even though Milly's predicament was tragic, the feelings her response to it evokes in us are not. We feel deep compassion for her plight, but we experience little terror at the thought of her situation. Her suffering is simply too passive—"fitting for the deuteragonist rather than for the protagonist of a major tragedy, for a Desdemona, not for an Othello" (*HJ*, 79). Yet, Matthiessen maintained, James was only reflecting the ethos of his age. In an era of rapid and unsettling change whose poignant effects were to be recorded by writers as various as Emily Dickinson, Sarah Orne Jewett, and Mark Twain, the more restricted form of the elegy was as close as anyone could come to full tragic expression. The point to be noted is that Matthiessen did not regard James's handling of tragedy as a deficiency. If the final chords that James was able to strike in this novel were essentially minor—"those of renunciation, of resignation, of inner triumph in the face of outer defeat" (*HJ*, 80)—*The Wings of the Dove* could still be accounted his masterpiece, "that single work where his characteristic emotional vibration seems deepest and where we may have the sense, therefore, that we have come to 'the very soul' " (*HJ*, 43). For all her delicacy and ultimate helplessness, Milly deserved to be regarded as James's "most resonant symbol for what he had to say about humanity" (*HJ*, 43), and in the characters surrounding her James exhibited his surest understanding of moral complexity.

Among the novel's other characters, Matthiessen was especially moved by James's portrait of Kate Croy, whom he saw as by no means the unscrupulous figure James had outlined in his notebooks. Kate was truly affecting because she, too, was a victim of circumstance; her most attractive qualities turned out to be those most vulnerable to misuse. Yet Kate's vitality, glamour, and strength of will could not have been delineated so vividly without the incisive contrasts James was able to draw. He compared Kate's qualities with Milly's greater frailty and gentleness and with Merton Densher's more passive, reflective, and fair-minded nature. In fact, James's handling of the triangular relationship of these three characters seemed nearly flawless to Matthiessen. Merton's sense of reality was a perfect foil for the air of charming enchantment which Susan Stringham and others built up around Milly, and Kate's grim pursuit of resources, her lucidity and tenaciousness, formed the necessary complement to Merton's seeming diffidence. Thus when the "wondrous silken web" (quoted, *HJ*, 74) in which Merton felt enmeshed was finally drawn taut, the disclosures that followed could be said to possess all the finality, at least for Merton, of tragic anagnorisis. Milly's horror of death, Kate's evil use of others, and Merton's sleazy compliance suddenly stood revealed for what they were. "Like the hero in any great tragedy," Matthiessen wrote, "he [Merton] has [finally] arrived at the moral perception of the meaning of what has befallen him" (*HJ*, 77).

The only major weakness Matthiessen could detect in the novel was that James, who had suspected the same thing himself, had spent so much time at the beginning on Kate and Merton that when he finally got round to Milly he had drastically to foreshorten his treatment of her. But James's decision to introduce Milly later on, and then indirectly, was inevitable, Matthiessen believed, because, owing to her passivity and vulnerability, she had to be understood and interpreted largely in terms of her effects upon other people. What James sacrificed in symmetry of structure he more than made up for in compression, intensity, and allusiveness. Indeed, the handling of Milly was part of James's purpose, according to Matthiessen. Having declared in his famous "summing up" that the "dramatic poem" seemed to be "the most beautiful thing possible," James, seeking in *The Wings of the Dove* to produce its prose analogue, succeeded so well that Matthiessen could account it James's signal masterwork and one of the supreme achievements in the form.

Subsequent critics, of course, have often disputed this claim by giving preeminence in the James canon to *The Golden Bowl*, but Matthiessen could not be swayed; not only was the later novel deeply flawed, but James had failed to see its deficiencies. The chief problems centered on James's understanding of his two main characters, Adam Verver, the American billionaire, and Adam's daughter Maggie, who lives comfortably at the beginning of the novel on her million a year. The very scale of their wealth, to say nothing of their subsequent spiritual triumph, posed problems that James had never had to face when dealing with characters confronted with defeat. It was largely a question of justifying the success of individuals who already were fabulously rich, a task requiring the utmost in tact, perspective, and irony; on Matthiessen's reading, James seems to have reserved most of his irony for his minor characters while taking his two central figures at face value.

Matthiessen could appreciate the care with which James had drawn Adam Verver as a man of new and almost inconceivable wealth, but he was troubled by the way James seemed unquestioningly to accept Adam. Painting him as almost a childlike innocent who was nonetheless able to amass one of the great American fortunes, James opened himself up, or so Matthiessen believed, "to the most serious charge that can be levelled against a great novelist, what Yvor Winters has instanced, in the case of *The Spoils of Poynton,* as the split between manners and morals, the lack of congruity between the environment which would have produced [such] a character and the traits which the author has imputed to him" (*HJ*, 89–90). The same problem was apparent in James's treatment of Maggie, though Matthiessen was reluctant to be as severely critical. It was not merely that James failed to perceive the darker prospect that Maggie's self-reliance would turn into something like an article of religious belief; it was also that he permitted her to acquire a sense of evil through the discovery of her husband's adulterous relationship with Charlotte Stant and then to employ the relationship for her own ends, while preserving intact a sense of her own innocence. These lapses suggested that James only half understood the relation between his major characters' private struggles and the broader social and cultural environment in which he placed them. To suppose that Adam Verver could become a billionaire and still remain naïve, merely because he was reared in an older and simpler America whose qualities tended to color his adult life, was to overlook the exploitative conditions in late nineteenth-century America which made possible the accumulation of vast wealth. And to assume that Maggie could have eventually turned evil to good account (while at the same time enjoying the taste of victory over her adversary), without even being touched by doing so, was to mistake innocence for the mask of it.

Matthiessen did not intend to undercut the merit of James's achievement in *The Golden Bowl.* He wanted only to set that achievement within the context of its obvious limitations so that appreciation could be focused on the relevant issues. For Matthiessen, those issues had to do with the positive values James could find in the world and the experience of the Ververs. According to Matthiessen's reading, the positive values attached to the two words "love" and "religion." By "love" Matthiessen seems to have meant Maggie's generosity of devotion which could be favorable likened to Milly Theale's; by "religion" he apparently referred to Maggie's strength of will which could stand comparison with Kate Croy's. In Maggie herself, these two values came to fullest expression in the great scene in the fifth book where she finally realized all that was at stake and all that she wished to retain. Her sudden temptation to denounce Charlotte publicly, which was precipitated by "the horror of finding evil seated all at its ease, where she had only dreamed of good" (quoted, *HJ*, 98), and which was dissipated only as she regained control of her will and resolved to overcome Charlotte's duplicity without destroying appearances or disrupting the serene equanimity of her father's life, expressed James's positive values most vividly. But despite his respect for James's artistic handling of these values, Matthiessen was quite critical. James did not see, for example, that the final resolution of the affair could only reduce the enormously attractive and poignant Charlotte Stant to little more than another brilliant addition to Adam Verver's collection, or that love alone was not enough to redeem Maggie's life, which must henceforth be spent in the company of the Prince, a man capable of little more significant than arranging his rare books and going to his club.

On the technical plane, James was unable to find the appropriate "objective correlative" for his theme. Whether consciously or not, Matthiessen reasoned, James had drawn upon the innocent affection in the close paternal and filial relationships that characterized his own family memories; but when he attempted to project these feelings "into a realm so unlike the one into which . . . [he] had been born, we . . . [reach] the breaking point of credibility" (*HJ*, 102). Lacking all heroic attributes save, perhaps, the freedom of aspiration conferred on them by their fabulous wealth, James's tale of the Ververs' success rang hollow. James had hoped to invest his book with a sense of those things, as he mentioned in his preface to *The American*, "that can reach us only through the beautiful circuit and subterfuge of our thought and desire" (quoted, *HJ*, 103); instead, he made it "finally a decadent book," Matthiessen argued, "in the strict sense in which decadence was defined by Orage, as 'the substitution of the part for the whole'" (*HJ*, 102).

In the remaining sections of his study, Matthiessen discussed three of James's other works—*The American Scene* (1907), which recorded James's impressions of the United States during a visit in 1904–05; *The Ivory Tower* (1917), unfinished at the time of James's death; and, in an appendix entitled "The Painter's Sponge and the Varnish Bottle," *The Portrait of a Lady* (1881), whose revisions reveal much about James's developing mastery of his craft. Yet it is fitting that Matthiessen, in his major concluding chapter, should have turned to a consideration of James's "religion of consciousness." Matthiessen wanted finally to define James's ultimate values, and in a frequently neglected essay, "Is There a Life after Death?" (which Matthiessen later included in *The James Family*), he believed that James had given those values their most mature expression.

In referring to James's religious beliefs, Matthiessen did not wish to convey the impression that there was a side to James less literary than philosophical or less aesthetic than theological. If James was consistent in anything, it was in his diffidence—if not downright opposition—to systems of any kind. Yet James believed that the most important question for a poet or a novelist, once he has reached full stride, is how he feels about life, and what, in sum, his philosophy is. A writer's view of the world he has so assiduously observed is always there to be inferred from his individual works, and James was prepared to go even further by saying that the details of those works are interesting only insofar as they illumine that informing vision. Hence, despite James's "indifference to dogma," as Eliot termed it, Matthiessen was convinced that Eliot had penetrated to the heart of James's religion by noting the paradoxical marriage between that indifference and "an exceptional awareness of spiritual reality" (quoted, *HJ*, 145). In fact, Matthiessen surmised that if James had come to maturity in an age such as Eliot's, he would have felt, as Eliot did, the need to attach himself to a traditional order of religious belief.

When James asked himself whether there is a life after death, he did so in a spirit of healthy curiosity. The only issue that death seemed to raise for him was whether one desired it as a welcome release from earthly existence or as the continuation and intensification of the pleasures of consciousness experienced during life. Matthiessen inferred James's preference from the language James used to describe the alternatives. In referring to life after death as a possible extension and refinement of a vivid sense of interest, of passion, of appreciation, which some men and women attain during life, James was invoking the same standards by which he judged most of his literary characters. Those standards included their capacity for aesthetic and moral imagination and their willingness to permit that same imagination free play in the lives of others. Since the development of this imagination represented something gained rather than something lost, James reasoned that such qualities are not likely to be snuffed out just when they have ripened into true virtues. On the basis of his own experience, it was much more logical to presume that beyond physical death there existed the possibility of a further development of conscious awareness and more subtle gradations of intellectual perception, "that all his life so far had given him just a glimpse of 'the unlimited vision of being' " (*HJ*, 147–48).

By "being," however, James did not mean that root ontological substance which, metaphysicians say, constitutes the ore of reality; he meant rather what Matthiessen describes as the "rich accumulations of experience" which are distilled from such ore once it has been brought to the surface of the mind, then refined by consciousness, and finally molded and shaped according to ethical commitments of one kind or another. For this reason Matthiessen found it necessary to describe James's formulation of immortality as more an aesthetic than a religious ideal, since it was less a product of the soul than of the mind. Being "loosely neo-Platonic," it was expressed most characteristically in the letter James wrote to his brother William at the time of Minny Temple's death, when he added the telling remark: "The more I think of her, the more perfectly satisfied I am to have her translated from this changing realm of fact to the steady realm of thought" (*HJ*, 147).

Matthiessen could not resist adding parenthetically that it was but a short step from the heightened consciousness of James's enviable observer, who can transmute evanescent facts into the imperishable medium of thought, to the hellish experience of Eliot's Teresias, who is doomed not only to foresee everything but also to foresuffer it, and who knows that all the fresh combinations and nuanced discriminations James projected into life after death may be only the eternal recurrence of meaningless patterns from the past. But the limitations of James's assumptions about religion were revealed even more starkly when brought into comparison with the fusion of the spiritual and the social which his own father had created. Even if James perceived correctly that his father's inclination toward abstraction tended to swallow up the individual and the concrete in the universal, Matthiessen still doubted that any revitalized consciousness of discrete particulars, such as the younger James wanted to substitute for it, could possibly survive "without a renewed synthesis of the sort that his father attempted" (*HJ*, 151). Matthiessen realized, of course, that the elder James's reliance upon such figures as Swedenborg and Fourier was too outmoded and eccentric to provide a sufficiently stable foundation for any new synthesis of religion and politics in the twentieth century. If anything like the elder James's synthesis of Christianity and democracy was to endure, Matthiessen was convinced that "the next synthesis must be more rigorously based in both political economy and theology, in the theology that recognizes anew men's radical imperfection, and in the radical political economy that insists that, whether imperfect or not, men must be equal in their social opportunities" (*HJ*, 151).

2

Interestingly enough, Matthiessen's next two books were in different ways attempts to continue this discussion. In *The James Family*, Matthiessen hoped to illumine the background from which Henry James's values had sprung by bringing them into direct contact with the different but not wholly unrelated set of values possessed, respectively, by his father, his sister, and his brother William. In *From the Heart of Europe* Matthiessen then sought, among other things, to clarify the nature of his own American politics and faith by recording his impressions during a six months' lecture tour in the summer and fall of 1947 at the Salzburg Seminar in Austria and at Charles University in Prague. Matthiessen's method in these two books was of course decidedly different. In the first book he made generous use of letters, diaries, and published writings to create a series of almost autobiographical portraits in which the various members of the James family spoke for themselves. In the second book he yielded to a more confessional impulse by adopting the device of a travel journal to speak for himself. Yet the two books go together. They are different ways of addressing the same problem, the problem that absorbed Matthiessen from the beginning to the end of his life: how to isolate, define, and repossess values from the past which can assist in shaping a more humane present and future. Hence *The James Family* and *From the Heart of Europe* represent two distinct but characteristic ways in which Matthiessen tried to fulfill the critical obligation, by seeking through an act of critical imagination, as Wallace Stevens might have said, what will suffice.

For our purposes, however, the latter book is the more germane. As a record of his own reflections during that critical international period just before Prague fell to the Russians, *From the Heart of Europe* is the most intimate and candid book Matthiessen ever wrote. He had been to Europe many times before —as a Yale freshman in 1920, as a Rhodes scholar in 1924, with Russell Cheney in search of Vermeers in 1931, and in 1938 just before the outbreak of war. This time, however, Matthiessen had returned to Europe less as a tourist in search of new experiences than as a seasoned traveler looking for added perspective on earlier ones. In the aftermath of World War II he felt a special urgency about renewing the understanding between peoples which transcends political differences and crosses ideological boundaries. His aim, he therefore confessed, was to think about "some of the things it means to be an American today" (*FHE*, 3), in the hope that his own reflections might facilitate the deepened cultural and human exchange that was absolutely essential if Americans and Europeans were to survive the tensions of the years ahead.

Matthiessen began his exercise in self-clarification with a description of present realities. After an illuminating account of his arrival in a Europe still scarred by the ravages of war and of his experiences at the seminar, where at least a few of these scars had begun to heal, Matthiessen turned back to recent political and intellectual life in America. What stood out most vividly in the years just preceding World War II was the sorry spectacle, as he put it, of writers and other intellectuals first shifting to radicalism and then shifting away from it with equal haste. The spectacle was both depressing and shameful because it illumined the shallowness of so much American political life. When writers like John Dos Passos and critics like Granville Hicks could now find refuge in an attenuated neoliberalism based upon eighteenth-century precedent, it was obvious that, however sincere their present desire to preserve the freedoms of liberal democracy, their earlier radicalism had never embraced the underlying realities that had dictated such a position in the first place. To Matthiessen it was clear that the situation had only worsened, that economic inequality, political injustice, and social oppression had become more pervasive and crippling during the intervening years, so that a commitment to some form of socialism was more compelling now than it had been in the 1930s. Thus he was driven to admit that if he were living in France he would be obliged to support the Communists, and that if he were living in England he would have found it natural to endorse the Labour Party.

These admissions provoked an ill-tempered response from the American press in 1948. They were too forthright for liberals and too un-American for conservatives. Irritated by the absence of any tone of self-recrimination, revisionists on the Left deplored Matthiessen's apparent lack of realpolitik while standpatters on the Right found evidence of fellow-traveling. Both responses were disingenuous in the extreme, since each revealed that typical closure of mind which Matthiessen's observations were designed to counteract. The fact that Matthiessen had made such admissions only to compare Europe with America, which had no viable socialist party, was disregarded. Few reviewers seemed willing or able to understand that Matthiessen's sole object was to suggest what was lacking in America, where radicalism was not a popular movement enjoying mass support, as in France and England, but merely a bloodless theoretical abstraction or a form of rigidly ideological sectarianism. The peppery little Harvard professor must be a Communist after all, despite his disclaimer, in the next several pages of *From the Heart of Europe,* that as a Christian he could not possibly be.

Matthiessen's reasons for not being a Communist were really very simple. A Christian by conviction as well as by upbringing, he believed that materialism is inadequate and that in the end man finds his fulfillment not by virtue of what he does for himself but by acknowledging his dependence upon others, and particularly upon God. As he put it,

I make no pretense of being a theologian, but I have been influenced by the same Protestant revival that has been voiced most forcefully in America by Reinhold Niebuhr. That is to say, I have rejected the nineteenth-century belief in every man as his own Messiah, along with the other aberrations of that century's individualism; and I have accepted the doctrine of original sin, in the sense that man is fallible and limited, no matter what his social system, and is capable of finding completion only through humility before the love of God. (*FHE*, 82)

In the intellectual climate of the postwar period, this declaration could as easily have confused the issue as resolved it. By 1948 Reinhold Niebuhr had become the theological standard-bearer for many disenchanted liberals who had taken to commuting from one political position to another; the notion of original sin was fast turning into a new intellectual call to arms to restore what Jefferson had referred to, with quite a different meaning, as "the ground we stand on"; and humility before the love of God was soon to become one of the better ways to promote that consensus view of ourselves which was already displacing all progressive, as well as radical, interpretations of the American past and present.[5] Any recourse to neoorthodoxy, with its strong emphasis upon human finitude instead of human freedom and upon self-discipline rather than self-liberation, could therefore be taken to be both obscurantist and conservative.

Matthiessen was well aware of this possibility. Many of his radical friends had often confessed their inability to comprehend his religions convictions, which must have seemed incongruous coming from a man with his firm social commitments. Yet Matthiessen could in turn attest to "a shallowness in their psychology whenever they . . . talked as though man was perfectible, with evil wholly external to his nature, and caused only by the frustrations of the capitalist system" (*FHE*, 82), because modern history provided a wealth of evidence to the contrary. How could one explain the demonism of Hitler or the cruelty of Stalin without recourse to an anthropology that saw man as both angel and devil? What was one to make of American history in the nineteenth and twentieth centuries if one expunged any hint that man himself was in part responsible for the way history had become the adversary? But Matthiessen had no need to draw upon such large, inchoate issues for his

[5] John Higham, "Beyond Consensus: The Historian as Moral Critic," *American Historical Review* 67 (1962): 609–25.

examples; the evidence that man is a complex intermixture of both good and evil was there for anyone to see in a Dante, a Shakespeare, or a Melville, and it served to confirm Matthiessen's own beliefs as a Christian.

Yet on one point—a crucial one for him—Matthiessen felt compelled to distinguish himself from most contemporary Christians. As he insisted,

> . . . I would differ from most orthodox Christians today, and particularly from the tradition represented by T. S. Eliot, in that, whatever the imperfections of man, the second of the two great commandments, to love thy neighbor as thyself, seems to me an imperative to social action. Evil is not merely external, but external evils are many, and some social systems are more productive of them than others. Thus my philosophical position is of the simplest. It is as a Christian that I find my strongest propulsion to being a socialist. I would call myself a Christian Socialist, except for the stale and reactionary connotations that the term has acquired through its current use by European parties. (*FHE,* 82)

Here Matthiessen was obviously differentiating himself from those who, like Eliot in his later years, espoused orthodoxy in religion, royalism in politics, and formalism in critical method. The point at issue was one Matthiessen had articulated a year earlier in his preface to the 1947 edition of *The Achievement of T. S. Eliot,* that "it is possible to accept the 'radical imperfection' of man, and yet to be a political radical as well, to be aware that no human society can be perfect, and yet to hold that the proposition that 'all men are created equal' demands dynamic adherence from a Christian no less than from a democrat" (*ATSE,* ix). It is worth noting that, however paradoxical the double allegiance to the religion of Christ and to the need for social action may have sounded to many literary intellectuals in the late 1940s, it was in no way inconsistent with the radical form of Protestantism which had been reinvigorated by Reinhold Niebuhr. Who but Niebuhr, for example, had coupled an awareness of man's crippling limitations with a relentless call for social reform, or yoked a tragic interpretation of man's nature and destiny to a social ethic based upon adjudicating the claims of all men to a more just and humane future? When Niebuhr wrote that "man's capacity for justice makes democracy possible" while "man's inclination to injustice makes democracy necessary," he was compressing into one pregnant statement virtually all that Matthiessen had learned about democratic possibilities from the American writers of the nineteenth century; and when Niebuhr claimed that evidence of the primal curse shows itself most clearly not in men's basest actions but rather in their noblest gestures, he was confirming all that Matthiessen had discovered about evil from his reflections on the literature of the past and from his participation in the politics of the present.

The purpose of such comparisons is not to say that Matthiessen was dependent upon Niebuhr for his double commitment as a Christian and a socialist, but merely to suggest that Matthiessen's commitments were neither unorthodox from a theological point of view nor illogical and self-contradictory from a philosophic point of view. His disclaimer notwithstanding, Matthiessen had good grounds for calling himself a "Christian Socialist" both within the Christian faith, at least in its most prominent contemporary expression, and within the more diffuse tradition of religious reflection native to the United States which he had worked so hard to uncover in *American Renaissance.*

Yet one can make too much of Matthiessen's consistency in such matters. Whatever support Matthiessen found in a theologian like Niebuhr (and presumably it was stronger than Matthiessen ever admitted), he still remained very much his own man theologically. For example, he departed sharply from Niebuhr in his view of the Soviet Union and of Marxism. Niebuhr interpreted Marxism as one of those empty faiths which, arising from the liberal ethos of the nineteenth century, lacked the ability to cope with the ineluctable fact of man's tragic life in history; he saw the Soviet Union as a nation that had elevated this illusory faith to the level of a religious absolute in order to pursue its own selfish and totalitarian ambitions. Matthiessen, by contrast, deemed the Russian Revolution of 1917 the most progressive event in the twentieth century and "the necessary successor to the French Revolution and the American Revolution and to England's seventeenth-century Civil War" (*FHE,* 82–3). Indeed, it was on precisely this issue that Matthiessen differentiated himself from most Christian socialists in *From the Heart of Europe,* arguing that the Russian Revolution simply completed the work of the French Revolution by showing how political revolution must be succeeded by economic revolution in order to complement the notion of man as citizen with the notion of man as laborer. To be sure, Matthiessen lamented the fact that the Russian Revolution had occurred in a country that was economically backward and possessed a long tradition of brutal and oppressive politics, but his obvious distaste for the excesses of the revolution did not deter him from applauding the principle for which it was fought and from which, in spite of "the grim pressures of dictatorship," the Russian people had not been deflected: "the right of all to share in the common wealth" (*FHE*, 83). Niebuhr clearly would have challenged this stand with all the impressive fieldpieces in his theological artillery, insisting that Matthiessen was unable to view the Russian political experiment with that same "sharp critical sense" for "excesses and limitations" (*FHE*, 14) which he had for so long focused on the American experience.

To take another example, if Matthiessen could believe with one part of his mind in the strict and powerful dialectics of Niebuhr's theology, which was constantly balancing such abstractions as freedom and finitude, good and evil, love and justice, moral man and immoral society, he could respond with the other to Wallace Stevens's poem, "Sad Strains of a Gay Waltz," suggesting "that here, in the contrast between a played-out tune and a new skeptical music which might spring from the very heart of our disbelief, lay one of the most resourceful 'ideas of order' for our broken time" (*FHE*, 179). The difference was not really over the question of certitude; Niebuhr, after all, had been able to speak meaningfully to many of the "cultured despisers of religion" in his generation precisely because he spoke humbly, as one who knows that the only true believers are those who are aware of the depths of their unbelief. The issue was rather one of coherence. Matthiessen was more willing to live in a state of intellectual and theological suspension than Niebuhr was; in fact, he believed that the ability to entertain two opposed ideas at the same time and still retain the capacity to function bespoke a higher degree of intellectual maturity than the tendency to seek reconciliation and resolution. To strive for intellectual closure, especially in relation to issues of ultimate import, was for Matthiessen to risk blurring distinctions that might well be more crucial and more illuminating than the sought-for unity of point of view; and it might also be more self-serving. Instead, Matthiessen aspired to be one of the people James spoke of on whom nothing is lost, even if this meant living with a certain measure of inconclusiveness and personal conflict. The alternative was not to live at all, and that Matthiessen was congenitally indisposed to accept until the agony of his own inner divisions became too intense for him to suffer and exploit simultaneously.

If Matthiessen was very much his own man theologically, he was even more so politically. As he makes clear in *From the Heart of Europe,* his interest in politics developed by accident and followed a course that was peculiarly personal. It all began, he relates, in an elementary course in economics he was required to take at Yale. Although he found the work dull and abstract, he decided to write a paper for extra credit as insurance against possible disaster in the final examination. By sheerest chance a book on the supplementary reading list, R. H. Tawney's *The Acquisitive Society,* caught Matthiessen's eye. The title called forth no particular associations, even though it suggested values he had grown up with as a boy and had become inured to at Hackley, but it was enough out of the ordinary to make him want to read the book. As it subsequently turned out, he could not have made a more fortunate choice. Tawney's book marked the beginning of Matthiessen's lifelong interest in social theory and remained as living to him, he once insisted, as anything but Shakespeare which he read in college.

It was Tawney's ideas about equality, particularly the notion that political equality must be based upon economic equality in order to ensure a full measure of social and individual freedom, which made a lasting impression on Matthiessen. Unless all men are given the right to the fruits of their labor, as Tawney argued, the Jeffersonian ideals of freedom and equality will become hollow and meaningless. Moreover, the concentration of wealth in the hands of a few, Tawney showed, can lead only to new forms of economic and political tyranny. It was but a short step from these convictions to the proposals for social reform Matthiessen encountered soon after in Henry George's *Progress and Poverty.* Before long, then, Matthiessen had swung the length of the political pendulum from tacit support of the Republican

Warren G. Harding to open avowal of the Socialist Eugene V. Debs. Spectacular as this shift of allegiance was, Matthiessen insisted that it was not simply a youthful act of protest. He supported Debs because he believed that Debs was right, and when as a Yale senior he finally heard Debs speak, an event he viewed as a turning point in his life, the man's bearing and presence confirmed his earlier decision. "His speech wasn't anything remarkable," Matthiessen later wrote, "for he was very tired. But white and worn-out as he looked, he still conveyed a broad dignity and warmth that showed me for the first time what a people's leader could be" (*FHE*, 75).

This almost parenthetical observation, mixed in with reflections on the development of what Matthiessen called his own "American politics," might easily be passed over if it did not so clearly reveal the peculiar strain of idealism which was to color all his political thinking and activity. As much as Matthiessen strove through politics to redress specific social ills and to effect the passage of more humane laws, he also viewed political involvement itself as a way of recovering specific qualities that might restore balance and wholeness to the national psyche. This truth was brought home to him most vividly one night in college. He had been teaching as a volunteer in a citizenship class at the New Haven Hungarian Club and had found the experience both challenging and rewarding. What struck him most was the way so many of his students, some twice his age, took with utter seriousness what he had always taken for granted. To them an education was something to be revered with almost religious awe and they paid their teacher the respect commensurate with his high office. Yet on the very last night of the course, when the class had been dismissed, his students overcame their reserve and invited him on a tour of the rest of the building. As it turned out, however, their real intent was to repair to the basement where each man had been fermenting his own private cask of prohibition wine. The ceremony that followed was simple but very moving. It consisted of little more than a sampling of several of the casks with a considerable show of feeling on all sides before they said their good-byes and departed. But as Matthiessen walked back to the Yale campus that evening, he recalled that "the stars seemed unusually bright. . . . I had felt in the natural and hearty comradeship of these men a quality that I was just beginning to suspect might be bleached out of middle-class college graduates. It was a kind of comradeship I wanted never to lose" (*FHE,* 73).

This kind of natural and earthy relationship with others on all levels of the social and economic ladder was what Matthiessen hoped and desperately needed to find through political association. More often than not, however, it eluded him. When he returned in 1925 from his Rhodes Scholarship in England, where he had been a member of the Oxford Labour Club, he was immediately struck by the lack of any real labor party in America, a party fully rooted in the needs and aspirations of the common people and drawing its leadership from within their ranks. In its place there was only Norman Thomas and his Socialists, and Thomas, however commendable his ideas, was too professorial in style ever to hold any real appeal for the masses. Consequently, Matthiessen was forced to compromise, always in ways that confounded his attempts to realize the deep sense of unity and of solidarity with others so necessary to his own psychic constitution. When Al Smith ran for the presidency in 1928, bringing with him "the earthiness of a seasoned popular campaigner" (*FHE,* 76), Matthiessen voted Democratic but with no real sense of identification with the party and its members. In 1932 he switched his support to the Socialists, even belonging to the party for a time, on the assumption that the Great Depression offered radicals an opportunity to regain the popular base they had developed under Debs. But he later admitted to having underestimated the strength of the reaction against Hoover and the progressive character of Roosevelt's first term. Roosevelt's campaign speeches had struck Matthiessen "as little more than the promises of a Harvard man who wanted very much to be President"; but when Roosevelt began to push through some of the legislation Norman Thomas and others had called for, Matthiessen "voted for him enthusiastically, though always from the left, until his death" (*FHE,* 76).

The problem was that being a Democrat "was not the same as having a party to belong to in the European sense, a labor party with a trade-union base to which an intellectual could adhere with the realization that he might learn the firsthand facts of economic organization from this contact, and could then, in turn, be of some use in helping to provide ideas of leadership" (*FHE*, 76). Further, the Democratic Party in America was a far cry from a grass-roots political organization fully representative in its makeup and genuinely participatory in its methods of operation. And so when Roosevelt died in 1945, Matthiessen turned to the Progressive Party, working tirelessly but happily for the election of Henry Wallace in 1948; he even delivered a seconding speech for Wallace's nomination at the convention. Matthiessen could not claim that Wallace was in all ways a people's candidate, but he did believe that Wallace had the people's best interests at heart. To him Wallace was "emphatically a successor in the Jeffersonian tradition, the great tradition of fearlessly introducing major principles into political discussion" (*FHE*, 85). If this was less than all one might wish, it was better than anything else on the horizon, and Matthiessen bent all his efforts in his last political campaign to getting Wallace elected or, failing that, to working for the spread of Wallace's ideas.

From the distance of more than a quarter of a century, it is clear that Matthiessen's work in national politics, though making him feel that he was executing some of his proper civic responsibilities, rarely provided him with a sense either that he was actually making any noticeable difference or that he was remaining in contact with the "democratic en masse." It was rather in serving local causes that Matthiessen felt his contributions mattered, and mattered most because they sometimes afforded him contact with people whose ways of life were very different from his own. It was as a member of the Executive Committee of the Massachusetts Civil Liberties Union, as a trustee of the Sam Adams School of Social Studies, and as an organizer of the Harvard Teachers' Union that Matthiessen achieved his greatest political effectiveness and found his deepest personal satisfactions. His participation in the founding and development of the Harvard Teachers' Union was particularly important to him. It not only provided him a much-needed sense of community amid the growing impersonality and fragmentation of Harvard; it also gave him and others a necessary feeling of solidarity with those beyond the perimeters of Harvard Yard.

Furthermore, because of the union's early decision to join the

American Federation of Labor, Matthiessen and his colleagues gained firsthand knowledge of how the American political system actually operates. His exposure to the problems of other locals, to the intricacies and the corruption of city government, and to the necessity of preparing and lobbying for bills before the state legislature counteracted much of the earlier streak of sentimentality once associated with his political idealism; he became a seasoned political infighter with a reputation for courage and moral rectitude. But his increasing shrewdness about political maneuvering, coupled with his stubborn refusal to be bribed or bullied into compromise on any issues he really cared about, brought with them disturbing consequences. As the decade of the forties progressed, Matthiessen was exposed to stiffening opposition from university administrators, unfavorable notices in the Boston dailies, anonymous phone calls in the middle of the night, and increasing alienation from many faculty colleagues. To be sure, Matthiessen was enough of a Westerner and maverick to enjoy a scrap with official Harvard and enough of a political realist to tolerate public censure. What hurt most, and seemed most inexplicable to him, was the resentment, suspicion, and even hostility from fellow academics. Could they not see that by refusing to concede the intimate relationship between education and politics, indeed, by refusing to be concerned as intellectuals about society's responsibility to accord an authentic place to the life of the mind, they were giving implicit aid and comfort to forces then on the ascendance in America, which would deny independent intellect any place at all in society? Desirous only of being left alone to pursue their specialized, academic interests, their unwillingness to be accountable to anything outside themselves was simply increasing the pressures of conformity. Even worse, in Matthiessen's opinion, they were running the risk, with little awareness of the consequences, of cutting themselves off from the intellectual's most valuable and indispensable resource, full participation in the life of the community.

For these reasons Matthiessen returned time and again, in *From the Heart of Europe,* to Walt Whitman, the central writer in the American tradition affirming the democratic faith. Whitman knew, in Matthiessen's estimation, what was missing from Emerson's conception of the individual; he realized that to assert the superiority of the isolated thinker was to sever one's bonds with what is common to the life of all. More than anyone else, Matthiessen believed, Whitman had done justice to the three elements in the French concept of democracy—*liberté, egalité,* and *fraternité.* Liberty and equality without the warmth of fraternity were cold constructs and empty abstractions which bore little or no relation to the pulsations of ordinary human life, whether that life was lived on the farm or in the urban jungle. Real freedom could not exist in isolation because without human contacts there could be no deeply shared existence. Freedom, as Whitman instinctively knew and Matthiessen echoed, comes only "through taking part in the common life, mingling in its hopes and failures, and helping to reach a more adequate realization of its aims, not for one alone, but for the community" (*FHE,* 90). The word that moved Whitman most deeply, his "great word," was "solidarity" (*FHE,* 90).

"Solidarity" in all its meanings—as a union of concerns within a group, as a community of interests transcending differences between groups, and as a name for that felt sense of unity, of human bondedness, which derives from such recognitions— brings us to the heart of Matthiessen's book. In his introductory remarks at the opening session of the Salzburg Seminar, intended as "a speech of fraternity rather than . . . of welcome" (*FHE,* 16), Matthiessen spoke of the occasion as historic, since it provided an opportunity "to enact anew the chief function of culture and humanism, to bring man again into communication with man" (*FHE,* 13). Referring to their situation as an "island of peace in a storm-crowded sea" (*FHE,* 14), he exhorted his fellow participants to take full advantage of the meetings "to penetrate," through the free exchange of opinions, "to new levels of understanding, to probe again the nature of man" (*FHE,* 13). By the time the seminar concluded, Matthiessen's highest expectations had been realized. The meetings provided the finest environment for teaching he had ever known, for "here was our Brook Farm; here was our ideal communistic experiment, where each—to borrow the words of a man who went farther than Fourier—gave according to his abilities, and received according to his needs" (*FHE,* 66).

All summer long, Matthiessen recalled, "our enchanted garden had seemed on the edge of a precipice" (*FHE*, 66). With the clouds of Hiroshima and Nagasaki darkening the horizon on one side and the menace of Russian expansionism looming on the other, they had worked to create a new sense of community and solidarity out of the bitter divisions of the past, but with no confidence that the future would honor it. "Yet at the heart of our disillusion," Matthiessen maintained, was the knowledge that he and his colleagues had recovered, through the often painful experience of self-exposure and self-criticism, a new faith in "the dignity and power of the intellectual":

Hardly more than a hundred men and women, some already worn beyond their years, we were nevertheless going back to our many countries with a renewed belief in the possibility of communication. We were carrying with us too the belief that there was much we could still do, by our speaking and writing, to cut through prejudice, to destroy the barriers of ignorance and hate that otherwise will destroy us all. (*FHE*, 66)

When the disastrous events of 1948, including the Communist take-over in Czechoslovakia, put so rude an end to many of Matthiessen's generous expectations, critics quickly found his optimism and faith easy targets for ridicule. Indeed, Matthiessen himself became increasingly despondent about the possibility of realizing these expectations once he returned to the United States. Nevertheless, in giving voice to faith and hope, Matthiessen not only captured the seminar's spirit but also personified it. His achievement is beautifully recognized in a loving reminiscence and tribute written by Alfred Kazin for the memorial issue of the *Monthly Review* shortly after Matthiessen's death. Kazin had been a lecturer at the seminar and, though little inclined to share all Matthiessen's political enthusiasms, was deeply moved by his example, by his need to find completion in the act of giving himself to those he cared for:

He was not only in every sense the leader of our enterprise—it was he particularly, by his personal generosity, his curiosity, his constant availability, the deeply felt and extraordinarily sympathetic relationships he formed with students of different countries and conflicting views, who personified the rich human interchange and re-opening of communication between American and European intellectuals that we sought from the Seminar.

But especially do I remember Matty reading Eliot to us at Salzburg. There was one day, near the end of the course, when he held the whole mass group of us in the library spellbound by the depth of emotion with which he read and expounded the last part of *The Waste Land.* I have never seen a lecture audience so moved, so happily aware that it was in contact with a man at his best, and whose greatest urge was to share with us the thing he loved. All that could be so wonderful in Matty flashed out upon our strangely mixed group that afternoon, binding us together in reverence for the creative spirit, transcending our nominal political differences—and all through his love of the poem, through the solemnity, the dignity, the marvelous inwardness with which he read. He was really free that day, completely in tune with himself, and he gave us all something that will always live in my mind as an example of the reconciliatory spirit at its most instinctive, its most truthful, its most loving—of Matty as in his deepest self he was, of Matty our Friend.[6]

The same reconciliatory spirit breathes through the pages of *From the Heart of Europe* and makes it far more than a travel diary; it is at once an act of self-definition and an essay in cross-cultural understanding. Matthiessen himself provided the best description of his aims for the book. After noting that "the responsibility of the artist is not to solve in advance the tensions of the society he lives in, but simply—yet this is a task for a lifetime—to give, to the full, experience as he has known it to be," Matthiessen concluded that the artist's indispensable role "is to keep alive the vital, delicate, and always menaced accuracy of communication, without which there can be no renewed discovery of man by man" (*FHE,* 58–59). Almost before the book was off the press, however, the delicate lines of communication which he had worked so hard to establish during his stay in Europe were threatened in ways that Matthiessen had not foreseen, making any "renewed discovery of man by man" more difficult than he could possibly have imagined.

3

Upon his return to America, Matthiessen awakened his first night at home "in a sudden sweat of fear" (*FHE,* 193). His six months away had given him a sense of perspective and renewal, but now he found himself "back in a very uncertain battle" (*FHE,* 193). He could not escape the feeling that the world was poised on the brink of disaster, and his experience in Europe,

6 *Monthly Review* 2 (1950): 283.

at least in retrospect, convinced him that time had run out for further compromises. The alternatives were war and international cooperation, and with a world at stake Matthiessen confessed to having acquired a new sense of the intellectual's responsibility. Now as never before it was imperative that the intellectual remain "as true as possible to what his own experience has taught him, and to speak for those truths as fully and fearlessly as he can" (*FHE*, 193).

It was in this mood of heightened political and social concern, with containment the official policy abroad and red-baiting on the rise at home, that Matthiessen decided to accept an invitation to deliver the Hopwood lecture at the University of Michigan. Convinced that literary criticism written in isolation from the actual theater of life was in danger of becoming "a kind of closed garden," Matthiessen hoped to convince his audience "that the land beyond the garden's walls is more fertile, and that the responsibilities of the critic lie in making renewed contact with that soil" (*RC*, 6). His title—"The Responsibilities of the Critic"—was a frank avowal of his intention. Instead of choosing a topic more appropriate to the prevailing critical mood—such as "The Limitations of Literary Criticism" or "The Liabilities of the Critic"—Matthiessen took a more aggressive approach.

The critic's first responsibility, Matthiessen said, was to possess a lively awareness of the works of art of his own time, regardless of his special period of competence. To know himself, and thus to be aware of his own biases and expectations regarding the past, the critic had to know the art of his own age. Knowledge of the present would also make for a true understanding of the past because, as Eliot had long maintained, "the past is not what is dead, but what is already living; and . . . the present is continually modifying the past, as the past conditions the present" (*RC*, 6). Matthiessen contended that "it is not possible to be a good critic of Goethe today without knowing Mann, or of Stendahl or Balzac without knowing Proust, or of Donne or Dryden without knowing Eliot" (*RC*, 6).

The other side of the coin was that a critic also had to know the past in order to comprehend the present. Such an observation may have been too obvious to bear repetition, but Matthiessen was convinced that the tempo of modern life had accelerated so rapidly that no tradition could be taken for granted. Unless we are willing to make a continual effort to repossess the past for ourselves, he was certain, we are in imminent danger of losing our sense of it altogether. In his words, "the proper balance, even for the critic who considers his field to be the present, is to bring to the elucidation of that field as much of the art of the past as he can command" (*RC,* 7).

Matthiessen found this balance admirably exhibited in the career of Paul Rosenfeld. A critic of contemporary music, Rosenfeld possessed a vast and enviable knowledge of the music of the past. Yet neither his love of the past nor his interest in the present prevented him from believing "that if our younger composers were to have a sense of possessing any audience, someone must make it his function to listen to them all" (*RC,* 7). In assuming this obligation, Rosenfeld risked appearing "thoroughly degraded" (*RC,* 7) to all those "intellectuals without love," as Auden described them, who had become victims of the modern tendency to overspecialize. Yet Rosenfeld's "generous openness to all the arts" (*RC,* 7) constituted a severe rebuke to those who supposed that the critic could carry out his chief responsibilities by walling himself off in specious enclaves of narrow competence. Indeed, Matthiessen argued that nothing could be more incapacitating. Whether such narrowness meant that critics knew little beyond their own fields of specialization or that they actually knew nothing at all, the example of Paul Rosenfeld made it difficult to imagine an alert critic lacking a genuine interest in, if not a mastery of, materials and techniques outside his own field. It was axiomatic with Matthiessen that "anyone understands his own discipline better if he is aware of some other subject and discipline" (*RC,* 8).

The critic, in addition to being aware of the arts of his own time, Matthiessen believed, must also become knowledgeable about the popular arts of the mass media. To many in his audience, this proposal must have sounded like sheer madness. The only people likely to take an active intellectual interest in popular arts were those who derived satisfaction from them. Or so it seemed from a perusal of the Sunday supplements, where pundits who specialized in such matters held forth. Matthiessen acknowledged that radio had done a fine job in educating countless millions to the sound of magnificent music, but the market-oriented arts of film and television served only as a constant reminder "of our immense potentialities and continual corruptions" (*RC*, 9). "Potentialities" versus "corruptions": this was precisely Matthiessen's point. The mass media, with their enormous power for public influence, gave critics but one choice: "either channel them to socially valuable ends or be engulfed by them" (*RC*, 8).

Given the starkness of this alternative, it is no accident that Matthiessen turned to William James and his image of the thinker as occupying a central position. It was Matthiessen's hope that James's image of the embattled intellectual might provide a fresh resource for critics who had grown dispirited in the face of ever-increasing challenges and distractions. Yet Matthiessen was forced to admit that it had become impossible "to take that image with the lightness that he [James] could":

Everywhere we turn in these few fateful years since the first atom bomb dropped on Hiroshima we seem menaced by such vast forces that we may well feel that we advance at our peril. But even greater peril would threaten us if those whose prime responsibility as critics is to keep open the life-giving communications between art and society should waver in their obligations to provide ever fresh thought for our own society. (*RC*, 9)

It was, of course, quite likely that many in his audience might find this whole discussion irrelevant to serious criticism of the arts, but Matthiessen vigorously disagreed: "The series of awarenesses which I believe the critic must possess lead ineluctably from literature to life, and I do not see how the responsible intellectual in our time can avoid being concerned with politics" (*RC*, 10).

By "politics" Matthiessen meant something much broader than the activities of parties or the problem of ideology in art; he intended to open up the whole question of cultural and historical context and the relation between social or economic fact and literary value. Even though he was a Christian rather than a Marxist, as he reminded his audience, and therefore had "no desire to repeat the absurdities" of the early 1930s "when literary men, quite oblivious theretofore of economics, were finding sudden salvation in a dogma that became more rigid the less they had assimilated it" (*RC*, 10), he still believed that some of the instincts of that earlier moment had been correct. In attributing to economic and political factors a primary role in social and cultural development, critics had vastly broadened the inquiry into an individual work of literature; they had demonstrated that the insights found in Marx and Engels could lead to a better understanding of the forces responsible for both the work and its author. Yet in spite of his own agreement with much of the Marxist analysis of social and cultural change, Matthiessen had no intention of claiming "that Marxism gives . . . an adequate view of the nature of man, or that it or any other economic theory can provide a substitute for the critic's painstaking discipline in the interplay between form and content in concrete works of art" (*RC*, 11). In raising again the question of a criticism informed by economic and social perspectives, his only point was "that analysis itself can run to seed unless the analyzing mind is also absorbed in a wider context than the text before it" (RC, 12).

Matthiessen had already mentioned two such contexts, or awarenesses, which constituted specific responsibilities of the critic, but he had a third one to add. It derived from the special character of the American experience, both preceding and following World War II, which he believed had widened the already substantial gulf between America and Europe. Whereas Europeans had suffered dictatorship, war, and occupation, Americans had suffered only war, and that, for most people, merely at second or third remove. Hence the stability of American social and political institutions before the war, America's privileged isolation during the war, and then her spectacular economic recovery immediately following it were breeding a dangerous, even perverse, sense of "false superiority" of the kind Matthiessen found so well expressed in Allen Tate's "Sonnet at Christmas":

> The American people fully armed,
> With assurance policies, righteous and harmed,
> Battle the world of which they're not at all. (Quoted, *RC*, 12)

The problem was to imagine how Americans might become part of the larger world, many of whose tribulations they had never experienced, and of how, in the face "of their vast special for-

tune," they might be prevented from "passing from innocence
to corruption without ever having grasped maturity" (*RC,* 14).
The answer suggested by Tate's lines was painfully clear to
Matthiessen:

Not by pretending to be something they are not, nor by being either proud
or ashamed of their vast special fortune. It does no good, for example, to adopt
the vocabulary of the Paris existentialists in order to emulate the crisis of
occupation which we have not passed through. The ironic lines of Tate's
"Sonnet at Christmas" suggest a more mature way of meeting experience.
None of us can escape what we are, but by recognizing our limitations, and
comprehending them, we can transcend them by the span of that knowledge."
(*RC,* 13)

It was in such terms that Matthiessen, in the Hopwood lecture,
envisaged the critic's most pressing responsibilities. His objective was not to diminish the critic's proper interest in the text
at hand, but rather to provide him with larger resources for
illuminating and evaluating it. And even when the critic's responsibilities might lead him beyond the work before him to
issues transcending it, Matthiessen was still not trying to make
criticism less than or other than literary, but only more fully so.
In urging the critic to consider simultaneously the arts of his
own time, the popular arts of mass society, and the relation
between America and the rest of the world, Matthiessen was
seeking to rescue criticism from the peripheries of life and return it again to the center. His main purpose was to recall critics
to the old Emersonian ideal—to make of their work nothing less
than an act of the whole of themselves.

4

This heroic ambition, to which Matthiessen gave himself so
completely, in the end got the best of him. Under the pressure
of increasing anxiety about the American future and a growing
obsession to make his work count for something, to make it
speak, however indirectly, to the present situation, Matthiessen
began to give way in his final book-length study, a biography
of Theodore Dreiser, to the impulse to stand and deliver. Because of his intense concern to demonstrate Dreiser's relevance,
Matthiessen was willing to dull the edge of his own critical instrument in order to make Dreiser's virtues stand out more

boldly and unambiguously. Dreiser was relevant and timely because of his long and torturous journey toward a more affirmative outlook on life and also because of his ultimate appreciation of the need for human community and solidarity. For Matthiessen the all-important fact was that Dreiser, however dark his early portraits of man's pathetic struggle against nature, never lost his capacity to empathize with the victim or to feel compassion for human weakness in all its expressions.

To be fair, one must add that there were other, less obvious reasons for Dreiser's importance to Matthiessen. Though no one (least of all Matthiessen) could disregard Dreiser's notoriously awkward style and his frequent failure to provide his ideas with adequate formal resolution, Matthiessen detected beneath such defects a solid core of substance. That substance derived not merely from the strength of Dreiser's material, but also from how he came by it and what he did with it. Dreiser's fiction, hammered out on the anvil of his own experience, sounded an unmistakable note of authenticity. He had had to struggle and suffer for his art, but he had not allowed himself to be brutalized or embittered in the process. Instead, he fought throughout to retain as generous a store of sympathy and compassion as life had measured out to him. "If genius is caring for human beings more than others know how to care," Dorothy Dudley remarked, "then Dreiser has genius," and Matthiessen agreed (quoted, *TD*, 81). The result was a body of fiction whose warm human concern often made up in integrity of purpose what it lacked in technical proficiency. The surface crudities of Dreiser's writing could not hide an elemental sense of life, a feeling for life's basic rhythms and emotions, which was larger and deeper than any of the patterns of thought or action in terms of which he tried to express it. H. L. Mencken best summed up this sense of life when he said that Dreiser's "aim is not merely to record, but to translate and understand; the thing he exposes is not the empty event and act, but the endless mystery out of which it springs" (quoted, *TD*, 122).

In following Mencken, Matthiessen was trying to revise the whole notion of naturalism as it applied to Dreiser, who, Matthiessen was convinced, had little interest in the theory of the novel. Nor was he obsessed with a desire to vindicate a special view of man and history. His instincts as a naturalist sprang rather from his growing fascination with "the broad processes of nature, and in making his fiction correspond with them" (*TD*, 120). One might easily criticize this aim as naïve, but one could hardly discount it as being frivolous. As a naturalist, Dreiser was less deeply moved by the things men can understand about themselves and their environment than by the things they cannot understand, and his chief goal as a novelist was to arouse compassion for anyone caught in the clutches of incomprehensible circumstances. Dreiser was a kind of "primitive, not unlike the occasional American sign painter who has found that he possessed the dogged skills to create a portrait likeness, and then has bent all the force of a rugged character to realize this verity" (*TD*, 60). Not really knowing how to adorn life in his fiction, Dreiser could only try to express it; through that endeavor he helped to forge an altogether new literary tradition.

Reading Dreiser's achievement in this way, Matthiessen argued that Dreiser's first novel, *Sister Carrie* (1900), for all its seeming originality at the time, was less than fully successful. The chief difficulty with Carrie Meeber was the very opposite of what Mrs. Doubleday supposed: she was not cut from a mold too far removed from the conventional and the ordinary, but rather, in her simple innocence, she was not unconventional enough. The only way Dreiser could evoke what he referred to as Carrie's "emotional greatness" was by dressing her out in a series of clichés, and when it came time to depict her affairs with Drouet and Hurstwood, he was afraid to break free of literary convention and show her truly moved by passion. Carrie thus remained too obvious a projection of Dreiser's own yearning for a realm of spirit he did not really understand, and as a result his picture of her never escaped sentimentality and foolishness.

The handling of Hurstwood was quite different, according to Matthiessen. Since Hurstwood did not call forth in Dreiser the same response of identification and desire, the novelist was able to maintain a more stable balance of sympathy and judgment in his treatment of him. Further, when Dreiser turned from Carrie to Hurstwood, he was not so easily tempted into forgetting that the only way to view a character realistically is to see him in terms of his whole environment. Dreiser was therefore able to make Hustwood's slow disintegration the most moving aspect of the book. By detailing all that Hurstwood's fall divests him of—family, friends, property, income, work, lodging, even will—Dreiser invested Hurstwood's decline with a significance far transcending his intrinsic worth as a person and made it a symbol of the fragility of all human existence.

Assuming that Hurstwood's demise was the heart of the novel, Matthiessen took the most significant episode to be the scene at Fitzgerald and Moy's where Hurstwood wavers back and forth before finally taking the money. In this scene the world lying back of the novel, a world of extreme insecurity without equilibrium or sense of permanence, is most brilliantly evoked. It is a world in which characters never meet, merely passing one another as they move off toward different, but always shifting, positions on the social scale. Matthiessen admitted that a novel portraying characters in that kind of world is likely to be "more impressive in its main sweep than in all its details" (*TD*, 86). Yet he was also convinced that the numerous criticisms of Dreiser's bumbling artlessness had all but obscured the passages where Dreiser, "like the journeyman painter," displays "a mastery of the plain style" (*TD*, 87). Such passages are most abundant at moments when the paths of various characters seem to cross for the last time. In these rare moments of fleeting contact, when the pathos of isolation was heightened by a temporary proximity, Dreiser's respect for the innate dignity of his characters as human beings was revealed in his willingness to let the poignancy of their situation speak for itself. Here it became apparent that Dreiser's essential attitude toward life was one of kindness. "Even at its worst," Matthiessen concluded, "life contains something which he, with full compassion for his beaten hero, will not reject, but will embrace with tenderness" (*TD*, 88).

In his next novel, *Jennie Gerhardt* (1911), Dreiser extended his attitude of compassion by applying it to a character whose fortunes were to rise rather than to fall. Dreiser wanted to center his attention on Jennie's "deepening awareness of what life does to people" (*TD*, 114), but he refused to be hurried in charting the course of Jennie's progress. Only by revealing the dogged but persistent movement of Jennie's mind, by making his story "conform," as he later put it, "to the large, truthful lines of life" (quoted, *TD,* 112), could he adequately represent her world and thus fulfill his ambition as a writer. But *Jennie Gerhardt* was not a flawless performance. Though Dreiser seemed to "offset his lack of invention with a gift for selection and massive rearrangement" (*TD,* 113), he was still reluctant to describe passion with realism, and he had difficulty in adhering to his central design. Once again, however, Matthiessen was willing to excuse Dreiser's limitations on the ground that within them the novelist had achieved a certain wholeness: by "writing out of what he himself had experienced, he could make others feel it" (*TD,* 113).

On the basis of this interpretation of Dreiser's first two novels, his three large novels on the highly successful business career of Frank Cowperwood should have proven failures, and Matthiessen was in no way disposed to dissent. Of the three—*The Financier* (1912), *The Titan* (1914), and *The Stoic* (1947)—only the first was at all successful. *The Titan* was flawed by a structure that was too static and a hero whom Dreiser could heighten only through excessive use of hyperbole and metaphor, and *The Stoic* lacked even *The Titan's* few redeeming features. Only in *The Financier* was Dreiser able to turn his hero into a thoroughly realized symbol and thus to record "not the professed but the actual forces of his time" (*TD,* 133). Thief as well as tyrant, villain as well as hero, Cowperwood represented much that Dreiser wanted for himself but could never attain. An egotistical and lawless individualist who embodied Spencer's law of "the survival of the fittest," Cowperwood was motivated not by grievance or frustration but rather by "an instinctive, unimpeded response to the expanding possibilities of the age" (*TD,* 136). Matthiessen could not accept Cowperwood's response with the unquestioning admiration that Dreiser could, but he was forced to acknowledge its degree of authenticity. When one compares *The Financier,* and even part of *The Titan,* with such contemporary works as David Graham Phillips's *The Master Rogue* (1905), Upton Sinclair's *The Metropolis* (1908) and *The Money Changers* (1908), Frank Norris's *The Pit* (1903), or even Robert Herrick's *The Memoirs of an American Citizen* (1905), one realizes how much more deeply Dreiser seemed to understand the American businessman than other novelists of the period.

Yet whatever the margin of Dreiser's success in comprehending the drives of an insider like Cowperwood, who gets to the top by dint of his energy and his lack of scruples, Matthiessen was convinced that Dreiser's real gifts lay in understanding the outsider, the victim, the pariah, or, in Dreiser's own words, "the sensitive and seeking individual in his pitiful struggle with nature—with his enormous urges and his pathetic equipment" (quoted, *TD,* 189). Dreiser returned to this figure in *An American Tragedy* (1925), the book that Matthiessen considered his masterpiece. Nowhere previously had Dreiser managed to achieve the same degree of detachment from a character so pathetic, a character so completely at the mercy of his environment that he is driven to the point of committing murder simply by having accidentally read a newspaper account of a drowning. This kind of situation could have stirred Dreiser's readiness to empathize, to pity what is merely hopeless, but in this novel his compassion was balanced with insight. He could write so movingly about Clyde Griffith's illusions because he realized how shabby they were, how incommensurate with the meretricious objects that fed them.

Dreiser still exhibited his old difficulty in portraying women. Although his treatment of Clyde's developing relationship with Roberta was as affecting as any love affair he had ever described, his explanation of Clyde's new attraction to Sondra Finchley was a disaster. The problem seemed to derive from the limitations of Dreiser's own experience. When he restricted himself to the kind of women he had known in his youth, he could be fairly convincing, but when he reached beyond a certain point on the social scale, he suddenly found himself out of his element and could only resort to clichés. Yet Dreiser's difficulties with Sondra Finchley were not sufficient to destroy the impression made by the book as a whole. The sections devoted to Clyde's awakening feelings of excitement and promise, and particularly the passages dealing with his experiences at the Green-Davidson, Matthiessen found generally admirable; and in response to the many charges brought against the last third of the novel, occupied solely with the trial and its aftermath, Matthiessen was content to quote Eisenstein, who said *An American Tragedy* was "as broad and shoreless as the Hudson, . . . as immense as life itself" (quoted, *TD,* 199).

Matthiessen was less interested in grading the novel on its perfection of form than in understanding its central values. Though he believed that the novel's overall proportions were essentially correct and that most of the smaller details were adequately realized, he was primarily concerned to pass judgment on the novel's character as American and its status as a tragedy. As to the novel being peculiarly American, he could cite many relevant details. Clyde's yearning for success was among the most approved of American ambitions, and his struggle displayed all the fierce elements of the competitive spirit. His rootlessness was in typical contrast with the more fixed patterns of European young people, and the "unthinking narrow moralism," both of Clyde's family and of Roberta's, constituted what Dreiser described as "excellent examples of that native type of Americanism which resists facts and reveres illusion" (quoted, *TD*, 202). There was also the refusal of American girls to associate with foreigners in the factory where Clyde worked, and the fact that the question of Clyde's guilt or innocence was eventually reduced to "a mere incident in the struggle between rival politicians" (*TD*, 202). But the primary factor determining Dreiser's choice of the word *American*, Matthiessen believed, was his strong emphasis on the importance of economic values. Dreiser could remember how passionately he had once desired to be wealthy, and Matthiessen points out that "he recalled how, furthermore, 'pride and show, and even waste, were flaunted in a new and still fairly virgin land—in the face of poverty and want not on the part of those who would not work, but the poverty and want of those who were all too eager to work, and on almost any terms' " (*TD*, 201). Dreiser had long since grown deeply critical of such values, but he understood the power of their allurement so well that he could write compassionately about those unable to resist their attractions.

To explain Dreiser's use of the word *tragedy* was more difficult. Dreiser had worked so diligently to undermine Clyde's heroic stature that there seemed to be nothing tragic about him at all. Lacking not only the power of will but also the element of free choice, Clyde's tragedy—if such it deserved to be called—could admit of no catharsis because it had no elements of real conflict. In writing about Clyde, Matthiessen suggests, Dreiser had simply tried to illustrate his belief "that man is 'a waif and an interloper in nature,' which desires only 'to work through him' and that he has 'no power to make his own way' " (*TD*, 205). Despite Dreiser's claim that this predicament constituted "the essential tragedy of life" (quoted, *TD*, 204–05), Matthiessen did not see how it could issue in tragedy in the traditional sense. Dreiser's novel therefore obliges one to make a distinction between tragic form, which it lacks, and tragic vision, which it possesses. "Dreiser has not shaped a tragedy in any of the traditional uses of the term," Matthiessen concluded, "and yet he has written out of a profoundly tragic sense of man's fate. He has made us hear, with more and more cumulative power, the 'disastrous beating' of the Furies' wings" (*TD*, 207)

In order to establish more clearly what elements in our national life were expressed by *An American Tragedy*, Matthiessen compared the novelist with Clarence Darrow, one of the book's most enthusiastic readers and one of Dreiser's longtime admirers. Matthiessen found that both Dreiser and Darrow united a pervasive skepticism with a belief in humane values. As Dreiser in *An American Tragedy* shared Darrow's "chief concern" with "society's immense fallibility in arriving at justice," so Darrow's "most condensed conclusion could have served as an epigraph for Dreiser's treatment of Clyde: 'I have always felt sympathy for all living things. . . . I have judged none, and therefore condemned none. I believe that I have excused all who are forced to live awhile upon the earth. I am satisfied that they have done their best with what they had' " (*TD*, 209).

Though Matthiessen did not comment on these values, it is difficult to see how he could have accepted them entire. His own view of man, heavily indebted to traditions that stress the evil within man as well as the evil without, makes it unlikely that he could have found satisfaction in Darrow's conviction, which laid the blame for man's suffering solely on externals. But Matthiessen's interest had changed. Whereas in an earlier period he would certainly have challenged the ethical superficiality of this blanket exoneration of human failure, now he wanted to demonstrate its rationale and measure its credibility. Realizing that the grounds for Darrow's curious admixture of skepticism and faith had become more tenuous and fragile since 1932, when *The Story of My Life* was published, Matthiessen felt that Darrow's values raised the question "of how long positive values can endure only as the aftershine of something that has been lost" (*TD*, 210).

This is the question that Matthiessen brought to a consideration of Dreiser's politics and philosophy, and, further, it is the question he believed had been chiefly responsible for driving Dreiser further toward the Left in social theory and closer to accepting transcendence in religion. Dreiser's course was by no means direct or unimpeded, but clearly he had traveled a considerable distance from the social and political views he had formulated after reading Spencer, Tyndall, and Huxley. Matthiessen believed the major turning points in Dreiser's attitudes were his visit to the Soviet Union in 1927, which resulted in *Dreiser Looks at Russia* (1928), and his long automobile trip across the United States in 1930, at the beginning of the Great Depression, which provided the material for *Tragic America* (1931). In the beginning Dreiser had insisted that stress on the inherent equality of all men was "one of the fundamental errors of our system of government"; later he swung around to the view that all men, regardless of their differing abilities, "should have equal *consideration,* not merely equal *rights,* before the law" (quoted, *TD*, 223). He had long since learned how destructive the lawless individualism of Frank Cowperwood could be, and he now realized that the goal of political justice would remain an illusion so long as wealth was concentrated in the hands of a few. His travels had provided him with fresh evidence that the American system was in danger of collapsing, and that threat encouraged him to put renewed faith in "the masses, from which much good has already come and will come in the future" (quoted, *TD*, 223).

Matthiessen did not duck the critical issue raised by Dreiser's stand in much of his later political writing. As the world moved closer to war, Dreiser frequently echoed Communist positions he little understood, and "often seemed very close to one of the worst danger points of our time—an unqualified acceptance of mass force for the good it can theoretically do" (*TD*, 231). What saved him from ever quite reaching it, Matthiessen believed, was his deepening commitment to equality, which convinced him that freedom requires a preservation of the rights not only of groups but also of individuals. As his political sense matured, therefore, Dreiser gave up pushing the claims of one against the other. The real problem, he eventually perceived, was to reconstruct society so as to ensure a measure of justice for both groups and individuals, a goal he believed could be realized only through socialism. How, then, was one to interpret Dreiser's decision to join the Communist Party? Matthiessen might have dismissed this gesture as one of the last acts of a foolish old man, but instead he tried to understand it against the background of the times, and in doing so shed further light on his own state of mind:

His major concern was the prevention of further wars, which he was convinced would destroy civilization. He had slowly learned the lesson that there could be no humane life in the United States until the inequities should be removed that had thwarted or destroyed so many of the characters in his fiction. He now believed that the next step was to do everything he could to break down the destructive barriers of nationalism, and to work for equity among all the peoples of the world. Otherwise there would be no world in which to live. (*TD*, 233)

Dreiser was pushed in the direction of communism because he had had to revise his feelings about man's place in relation to the cosmos. In one sense, of course, his attitudes remained consistent. Even though he thought of himself as a naturalist, he had no "fixed philosophy" he wanted to illustrate in his fiction, and he remained largely ignorant of the specific theoretical tenets of a program such as Zola's. The term "naturalist" applied to Dreiser, Matthiessen insisted, only because he, like Melville, was absorbed in the question of man's relation to nature: "This is what gave Dreiser's books their peculiar breadth: they are universal, not in their range of human experience, but in the sense that an only partly known universe presses upon and dominates his searching consciousness of what happens to all his characters" (*TD*, 236).

Matthiessen acknowledged, however, that in another sense Dreiser's basic attitudes underwent substantial alteration. From his earlier rejection of belief in a purposeful universe, he moved to an almost mystical acceptance of cosmic wholeness; this new interest in life's unity led to renewed emphasis upon the need for solidarity with men as well as with nature. Matthiessen brought out the obvious parallel with Whitman at this point, but the comparison he drew with Thoreau is even more illuminating. Dreiser appreciated Thoreau because of his refusal to limit life to a mechanical process and his unwillingness to subordinate the individual to the group. In Matthiessen's reconstruction, Thoreau seems to have answered Dreiser's simultaneous need to believe in an "unconquerably limitless universe" that exercises "a universal and apparently beneficent control . . . however dark and savage its results or expressions may seem to us at times" (*TD,* 240), and to believe that the best society is one that preserves the widest freedom of opportunity for its individual members. That these two commitments were not capable of reconciliation was of no apparent consequence to Dreiser. His lack of sophistication in processes of formal thought saved him, just as it had saved Whitman before him, from perceiving the barriers that might logically oppose his effort to synthesize discordant realms of experience. As Matthiessen wisely remarked, "the only kind of coherence that one can find in such diverse and apparently contradictory pursuits is in the unity of personality behind them" (*TD,* 240). For Dreiser, that unity remained firm all the way down to his last novel.

That *The Bulwark* (1946) was different from Dreiser's earlier novels could not be denied. Its artless, almost wooden, prose, its bare chronological structure, its lack of social documentation, and its explicitly religious ethos immediately gave it a reputation as a mutant in the Dreiser canon. Though *The Bulwark* could not stand comparison with *Sister Carrie* or *An American Tragedy,* Matthiessen felt that Dreiser had at least discovered a new form for what he wanted to say. A symbolic rather than a naturalistic novel, *The Bulwark* was authentic the way a parable is—as the expression of a simple, even primitive, truth. Solon Barnes, the novel's "bulwark" against change, was obviously Dreiser's chief symbol, and "the central truth that he wanted to affirm through Solon was that living authority lies not in the harsh judging mind but in the purified and renewed affections of the heart" (*TD,* 249). Matthiessen never doubted for a moment that Dreiser's directness in trying to express this truth in *The Bulwark* was a far cry from the bleak and anguished statements in many of his earlier novels, but he was also convinced that the truth itself had been there all along: "Like Melville in the forty years from *Moby-Dick* and *Pierre* to *Billy Budd,* he had progressed from a bitter questioning of the universe to a more serene acceptance—and yet his deepest burden was still compassion over all that remained inscrutable" (*TD,* 249).

Matthiessen had to take this development seriously because it coincided with many of his own deepest convictions. Dreiser had finally come to stand pretty much where Matthiessen himself wanted to stand, and Matthiessen could not resist displaying his gratitude by treating Dreiser's spiritual odyssey as more noteworthy and relevant than it actually was. The important point for Matthiessen, however, was not where Dreiser eventually wound up but how he got there. Lacking both education and talent, Dreiser had been forced to rely solely upon experience and had thus arrived at this position strictly on his own. For writing only what he knew to be true and for remaining true, even at the expense of clumsiness, only to what he actually knew, Matthiessen viewed Dreiser's life as well as his work as exemplary, a point of illumination and even of hope in a steadily darkening world.

Yet there is no gainsaying that it may have cost Matthiessen dear to accept this view. A former friend has suggested in private that Matthiessen's work on the Dreiser book is what finally drove him to suicide. Even if this theory is rejected as implausible, *Theodore Dreiser* still furnishes evidence that Matthiessen was losing what Hemingway referred to as "the old thing, the holding of his purity of line through the maximum of exposure." In spite of his clear understanding of Dreiser's strengths, Matthiessen could no longer explain them in wholly convincing terms. It is not that he was wrong about Dreiser's power deriving, as Dorothy Dudley put it, from his "genius for caring," or about Dreiser's virtues being those of a journeyman painter, only that his discussion of such issues had lost their edge and bite, as though he was seeking to convince himself that Dreiser did indeed possess such attributes while he was trying to describe them. And when Matthiessen moved on to comparisons of Dreiser and Melville or Dreiser and Thoreau or even Dreiser and Whitman, he overlooked the equally crucial points of contrast which in earlier years he would have used as a tool of measurement and evaluation.

Theodore Dreiser displays clear signs of Matthiessen's increasing strain and fatigue. In the suicide note Matthiessen left behind at the Manger Hotel near Boston's Old North Station, he spoke of having suffered severe attacks of depression over the past several years which left him feeling that he could no longer be of use either to his profession or to his friends.[7] This was a desperate conclusion but wholly in character, for it shows what finally resolved Matthiessen to take his own life. It was not the pessimism of Dreiser's early novels from which, admittedly, he had such difficulty shaking free, or the darkening world situation which he conceded to be an influence upon his present state of mind, or the fear of public exposure as a Communist sympathizer or a homosexual, or his heightened sense of isolation from the mainstream of American life, or even the loss of devoted and beloved friends; rather, his suicide stemmed from the combined effect of all these sources of anxiety, which prevented him from maintaining any longer the delicate balance of forces within himself, and which consequently made it impossible for him to bring all of himself to his life and work, to make his criticism an act of the whole man.

Matthiessen's decision to commit suicide was a tragic decision, but not a wholly despairing one. In deciding to terminate his own suffering, he was not giving up but only giving in; he was yielding to the agonizing realization that he could no longer function in the face of problems at once personal, political, and professional as he felt he should and must. His dying, like his living, was an attempt to remain true to his deepest sense of himself. And by striving to remain true, to be one of those who, as Coleridge says, "really know their knowledge," Matthiessen made his life come full circle with his work. He attested once again to the Emersonian integrity of being which he himself could finally achieve, if at all, only in death.

---

[7] For the complete suicide note, see Rackliffe, "Notes for a Character Study," pp. 259–60.

CHAPTER SIX

The Nature and Quality
of Matthiessen's Achievement

The critic's business is, I think, not the avoidance of subjectivity, but its purification; not the shunning of what is disputable, but the cleansing and deepening of the dispute. As a teacher he is involved in a task which would appear impossible by the standards of the scientific laboratory: to teach what, strictly speaking, cannot be taught, but only "caught," like a passion, a vice or a virtue. This "impossibility" is the inspiration of his work. There are no methods that comprehend his subject; only methods, perhaps, that produce the intellectual pressure and temperature in which perception crystallizes into conviction and learning into a sense of value.

> Erich Heller
> *The Disinherited Mind*

IF THE ultimate value of a critic lies in the maturity and prescience of his judgments, F. O. Matthiessen's reputation as a critic of American life and letters is secure. As early as 1929 he perceived a need for the kind of inquiry into the Puritan origins of American culture which has since been handsomely provided by Samuel Eliot Morison, Perry Miller, Kenneth Murdock, Edmund Morgan, Daniel Boorstin, and a host of others. Matthiessen's conviction—for which he was indebted to Frederick Jackson Turner—that the frontier was an important factor in the making of the American mind was ably confirmed by the pioneering work of Henry Nash Smith and later extended by such critics and historians as Leo Marx, John William Ward, and Edwin Fussell. Finally, Matthiessen's desire to see literary movements treated as integral responses to the spirit of their times has been fulfilled many times over in the work of scholars like Adrienne Koch, R. W. B. Lewis, Alfred Kazin, Frederick J. Hoffman, Werner Berthoff, Harry Levin, Roy Harvey Pearce, Jay Martin, and Larzer Ziff, to name only a few.

Matthiessen's prescience, however, extended far beyond his ability to predict the future of American scholarship. His unusual powers of foresight enabled him to recognize the importance of major writers long before they had achieved anything like serious recognition. Although the term "American renaissance" has now become part of the lingua franca of American criticism, neither the period itself nor its seminal figures were seen in any but the dimmest outlines before 1941, when Matthiessen's book of that title was published. Six years earlier Matthiessen had published his pioneering study of T. S. Eliot which did so much to revise critical theory and taste during the late 1930s and early 1940s; in 1944, three years after the appearance of *American Renaissance,* Matthiessen brought out the first of his three books on Henry James, which helped initiate the James revival of the late 1940s and contributed heavily to the growing interest in the theory of fiction. Yet Matthiessen's extensive work on craftsmen like James and Eliot did not blind him to the lesser virtues of a Sherwood Anderson or a Theodore Dreiser, the latter serving as an important link for Matthiessen between the generation of Hawthorne and Melville and the generation of the great moderns.

Moreover, during World War II and after, when the primary critical attention of the country was focused abroad and its taste so often fixed upon the major talents, Matthiessen continued to reveal a remarkable sensitivity to authentic minor figures like John Crowe Ransom and Katherine Anne Porter, who were transmitting, as Matthiessen said of Miss Porter, in a less conspicuous but no less scrupulous way, a sense of "that true and human world of which the artist is a living part" (*RC,* 71). Even earlier, during the middle and late thirties, Matthiessen was one of the few American critics who realized the limited but unquestionable social significance of regionalists like Willa Cather and Sarah Orne Jewett. Both these writers were able, through a patient mastery of their craft, to convey a sense of what was about to be lost as America was suddenly transformed from a rural, agrarian nation into an urban, industrial society.

Independence of mind and catholicity of taste were the hallmarks of Matthiessen's best criticism. A direct result of his firm commitment to imagination, sympathy, perspective, and balance, they issued in that manifold sense of variousness, complexity, and difficulty which, as Lionel Trilling has so ably argued,[1] have always been the distinguishing attributes of the truly liberal mind. What Matthiessen was continually striving for in his usually forceful, sometimes halting, but always circumspect prose was that constant modulation of perception and judgment which he considered one of the critic's essential virtues. Like Arnold before him, Matthiessen was of the opinion that the critical imagination should be *ondoyant et divers.*

Taken together, these convictions gave Matthiessen's criticism an extraordinary flexibility and scope, which accounts not only for the variety of materials he was willing to consider but also for the different kinds of criticism he brought to bear upon them. As a critic who shared the modern predisposition to view literature as primarily a thing of words, Matthiessen practiced the close linguistic analysis of fiction, as well as of poetry, which has become the staple of the intrinsic critic. Yet, believing that carefully modulated prose and beautifully rhythmic poetry both depend for their force upon something more than a writer's way with words, he pushed the analysis of rhetoric and diction further than most intrinsic critics. Rhythm in poetry depended, for Matthiessen, upon a writer's sense of physical and emotional movement in the life around him. Thus an analysis of rhythm inevitably led to a description of a writer's sense of his own age and its particular tempo. A feeling for words and their possible uses presupposed a writer's awareness of the tradition in which those words acquired their primary connotations and a sense of the circumambient possibilities which might permit them to acquire new ones. Hence an examination of an artist's language required an investigation of his awareness and reappropriation of the historical tradition to which he was indebted, and, beyond that, a close inspection of the cultural conditions that might have conspired to release him from the burden of that tradition.

But Matthiessen did not stop here. If he assumed with modern criticism in general that literature can be understood only in

[1] See preface to *The Liberal Imagination* (Garden City, N.Y.: Doubleday Anchor Books, 1957), pp. vii–xiii.

terms of principles and aims intrinsic to its own mode of being, he was convinced that literature cannot be evaluated—as it must be if the critic is to execute his full responsibility—without an appreciation of the conditions that, as it were, generated those principles and aims. Each specific work must be comprehended in terms of its own context, where context is taken to mean something acquired instead of given, something organic and vital instead of static and lifeless—in short, something that arises out of particular needs and is created to fulfill specific purposes. Such an assumption encouraged Matthiessen to employ the widest possible variety of critical approaches to particular texts: the economic to Melville's *Redburn;* the political and psychological to Hawthorne's *The House of the Seven Gables;* the philosophical to Dreiser's later novels; the rhetorical and linguistic to Emily Dickinson's poetry; the theological and metaphysical to Eliot's later poetry and Melville's *Moby-Dick;* the biographical and historical to Sarah Orne Jewett and, later, to the James family; the sociological and textual to modern American poetry; and, finally, the mythic and archetypal to account fully for the achievement of the mid-nineteenth-century American literary renaissance. Matthiessen's use of each of these modes of approach arose out of what he took to be the requirements of the subject at hand. Yet he refused to make special claims for any one of them. They were tools of analysis and nothing more, implements in the service of coming to grips with particular works by placing them as accurately and completely as possible both within their own contexts as well as within ours.

Matthiessen's emphasis upon the critic's obligation to the text itself and to the necessity of recovering it for contemporary appropriation indicated something more than a pragmatic approach to literary criticism. His twofold purpose flowed with perfect consistency from his deepest assumptions about the nature of literature and issued in his strongest convictions about the responsibilities of criticism. Works of literature, to him, were not mere objects to be valued exclusively for their own sake but also for what, in our appreciation of them, they might still become if, through an act of historical repossession, we could perceive their unspent potential. The individual text was at once a symbolic artifact and also a kind of resource which retained an element of vitality to communicate to the present. And if individual works of literature thus conceived should by their very nature lead us toward life rather than away from it, then the most fully responsive and penetrating criticism should possess an underlying social and political relevance. As there was no ultimate conflict for Matthiessen between art and experience, so there could be no absolute distinctions between a purely literary criticism on the one hand and a more general social, cultural, and moral criticism on the other.

These assumptions gave to Matthiessen's best work an unusual power and relevance, not because he was always successful in unifying them, but rather because he had learned, though only after considerable experimentation and much painful experience, how to exploit and utilize the tensions among them. There was a taut energy of perception in his criticism, an uncompromising honesty and truthfulness, which set it in a class apart. Wanting no blurred edges, no cheap compromises, no easy solutions, Matthiessen simply "steeled himself," as Leo Marx once said, "to speak from as deep in his heart as he knew how to reach,"[2] and if what he found there occasionally lacked clarity or complete consistency, it more than made up for such defects in candor, seriousness, and lack of remoteness. Matthiessen was one of those rare critics who is willing to risk personal and intellectual disruption for the sake of doing full justice to recalcitrant and even hostile materials, but he also shared with Yeats the view that "Belief makes the mind abundant."[3] It was this unique combination in him of vulnerability and confidence, of openness and conviction, which made his writing so singular an experience to read, which gave it integrity and nobility at the same time. Other critics might be more learned, more sophisticated, or more polished, but few were so wise, so capacious, or so sensitive in registering their own divided responses to the work before them. Matthiessen would not permit his own imagination of large concerns to blind him to what were often uncongenial and contradictory facts; by the same token, he was equally reluctant to allow his awareness of those frequently in-

[2] Leo Marx, "The Teacher," *Monthly Review* 2 (1950): 211.
[3] Quoted by Alfred Kazin, *On Native Grounds* (Garden City, N.Y.: Doubleday Anchor Books, 1956), p. 349.

tractible facts to deter him from placing all his criticism at the service of a unified core of humane values.

The question still to be raised is whether Matthiessen had to pay too subtle a moral price for his various commitments, and whether he was, as George Abbott White has recently queried, guilty of certain lapses in moral vision.[4] For example, how, White asks, following a line of questioning first opened up by Granville Hicks, could Matthiessen the socialist, the radical democrat, "have the regard (even fear) for Eliot that he did. Eliot, let us say it plainly, with his very bad politics?"[5] The simplest answer would be that Matthiessen made the same distinctions Eliot did between the man who suffers and the poet who writes and therefore did not find it necessary to share the poet's beliefs in order to appreciate his poetry. But this answer would really beg the question, for Matthiessen never preserved these distinctions as carefully as Eliot insisted one should when he first articulated them, and then Eliot, in turn, eventually abandoned or at least modified them in both his later criticism and his later poetry. The fact is (as I have tried to show in chapter ii) that Eliot's early critical position created real problems; many of the ideas he had first used to support a flexible and broadly organicist orientation could easily be turned upside down to uphold a doctrinaire formalism based not only on bad politics but also on bad religion. Nonetheless, Matthiessen's lapse in this instance was not so much moral as intellectual; he simply failed to perceive the connection between Eliot's earlier ideas, which he immediately embraced as a counterforce to contemporary critical excesses, and the unattractive later ideas which, when the time came round, he firmly rejected.[6]

[4] See George Abbott White, "Ideology and Literature: *American Renaissance* and F. O. Matthiessen," *Tri-Quarterly* 23/24 (1972): 430–500. Although this essay did not come to my attention until I had nearly completed my work, I still owe White a considerable debt. His close interweaving of biography, exposition, and commentary provided me with an excellent model to emulate (to say nothing of several important facts that had escaped my notice); and in his incisive, provocative analysis, sympathetic as it is, of Matthiessen's moral lapses, he challenged me to sharpen the focus of my own somewhat divergent interpretation.

[5] *Ibid.*, p. 489.

[6] Insofar as I understand him, White tries to explain at least part of Eliot's influence over Matthiessen by suggesting that Matthiessen, as a homosexual and an Episcopalian, shared Eliot's typically Anglican feeling of revulsion for the physical, particularly for heterosexual union. Noting the variety of ways in which Eliot depicts the sexual act "as

A more significant point is that Matthiessen had his own reasons for considering Eliot important as both critic and poet,
reasons that had little to do with either religious orthodoxy or
political conservatism. Matthiessen felt deeply that Eliot, whatever his professed beliefs, possessed an unerring grasp of certain essentials. The Eliot whom Matthiessen revered, and who
had so strong an influence on his career, was the writer who
strove in all his work to effect through form as well as theme
such reconciliation of opposites as was possible to one whose
world seemed, on Matthiessen's reading, "increasingly threatened with new dark ages" (*ATSE,* 195). No matter what his
articles of faith, then, Matthiessen's Eliot remained preeminently the tragic Eliot, whose chief value resided in his unflinch-
ing analysis and acceptance of human limitations. But in this
acceptance Matthiessen detected no trace of political or moral
acquiescence. If the tragic writer deserved any epithet, so far as
Matthiessen was concerned, he had to be called a radical in the
fullest sense of the word:

> The value of the tragic writer has always lain in the uncompromising honesty
> with which he has cut through appearances to face the real conditions of man's
> lot, in his refusal to be deceived by an easy answer, in the unflinching, if
> agonized, expression of what he knows to be true. The effect of such integrity
> is not to oppress the reader with a sense of burdens too great to be borne,

---

the most disgusting possible event in which two human beings could participate" (*ibid.,*
p. 494), White asserts that Eliot's amalgam of fear and guilt "radiated an authority that
was in some deep sense determining" for Matthiessen as well (*ibid.,* p. 495). Aside from
the fact that time and again Matthiessen praised a poet like Whitman for having re-
deemed the experience of the physical and especially the sexual as subjects worthy of
serious literary treatment, I wonder if any amalgam of fear and guilt which Eliot and
Matthiessen conceivably might have shared can be said to have stemmed from their
mutual relation to Anglicanism. Sexual anxiety, to be sure, comes in a variety of shapes,
sizes, *and* denominations, but the Anglican church has not been traditionally known as
one of its sponsors. Indeed, the Anglican tradition might well have proven an important
emotional as well as spiritual resource for Matthiessen—if he ever really shared the kind
of prudery White finds in Eliot—precisely because it placed a positive rather than a
negative interpretation upon the physicality of human existence. As the Christian doctrine of the Incarnation—the dogmatic keystone of whatever theological position one
can derive from the Anglican form of Protestantism—expressed it, God so loved the
world, not that he sent his own Son to serve as a sacrifice for its sins, or that he might
offer his Son as a vicarious payment for man's guilt in originally disobeying him, but
rather that he might, in the person of his Son, take upon himself the world's very flesh
and blood in order to show man that the only way to salvation is through the concrete
and the actual and not in flight from them.

but to bring him some release. For, if it is part of the function of every great artist to transform his age, the tragic writer does so not by delivering an abstract idealization of life, but by giving to the people who live in the age a full reading of its weakness and horror; yet, concurrently, by revealing some enduring potentiality of good to be embraced with courage and with an ecstatic sense of its transfiguring glory. Through the completeness of his portrayal of the almost insupportable conditions of human existence, he frees his audience from the oppression of fear; and stirring them to a new heart by his presentation of an heroic struggle against odds, he also enables them to conceive anew the means of sustaining and improving their own lives. Only thus can he communicate both "the horror" and "the glory." (*ATSE*, 107)

A yet more serious charge of moral lapse was made by Frederick C. Stern in his fine unpublished dissertation, "The Lost Cause: F. O. Matthiessen, Christian Socialist as Critic." The charge is more serious if only because it is more difficult to answer in a fully satisfactory way; it appeals to prejudices so deeply ingrained in the modern mind that they seem almost beyond challenge. Stern's basic argument, and one in which many others concur, is that the chief sources of Matthiessen's view of life and letters—Christianity, socialism, and tragedy— were inherently incompatible, and that, further, Matthiessen's beliefs as a Christian frequently interfered with his judgments as a critic, particularly as a critic of tragedy. Stern's charge is not restricted to the contention that Matthiessen's claims about the existence of something like Christian tragedy may have rested on shaky historical and theoretical grounds; he goes further, suggesting that Matthiessen's allegiance to interpretations of life as mutually exclusive as Christianity and tragedy was wrong from the start, since the former puts a positive interpretation on precisely those facts that the latter cannot. The issue is not whether Matthiessen was occasionally tempted to load the dice, so to speak, to read certain works more affirmatively than a close reading of them may have warranted; rather, it is whether Matthiessen was not in some deep and personally destructive way self-deceived, struggling to reconcile in his criticism two views of experience he knew—or should have known—with his heart to be utterly opposed.

Such an argument is not entirely without foundation. Matthiessen's reading of *Billy Budd*, for example, as "a reassertion of the heart" seems strained and unconvincing just insofar as it appears to reflect the position where Matthiessen wanted Melville to come out. Melville had to find his way through to the other side of cynicism and despair, it could be argued, almost because as a Christian Matthiessen was unable to contemplate the possibility that he had not. Or, again, Matthiessen was compelled to find beneficial, even redemptive, effects flowing from the suffering of so many of Hawthorne's characters simply because he could not himself accept a world in which suffering was without moral significance. These examples, and one could probably find others, provide some evidence that Matthiessen was guilty of lapses in judgment which were the result of his occasional tendency to allow his critical judgments to be dictated by his beliefs, but they in no way show that such critical lapses derived from a more fundamental flaw in Matthiessen's moral vision. If he was from time to time guilty of placing too affirmative an interpretation on works that were essentially pessimistic, he was certainly not deceived either personally or intellectually by his attempt to comprehend both the tragic and Christian elements within such works. To suppose that Christianity assumes a world in which all suffering is deserved and all events are preordained and fundamentally just is as fatally misleading and historically inaccurate as to argue that tragedy assumes a world in which the deepest suffering is unmerited and the most important events are unjust and arbitrary. As tragedy admits of more than one kind or form, so Christianity admits of more than one theology or view of the whole.[7]

More important, however, Matthiessen knew that Christianity has its tragic component just as tragedy has its redemptive. The Christian, as he stressed in his discussion of the later Eliot, is no more adept at overcoming or escaping or transcending the human condition than the next man. He simply has a slightly better chance of surviving that condition if he is willing to pay the price—a price, as Eliot insisted in *Four Quartets,* "Costing not less than everything."[8] The choice, as Eliot posed it, is simple but stark: "We only live, only suspire / Consumed by either fire

---

[7] For an excellent discussion of this issue, see Dorothea Krook, *Elements of Tragedy* (New Haven: Yale University Press, 1969), esp. pp. 253–71.

[8] T. S. Eliot, "Little Gidding," in *The Complete Poems and Plays, 1909–1950* (New York: Harcourt, Brace, 1952), p. 145.

or fire."[9] Such a choice, which Eliot called "an occupation for a saint,"[10] could be viewed as the tragic hero's occupation as well, only changed because the saint, unlike the tragic hero, may be said to receive by an act of grace a return on his investment, which he in no sense deserves. But like the tragic hero, he has no guarantee on his "something given / And taken, in a lifetime's death in love, / Ardour and selflessness and self-surrender."[11] The Christian hero, like his counterpart in tragedy, must simply learn with Eliot's Becket that "action is suffering and suffering is action"[12] and wait for the rest, for whatever may follow "prayer, observance, discipline, thought and action," for "hints and guesses, / Hints followed by guesses."[13]

Matthiessen would not have denied that "hints and guesses" are more than most tragic heroes ever attain. The Christian hero, like Eliot's saint, was a figure who gained as well as lost, and whose gain was seen as a direct result of his willingness to lose; but many tragic heroes lost more than they gained, and their loss was the more terrible because they were willing to risk everything to gain anything. Yet Matthiessen was convinced that there was gain as well as loss even in the blackest of tragedies, for "otherwise," he wrote in another context, "we would not have so much use for poets, the secret of whose power over us lies in the way they provide most consolation when, in a *Lear* or an *Oedipus,* they are most tragic. They bring us back to a love of life by a deepened acceptance of men's constant desperate ruin, and, in the face of that, of man's heroic capacity for no less constant renewal" (*FHE,* 50).

It was this twin emphasis upon "men's constant desperate ruin" and "man's heroic capacity for no less constant renewal" which provided Matthiessen with the point of contact between all that he meant by Christianity and all that he meant by tragedy. In addition, this twin emphasis constituted the basic anthropological insight in which he rooted his own peculiar form of socialism. Grounded in a sense of life which was at once realistic and hopeful, this bipolar vision represented a balanced

[9] *Ibid.,* p. 144.
[10] "The Dry Salvages," in *ibid.,* p. 136.
[11] *Ibid.*
[12] *Murder in the Cathedral,* in *ibid.,* p. 182.
[13] "The Dry Salvages," in *ibid.,* p. 136.

view that Matthiessen believed was as far from misplaced optimism as from the alternative of despair. That Matthiessen finally found it impossible to maintain this balance for himself only heightens the importance he attached to it. Few other critics of his time were so conscious of its importance or so sensitive to the threats against it; no other critic fought harder to sustain it or paid a heavier price for its ultimate breakdown.

To say that Matthiessen's effort was ultimately attended by failure is not, however, to suggest that it was in vain. Beyond his incalculable influence upon students, colleagues, and friends, Matthiessen left a critical legacy best understood as the work, in Bruno Bettelheim's fine phrase, of an "informed heart." But the last word deserves to remain with Henry James, who once differentiated the genuine article from its many pale imitations by saying that the true critic is one capable of lifting "perception" to "the pitch of passion." This, ultimately, was Matthiessen's achievement. Until the end he was able to draw so much of his own and of his culture's experience into his criticism that his criticism contributed a new form to our cultural experience. Without Matthiessen's "pitch of passion," modern criticism would have lost something of its depth of perception and the American tradition would have been deprived of one of its "still undiminished resources."

Bibliography of the Works
of F. O. Matthiessen *

BOOKS

Sarah Orne Jewett. Boston: Houghton Mifflin, 1929.

Translation: An Elizabethan Art. Cambridge: Harvard University Press; London: Oxford University Press, 1931.

The Achievement of T. S. Eliot: An Essay on the Nature of Poetry. Boston: Houghton Mifflin; London: Oxford University Press, 1935. New and enl. ed., with chapters on the plays and *Four Quartets.* New York, London, Toronto: Oxford University Press, 1947. 3rd ed., with additional chapter by C. L. Barber. Galaxy Books; New York: Oxford University Press, 1959.

American Renaissance: Art and Expression in the Age of Emerson and Whitman. New York, London, Toronto: Oxford University Press, 1941.

Henry James: The Major Phase. New York: Oxford University Press, 1944.

Russell Cheney, 1881–1945: A Record of His Work. Published for the Memorial Exhibition, 1946–1947. Subsequently issued in New York by the Oxford University Press, 1947.

The James Family: Including Selections from the Writings of Henry James, Senior, William, Henry, and Alice James. New York: Knopf, 1947.

From the Heart of Europe. New York: Oxford University Press, 1948.

* This bibliography is a compilation of two bibliographies prepared by C. L. Barber: "A Preliminary Bibliography of F. O. Matthiessen," *Monthly Review* 2 (1950):316–22; "A Supplementary Bibliography of F. O. Matthiessen," *Monthly Review* 4 (1952):174–75. It is printed here by permission of C. L. Barber and Paul M. Sweezy. For convenience, I have followed the same divisions Barber used. The bibliography does not include work Matthiessen published as an undergraduate.

Theodore Dreiser. New York: William Sloane Associates, 1951.
The Responsibilities of the Critic: Essays and Reviews by F. O. Matthiessen. Sel. John Rackliffe. New York: Oxford University Press, 1952.

BOOKS EDITED

Stories of Writers and Artists, by Henry James. New York: New Directions, 1944.
Herman Melville: Selected Poems. "The Poets of the Year." Norfolk, Conn.: New Directions, 1944.
The American Novels and Stories of Henry James. New York: Knopf, 1947.
The Notebooks of Henry James. With Kenneth B. Murdock. New York: Oxford University Press, 1947.
The Oxford Book of American Verse. New York: Oxford University Press, 1950.

CONTRIBUTIONS TO COLLABORATIVE WORKS AND ANTHOLOGIES

"James Fenimore Cooper, Class of 1806: Novelist and Critic"; "Alphonso Taft, Class of 1853: Lawyer and Statesman"; "Oliver Wolcott, Class of 1778: Secretary of the Treasury in Washington's Cabinet." In *The Memorial Quadrangle: A Book about Yale.* Comp. Robert Dudley French. New Haven: Yale University Press; London: Oxford University Press, 1929. Pp. 162–71, 306–10, 362–66.
"New England Stories." In *American Writers on American Literature,* by thirty-seven contemporary writers. Ed. John Macy. New York: Liveright, 1931. Pp. 399–413.
"Sarah Orne Jewett." In *Dictionary of American Biography.* Vol. 10. New York: Scribner's, 1933. Pp. 70–72.
"Hart Crane." In *Dictionary of American Biography.* Vol. 21, Supplement One. New York: Scribner's, 1944. Pp. 206–8.
"The Ambassadors." In *The Question of Henry James.* Ed. F. W. Dupee. New York: Henry Holt, 1945. Pp. 218–35.
"That True and Human World." In *Accent Anthology,* selections from *Accent,* 1940–1945. Ed. Kerker Quinn and Charles Shattuck. New York: Harcourt Brace, 1946. Pp. 619–23.
"On Hawthorne's 'Young Goodman Brown' "; "On Whitman's 'When Lilacs Last in the Dooryard Bloom'd.' " Excerpts from *American Renaissance* in *Readings for Liberal Education.* Ed. L. G. Locke, W. M. Gibson, and G. Arms. New York: Rinehart, 1948. Vol. 2, pp. 495–96, 543–47.
"The Sense of His Own Age." Excerpt from *The Achievement of T. S. Eliot* in *T. S. Eliot: A Selected Critique.* Ed. Leonard Unger. New York: Rinehart, 1948. Pp. 221–35.
"Edgar Allan Poe"; "Poetry" (during the twenty-five years before 1940). In *Literary History of the United States.* Ed. Robert E. Spiller and others. New York: Macmillan, 1948. Pp. 321–45, 1335–57.
"An Opinion." In *The Case of Ezra Pound,* by Charles Norman. With opinions by Conrad Aiken, e. e. cummings, F. O. Matthiessen, William Carlos Williams, Louis Zukofsky. New York: Bodley Press, 1948. Pp. 57–59.

"The Pattern of Literature." In *Changing Patterns in American Civilization,* by Dixon Wecter and others, with preface by Robert E. Spiller. Philadelphia: University of Pennsylvania Press, 1949. Pp. 33–57.

"Emerson, Thoreau, Melville, and Whitman: Their Challenge to Writers Today." In chap. xiii, "The Writers Debate Tolstoy's Classic Theme," in *Speaking of Peace.* Ed. Daniel S. Gillmor. New York: National Council of the Arts, Sciences, and Professions, 1949. Pp. 78–79.

"Introduction." In *Fingerboard,* by Marshall Schacht. New York: Twayne Publishers, 1949.

ARTICLES

"[Four reports on life at Oxford] by F. O. Matthiessen, 1923 Oxford Rhodes Scholar." *Yale News,* vol. 47, no. 36 (6 Nov. 1923); no. 59 (4 Dec. 1923); no. 86 (22 Jan. 1924); no. 106 (19 Feb. 1924).

"Michael Wigglesworth: A Puritan Artist." *New England Quarterly* 1 (1928): 491–504.

"The Great Tradition: A Counterstatement." *New England Quarterly* 7 (1934): 223–34.

"The New Mexican Workers' Case." *New Republic* 82 (1935):361–63.

"For an Unwritten Chapter." [Discussion of *Murder in the Cathedral.*] *Harvard Advocate* 125 (1938):22–24.

"A Year of the *Kenyon Review.*" *American Oxonian* 27 (1940):83–85.

"A Teacher Takes His Stand." *Harvard Progressive* (Sept. 1940):12–14.

Statement on Wallace Stevens. *Harvard Advocate* 127 (1940):31.

"The Crooked Road." [On the development of Yeats.] *Southern Review* 7 (1941):455–70.

"Eliot's Quartets." *Kenyon Review* 5 (1943):161–78.

"No More Colleges for the Duration." *The Bridge of Eta Kappa Nu* 40 (Nov. 1943):2.

"The Humanities in Wartime." *The 1943 Harvard Album* (1943):33–37.

"James and the Plastic Arts." *Kenyon Review* 5 (1943):533–50.

"Higher Education after the War: A Symposium." With O. O. Carmichael, Virgil M. Hancher, and John W. Nason. *American Oxonian* 31 (1944):75–78.

"Henry James' Portrait of the Artist." *Partisan Review* 11 (1944):71–87.

"The Painter's Sponge and Varnish Bottle: Henry James' Revision of *The Portrait of a Lady.*" *American Bookman* 1 (1944):49–68.

"Harvard Wants to Join America." *New Republic* 113 (1945):220–21.

"The Problem of the Private Poet." [On Emily Dickinson.] *Kenyon Review* 7 (1945):584–97.

Statement. *Yale Literary Magazine* 112 (Spring 1946):18.

"Poe: An Essay." *Sewanee Review* 54 (1946):175–205.

"American Poetry, 1920–1940." *Sewanee Review* 55 (1947):24–55.

"Primarily Languge." [An article in "Homage to John Crowe Ransom . . . in honor of his Sixtieth Birthday."] *Sewanee Review* 56 (1948):391–401.

"John Crowe Ransom." *The Wind and the Rain* 5, no. 3 (1948–49):172–77. Same as "Primarily Language," *Sewanee Review* (1948), except for the omission of the three opening paragraphs.

"Phelps Putnam, 1894–1948." *Kenyon Review* 11 (1949):61–82.

"The Responsibilities of the Critic." *Michigan Alumnus Quarterly* 55 (1949): 283–92.

"Needed: Organic Connection of Theory and Practice." *Monthly Review* 2 (1950):7.

"Theodore Spencer, 1902–1949." *Contemporary Poetry* 10 (1950):36–38.

REVIEWS

"A Monument to Howells." *New Republic* 58 (1929):284–85. *Life and Letters of William Dean Howells,* ed. Mildred Howells.

"New Standards in American Criticism." *Yale Review* 18 (1929):603–4. *The Reinterpretation of American Literature,* ed. Norman Foerster; *American Criticism,* by Norman Foerster.

[Review of] *The Day of Doom . . . with Other Poems,* by Michael Wigglesworth. Ed. K. B. Murdock. *New England Quarterly* 2 (1929):512–13.

"Sherman and Huneker." *New Republic* 61 (1929):113–15. *The Life and Letters of Stuart P. Sherman,* by J. Zeitlin and H. Woodbridge; *Essays by James Huneker,* Ed. H. L. Mencken.

"The Isolation of Hawthorne." *New Republic* 61 (1930):281. *Hawthorne,* by Newton Arvin.

"A Critic of Importance." *Yale Review* 20 (1931):855–56. *Axel's Castle,* by Edmund Wilson.

[Review of] *The Life of Emerson,* by Van Wyck Brooks. *New England Quarterly* 5 (1932):819.

[Review of] *Selected Poems of William Vaughn Moody,* ed. Robert Morss Lovett. *New England Quarterly* 4 (1931):797–801.

"Mark Twain and the Jameses." *Yale Review* 22 (1932):605–9. *Mark Twain's America,* by Bernard De Voto; *The Three Jameses,* by C. Hartley Grattan; *Theater and Friendship,* by Elizabeth Robins.

[Review of] *The Great Tradition,* by Granville Hicks. *Atlantic Monthly* 152 (Dec. 1933):16+.

[Review of] *The Liberation of American Literature,* by V. F. Calverton. *New England Quarterly* 6 (1933):190–95.

[Review of] *The Life of Moses Coit Tyler,* by Howard Mumford Jones. *New England Quarterly* 7 (1934):744–50.

"Yeats and Four American Poets." *Yale Review* 23 (1934):611–17. *Talifer,* by Edwin Arlington Robinson; *Give Your Heart to the Hawks,* by Robinson Jeffers; *Now with His Love,* by John Peale Bishop; *Poems, 1924–1933,* by Archibald MacLeish; *Collected Poems,* by W. B. Yeats; *The Winding Stair,* by W. B. Yeats.

"T. S. Eliot's Drama of Becket." *Saturday Review of Literature* 12 (12 Oct. 1935): 10–11. *Murder in the Cathedral,* by T. S. Eliot.

"Society and Solitude in Poetry." *Yale Review* 25 (1936):603–7. *King Jasper,* by Edwin Arlington Robinson; *Theory of Flight,* by Muriel Rukeyser; *The Iron*

Hand, by Stanley Burnshaw; *Solstice and Other Poems,* by Robinson Jeffers; *Ideas of Order,* by Wallace Stevens.

[Review of] *The Flowering of New England,* by Van Wyck Brooks. *New England Quarterly* 9 (1936):701–9.

[Review of] *Pedlar's Progress: The Life of Bronson Alcott,* by Odell Shepart. *New England Quarterly* 10 (1937):584–91.

[Review of] *Anthology of Verse from the Yale Literary Magazine, 1836–1936,* ed. A. R. Bellinger. *New England Quarterly* 10 (1937):807–8.

"W. B. Yeats and Others." *Southern Review* 2 (1937):815–34. *The Oxford Book of Modern Verse, 1892–1935,* chosen by W. B. Yeats; *On This Island,* by W. H. Auden; *Poems, 1911–1936,* by John Hall Wheelock; *New Poems,* by Frederick Mortimer Clapp; *The Golden Fleece of California,* by Edgar Lee Masters; *Road to America,* by Frances Frost; *The Deer Come Down,* by Edward Meismiller.

"A Review of Recent Poetry." *Southern Review* 3 (1937):368–91. *Twelve Poets of the Pacific* (Yvor Winters, Janet Lewis, Clayton Stafford, Howard Baker, Henry Ramsey, Achilles Holt, J. V. Cunningham, Barbara Gibbs, Don Stanford, James Atkinson, Richard Finnegan, Ann Stanford); *Not Alone Lost,* by Robert McAlmon; *Hounds on the Mountain,* by James Still; *American Frontier,* by Elisabeth Peck; *Ornament of Honor,* by E. H. R. Altounyan; *In Sight of Mountains,* by C. A. Millspaugh; *Poems, 1929–1936,* by Dudley Fitts; *The Fall of the City,* by Archibald MacLeish; *Conversation at Midnight,* by Edna St. Vincent Millay.

[Review of] *Thirty-Six Poems,* by Robert Penn Warren. *American Oxonian* 24 (1937):94–97.

"An Absolute Music." *Yale Review* 27 (1938):173–75. *Hart Crane,* by Philip Horton.

[Review of] *Poems,* by Louis MacNeice. *Partisan Review* 4 (1938):56–60.

"In the Tradition from Emerson." *New Republic* 94 (1938):279–280. *The Triple Thinkers,* by Edmund Wilson.

"Record of Our Education." *New Republic* 95 (1938):285. *Literary Opinion in America,* ed. Morton Dauwen Zabel.

"Walt Whitman's Opinions." *New Republic* 97 (1938):50–51. *Whitman,* by Newton Arvin.

"Towards Our Understanding of Elizabethan Drama." *Southern Review* 4 (1938):398–428. *Shakespeare,* by John Middleton Murry; *The Enchanted Glass: The Elizabethan Mind in Literature,* by Hardin Craig; *Shakespeare's Young Lovers,* by E. E. Stoll; *I, William Shakespeare,* by Leslie Hoston; *Christopher Marlowe: The Man in His Time,* by John Bakeless; *Drama and Society in the Age of Jonson,* by C. L. Knights; *What Happens in Hamlet,* by J. Dover Wilson; *Prefaces to Shakespeare: Third Series: Hamlet,* by Harley Granville-Barker; *John Gielgud's Hamlet: A Record of Performance,* by Rosamond Gilder; *Shakespeare's Imagery and What It Tells Us,* by Caroline Spurgeon; *The Mediaeval Heritage of Elizabethan Tragedy,* by Willard Farnham; *Death and Elizabethan Tragedy: A Study of Convention and Opinion in the Elizabethan Drama,* by Theodore Spencer; *Shakespeare's Philosophical Patterns,* by Walter Clyde Curry.

"Footprints in the Sands." *Saturday Review of Literature* 19 (10 Dec. 1938) 7.

Young Longfellow, 1807–1843, by Lawrence Thompson.

[Review of] *U.S. One: Maine to Florida,* prepared by the Federal Writers' Project of WPA. *New England Quarterly* 12 (1939):178.

"A Good Workman." *Kenyon Review* 1 (1939):453–57. *Collected Poems, 1922–1938,* by Mark Van Doren.

"Thoreau Reconsidered." *Yale Review* 29 (1939):416–18. *Thoreau,* by Henry Seidel Canby.

[Review of] *"I Hear America . . ." Literature in the United States since 1900,* by Vernon Loggins. *American Literature* 11 (1939):224–26.

"The Best Critic of Her Day?" *New Republic* 105 (1941):314. *The Writings of Margaret Fuller,* ed. Mason Wade.

[Review of] *Edwin Arlington Robinson,* by Herman Hagedorn. *American Literature* 12 (1941):509–12.

"Twain into Clemens." *New Republic* 107 (1942):179. *Mark Twain at Work,* by Bernard DeVoto.

"The Economic Novel." *New Republic* 107 (1942):324–25.

[Review of] *The New Criticism,* by John Crowe Ransom; *The Intent of the Critic,* by Edmund Wilson, Norman Foerster, John Crowe Ransom, W. H. Auden. Ed. Donald A. Stauffer. *American Oxonian* 29 (1942):97–102.

[Review of] *Irving Babbitt: Man and Teacher,* ed. F. Manchester and and Odell Shepard; *Spanish Character and Other Essays,* by Irving Babbitt. *New England Quarterly* 15 (1942):142–46.

"Old Methods, New Horizons." *Partisan Review* 9 (1942):422–26. *The Wind Blew from the East: A Study in the Orientation of American Culture,* by Ferner Nuhn; *Writers in Crisis: The American Novel between Two Wars,* by Maxwell Geismar.

[Review of] *On Native Grounds,* by Alfred Kazin. *New England Quarterly* 16 (1943):326–28.

"A New York Childhood." *Partisan Review* 10 (1943):292–94. *Genesis: Book One,* by Delmore Schwartz.

"Milton and Our War." *New Republic* 108 (1943):674–75. *Chariot of Wrath,* by G. Wilson Knight.

"Education after the War." *New Republic* 110 (1944):121–22. *Liberal Education Reexamined,* by Theodore M. Greene and others.

"A Poet as Critic." *New Republic* 110 (1944):568. *The Shield of Achilles,* by Horace Gregory.

"Our First National Style." *New Republic* 110 (1944):353–55. *Greek Revival Architecture in America,* by Talbot Hamlin.

"Not All New, Some Good." *New Republic* 111 (1944):435–37. *New Poems: 1944,* ed. Oscar Williams.

[Review of] *Study Out the Land,* by T. K. Whipple. *American Literature* 16 (1944):157–59.

"Pilgrimage to the Distant Past." *New York Times Book Review* (1 Oct. 1944): 1+. *The World of Washington Irving,* by Van Wyck Brooks.

"The Innocent Eye." *New Republic* 111 (1944):530–2. *William Sidney Mount,* by

Bartlett Cowdrey and H. W. Williams, Jr.; *Winslow Homer,* by Lloyd Goodrich.

"American Poetry Now." *Kenyon Review* 6 (1944):683–96. *The Giant Weapon,* by Yvor Winters; *The Seven Sleepers,* by Mark Van Doren; *An Act of Life,* by Theodore Spencer; *A Wreath for the Sea,* by Robert Fitzgerald; *1 X 1* by e. e. cummings; *Selected Poems,* by Robert Penn Warren; *V-Letter,* by Karl Shapiro.

"Some Philosophers in the Sun." *New York Times Book Review* (31 Dec. 1944):1 +. *Cannery Row,* by John Steinbeck.

"Tennyson." *New York Times Book Review* (28 Jan. 1945):4. *A Selection from the Poems of Alfred Lord Tennyson,* with an introduction, by W. H. Auden.

"Fragmentary and Whole." *New Republic* 112 (1945):232–33. *The Wedge,* by William Carlos Williams; *The Soldier,* by Conrad Aiken; *The Winter Sea,* by Allen Tate.

[Review of] *Puritanism and Democracy,* by Ralph Barton Perry. *PM* (21 Jan. 1945):15–16.

[Review of] *Western Journals of Washngton Irving,* ed. John Francis McDermott. *Nation* 160 (1945):22.

"Portrait of the Literary Scholar." *Saturday Review of Literature* 28 (9 June 1945):14. *Literary Study and the Scholarly Profession,* by Hardin Craig.

[Review of] *The Leaning Tower,* by Katherine Anne Porter. *Accent* 5 (1945): 121–23.

"A Classic Study of America." *New York Times Book Review* 5 (15 April 1945): 1+. *Democracy in America,* by Alexis de Tocqueville. Ed. Phillips Bradley.

"The Essays of Arthur Koestler." *New York Times Book Review* (27 May 1945): 1+. *The Yogi and the Commissar, and Other Essays,* by Arthur Koestler.

[Review of] *Hawthorne the Artist,* by Leland Schubert. *New England Quarterly* 18 (1945):265–68.

"Whitman: His Poetry and Prose." *New York Times Book Review* (29 July 1945): 1+. *The Portable Walt Whitman,* selected and with notes by Mark Van Doren.

"On the Confusions in Poetry." *New York Times Book Review* (28 Oct. 1945): 1+. *Essay on Rime,* by Karl Shapiro.

"Not Quite the Real Thing." *New Republic* 113 (1945):766–68. *The Short Stories of Henry James,* ed. Clifton Fadiman.

"God, Mammon and Mr. Dreiser." *New York Times Book Review* (24 March 1946):1+. *The Bulwark,* by Theodore Dreiser.

"James T. Farrell's Human Comedy." *New York Times Book Review* (12 May 1946):1+. *Bernard Clare,* by James T. Farrell.

"Refugees from America." *New Republic* 114 (1946):739–40. *Southern California Country,* by Carey McWilliams.

"A New Appraisal of Shelley." *New York Times Book Review* (5 Jan. 1947):5. *Shelley: A Life Story,* by Edmund Blunden.

"Wallace Stevens at 67." *New York Times Book Review* (20 April 1947):4. *Transport to Summer,* by Wallace Stevens.

"L. C. Knights' Essays on Critics and Criticism." *New York Times Book Review*

(15 June 1947):4. *Explorations: Essays in Criticism Mainly on the Literature of the Seventeenth Century,* by L. C. Knights.

"About Paul Rosenfeld." *New York Times Book Review* (2 May 1948):6. *Paul Rosenfeld: Voyages in the Arts,* ed. Jerome Mellquist and Lucie Wiese.

"The Real Education." *New Republic* 119 (1948): 30–31. *The Young Henry Adams,* by Ernest Samuels.

[Review of] *A Bibliography of the Published Writings of Sarah Orne Jewett,* comp. Clara Carter Weber and Carl J. Weber. *Colby Library Quarterly,* ser. 2, no. 12 (1949):198–201.

"Classic Models for Modern Critics." *New Republic* 120 (6 June 1949):21–22. *Lectures in Criticism,* by R. P. Blackmur, Benedetto Croce, Henri Peyre, John Crowe Ransom, Herbert Read, Allen Tate. Bollingen Series XVI.

UNPUBLISHED

"Oliver Goldsmith as Essayist and Critic." B. Litt. thesis, Oxford. in Cambridge, Mass., 1925.

Index